EX AUDITU

An International Journal of Theological Interpretation of Scripture

Volume 19 2003

Ex Auditu is published annually by Pickwick Publications, 215 Incline Way, San Jose, California, 95139-1526, USA.

Subscriptions
- Individuals:
  - U.S.A. - $17.00
  - Canada - $15.00 (in U.S. Funds)
  - All other countries - $18.00 (in U.S. Funds)
  - Students - $12.00
- Institutions:
  - U.S.A. - $30.00
  - Canada - $25.00 - (in U.S. Funds)
  - All other countries - $30.00 (in U.S. Funds)

This periodical is indexed in the *ATLA Religion Database,* published by the American Theological Library Association, 250 S. Wacker Dr., 16th Flr., Chicago, IL 60606, E-mail: atla@atla.com, WWW: http://www.atla.com/; *Internationale Zeitschriftenshau für Bibelwissenschaft*; *Religious and Theological Abstracts;* and *Old Testament Abstracts.*

Please address all subscription correspondence and change of address information to Pickwick Publications.

ISSN 0883-0053

EX AUDITU

An International Journal of Theological Interpretation of Scripture

THE EDITORIAL BOARD MEMBERS AND CONSULTANTS represent various disciplines and denominations. Theological Interpretation of Scripture is a task to be taken seriously by scholars who are committed to the Christian faith and tradition. However, as one editorial consultant stated: "let people gradually get used to the idea that a sane hermeneutics is both oriented in advance toward agreement/consent and is simultaneously exigent, discriminating, critical."

EX AUDITU

Volume 19 2003

CONTENTS

ANNOUNCEMENT OF THE 2004 SYMPOSIUM

North Park Theological Seminary in Chicago, Illinois, is pleased to announce that the twentieth Symposium on the Theological Interpretation of Scripture will take place September 23–25, 2004. The Symposium will start at 7:00 p.m. on September 23 in Nyvall Hall and will extend through a Saturday afternoon worship service on September 25.

The theme in 2004 will be Judgment, i.e., the Judgment of God, not that of humans. The following persons have agreed to make presentations:

Richard Bauckham, University of St. Andrews, New Testament
Stephen Long, Garrett-Evangelical Theological Seminary, Theology
Gordon McConville, University of Gloucestershire, Old Testament
John E. Phelan, Jr., North Park Theological Seminary, New Testament
Clark Pinnock, McMaster Divinity School, Theology
Emerson Powery, Lee University, New Testament
Pam Scalise, Fuller Theological Seminary Northwest, Old Testament
Paul Scott Wilson, Emmanuel College, University of Toronto, Preaching
Randall Zachman, University of Notre Dame, Church History

Persons interested in attending the sessions should write before September 1 to:

Ms. Guylla Brown
North Park Theological Seminary
3225 W. Foster Avenue
Chicago, Illinois 60625

Meals may be taken at North Park and assistance can be provided in finding nearby lodging.

ABBREVIATIONS

AB	Anchor Bible
ABD	*Anchor Bible Dictionary*
BDAG	Bauer, W., F. W. Danker, W. F. Ardnt, and F. W. Gingrich, *Greek-English Lexicon of the New Testament and Other Early Christian Literature*
CTS	Calvin Translation Society edition of Calvin's commentaries.
DSD	*Dead Sea Discoveries*
ELCA	Evangelical Lutheran Church of America
ESV	English Standard Version
ExAud	*Ex Auditu*
ICC	International Critical Commentary
Int	*Interpretation*
JB	Jerusalem Bible
JBL	*Journal of Biblical Literature*
JBR	*Journal of Bible and Religion*
JETS	*Journal of the Evangelical Theological Society*
JSNT	*Journal for the Study of the New Testament*
JSOT	*Journal for the Study of the Old Testament*
JSNTSup	Journal for the Study of the New Testament: Supplement Series
LXX	Septuagint
NIDNTT	*New International Dictionary of New Testament Theology*

NJB	New Jerusalem Bible
NovTSup	Novum Testamentum Supplements
NRSV	New Revised Standard Version
NTS	*New Testament Studies*
RB	*Revue biblique*
REB	*Revised English Bible*
RSV	*Revised Standard Version*
SP	Sacra pagina
SR	*Studies in Religion*
TDNT	*Theological Dictionary of the New Testament*
VTSup	Vetus Testamentum Supplements
WBC	Word Biblical Commentary

INTRODUCTION

Quite possibly the question of the authority of Scripture is more pertinent in the life of the church now than it ever has been. Do we give an acquiescent nod to Scripture, or possibly point to it as a historic icon, or do we actually allow Scripture to confront and regulate our lives, as difficult as that sometimes is? If I am not mistaken, the society's attitude toward the Bible has changed significantly within the past decade or so. Whereas before a commitment to the authority of Scripture was viewed as quaint or possibly even commendable, although strange, now such a commitment is often viewed as misguided, uninformed, and possibly even dangerous. Why would people want to grant authority—whatever that might mean—to an ancient book with strange ideas? Does the Bible get to define who we are, and if so, why?

The articles from North Park's 2003 symposium discuss the complexities of talking about the authority of Scripture. Any discussion of this subject is not just a treatment of one's stance toward the Bible. Very quickly issues of canon, hermeneutics, Christology, church tradition, and a variety of other subjects demand attention, as is evident in the articles that follow. By the nature of the case, the authority of Scripture is not one thing. The authority of a narrative is not the same as the authority of a psalm or a proverb or a letter. The reasons for granting authority to Scripture are varied as well, and different connotations of authority exist.

For example, people often distinguish between extrinsic and intrinsic authority. Richard Bauckham helpfully applies this distinction to the discussion of the authority of Scripture. (See "Authority and Scripture," in *God and the Crisis of Freedom: Biblical and Contemporary Perspectives*, Louisville: Westminster/John Knox, 2002, 50–77, esp. 56–58.) Extrinsic authority is lodged not in the validity of the opinion itself but in something or someone external who is qualified or who is legitimated by office to give an "authoritative" judgment. Intrinsic authority rests on the truthfulness and persuasiveness of the opinion in its own right, not on the judgment of some person or institution. Both kinds of authority are operative in most of life, even when we say we reject authority, as our society likes to do. Both are operative also with regard to Scripture and rightly so. We usually read Scripture because someone else, often an "authority figure," said Scripture has authority and should be read—an external authority witnessing to an intrinsic authority. Also, the church rightly insists that Scripture *alone* has the right to define us, even when we do not mean *really* alone. Further,

Scripture contains truth claims about its own contents as a Word from God. Such extrinsic claims concerning authority are natural and necessary, but ultimately more significant is intrinsic authority, the inherent persuasiveness of the truthfulness of the statements made. Some people never move past acknowledging Scripture's extrinsic authority, but surely what is most pertinent and life changing is a recognition of Scripture's intrinsic authority, when people no longer believe because they should but because they do.

In the end we are not talking about the authority of Scripture so much as we are talking about the authority of the God revealed in Jesus Christ and the conviction that the scriptural documents do indeed uniquely show us who this God is, what God has accomplished, and what we are to be in response. The verse selected for the cover reminds us that authority ultimately resides in the incarnate Word, even though it is only through the written Word that his identity and character is known.

The symposium brings together people from various traditions and does not attempt to get them to make uniform statements. The discussions this year, even more than usual, were lively, engaging, and compelling, and the fellowship and worship were enjoyable contributions to our common life in Christ. With the diversity of views expressed, statements made, of course, reflect the views of the authors, not necessarily those of the editor, the publisher, or North Park—just to make the necessary disclaimers.

Thanks is expressed once again to the presenters and respondents who made a significant investment in the life of North Park. The friendship of these people is a privilege. We also thank all those in attendance for their interest and contribution to the discussions. As has been the case in recent years, this journal was typeset using the word processor *NotaBene*, and gratitude is expressed to the good people at *NotaBene* for their continued, generous help. Special thanks is expressed to Rebekah Eklund, who *volunteered* to proofread the journal, and to Guylla Brown from North Park's staff, without whom the symposium would not be possible.

Klyne Snodgrass
The Editor

READING THE BIBLE WHOLE IN A CULTURE OF DIVIDED HEARTS

RAYMOND C. VAN LEEUWEN

The authority of Scripture has become a seemingly intractable problem. The solution to this problem is not to be sought simply in better theological analysis or in assertions that the Bible is God's Word. The problem of the Bible is the problem of humanity in rebellion, opposed to the Word and Spirit, alienated from God in Christ, confused about good and evil, and needing conversion and fundamental reorientation to the Way of life. It is also the problem of a church accommodated to the cultural categories of the world around it and without adequate theories of how literary artworks, including the Bible, represent reality and communicate their meaning. Thus, we cannot make our discussion merely a matter of the Bible and theology—for the issues that concern us are inextricably entwined with the great and complex problems of culture and society worldwide and locally, of persons, families, groups, institutions, and nature in all their mutual relations. "Ask not for whom the bell tolls, it tolls for thee." Our discussions need to be engaged with the world in which we live and self-aware of the sort of people we are—all in relation to God (Rom 11:36).

Saint Augustine divided the world into those who were citizens of the "City of God" and those who gave their allegiance to the "Earthly City." My concern is that the citizens of God's City have divided loyalties, give allegiance to two kingdoms, and are walking under the opposed powers of Spirit and Flesh, God and Mammon. The dividing line between the world (in the negative sense) and the church is not simply between us and them; the conflict between spiritual forces runs right through the heart of every believer, and our very bodies are battlegrounds for the rule of Christ as opposed to darkness. The problem is not merely individual; it affects our corporate existence in Christian organizations and public institutions of all sorts. It affects Christian action in the public spheres of life.

The problem of the Bible is the problem of the church, which is in disarray, often in conflict with biblical principles,[1] and with more than 33,820 "denominations" and paradenominations worldwide.[2] We are far from the reality prophesied in Jeremiah, "I will give them *one heart and one way* to fear me all the days, for their good and their children's" (32:39). This not-yet-fulfilled promise points both to the deepest inner source of human actions, thoughts, and aspirations, the biblical "heart,"[3] and also to the "way" that human beings live in the world, that is, the way they do things as persons, families, and groups. It is the conviction of this essay that the Scriptures are the ultimate authority by which humans may judge whether their heart and way are shaped by Christ and his Spirit or not.

My purpose here is not to try to solve the world's problems; the gospel tells us that only God in Christ can do that. My purpose is to focus on the nature and use of God's written Word. I begin by noting our contemporary cultural and ecclesiastical crisis and continue by revisiting the great text 2 Tim 3:15–17, which famously tells us what the Bible is good for. Finally, I look at what sort of book the Bible is, that it can do those things described in 1 Timothy. In this regard, *I focus on the Bible as the one true metanarrative or universal story and as a creational wisdom book.* My interests are "practical" and, though I highly regard that area of human action we call "theory," theory is not my primary concern. What begs our attention as the larger context for theorizing, preaching, teaching, and writing is this: clergy and laity alike need to actually read and study Scripture so that it sets the agenda for our present existence, rather than letting our own local worldview and concerns set the agenda for God.

THE CONTEMPORARY CULTURAL CRISIS: THE PROBLEMATIC CONTEXT IN WHICH WE READ THE BIBLE

In the modern West the question of Scripture's character and authority came to be framed in terms of profoundly mistaken Enlightenment assumptions, unfortunately shared by liberals and conservatives alike.[4] In general, churches contributed to or accepted the developing scientism[5] and historical positivism around them, and even orthodox churches tried to make the Bible, in quasi-docetic fashion, into a "scientific" or modern historical document, satisfying the standards of the modern imagination and ignoring those of Scripture.[6] So doing, they distorted the Bible and made it more difficult to understand the decidedly nonmodern modes in which the Bible communicated the truth about reality.[7] Consequently, both evangelical and mainline churches painted themselves into untenable intellectual corners, since to frame a question wrongly is to deny oneself the possibility of appropriate answers. In this matter, the church was more shaped by the world around it (Rom 12:2) than by truth, reality, and the Bible itself. No less than when the church condemned Galileo, the modern church made it difficult for intellectually responsible people to accept the Bible as true, let alone as God's authoritative word for life. In each case, leaders of the church seemed unaware that they imposed upon Scripture cultural assumptions that were false to reality and to the Bible itself. When these assumptions were shown to be false and the science correct, Scripture became literally incredible for many intelligent, educated people. That this problem is still with us is evident from the anti-intellectual fear of education on the part of many Christians and the frequency with which our best and brightest youth leave the church when they attend our great secular universities. Many evangelicals fear that they have no answers to the problems raised by modernity and its science.

Another aspect of the decline in the Bible's functional authority was the misuse Christians made of the Bible to give warrant to contradictory and often wicked personal and public schemes, including centuries of anti-Judaism and dubious "religious" wars.[8] For example, the British historian Christopher Hill has documented the use of the Bible for contradictory political purposes in the seventeenth century British revolution. In that tumultuous time each party claimed the Bible as divine warrant for their own desires and deeds. Revolutionaries appealed to the Geneva Bible while monarchists promoted the Authorized Version.[9] Consequently, by 1660 the Bible in England had declined markedly in authority as a book to guide public conduct in civil and political affairs even though the bulk of the populace remained personally Christian.[10] In America the wicked history of slavery—based on a twisted, self-serving "Christian" misuse of the Bible—fostered a culture wide, complex reaction that contributed to the exclusion of Scripture's voice from "secular," public matters.[11] In such ways, among others, the Bible and its gospel were nullified, domesticated, or privatized. I am not arguing here that non-Christians should be called to obey Scripture but that Christians are. Nor am I arguing that Christians should enter public debates with direct appeals to Scripture but rather with biblically shaped insight into the common reality and circumstances we all inhabit.

My point is that Christians who claimed the warrant of Scripture for their deeds too often did evil deeds that discredited themselves, the Scriptures, and the God of Scripture—precisely because they did not approach Scripture with the attitude of Samuel: "Speak, Lord, for your servant (obediently) hears" (1 Sam 3:9–10). And too often they evaded responsibility for their own (mis)interpretations by epistemological theories that declared their readings to be merely "literal," thus, noninterpretative. For example, American Christians claimed "biblical" warrant for their sinful institution of slavery, even while violating biblical restraints on the evils of slavery.[12] Again, to ask a counterfactual question, if the church in France had obeyed biblical principles of righteousness and justice during the monarchy, would the French Revolution have taken a different course or even occurred at all?

The problem of the Bible is also the problem of the church because Christians in America and Europe have wittingly and unwittingly accepted a worldview that says their religion is a private, "spiritual" matter of the heart, a subjective matter of personal values that have no claim on the real world. This collective, gnostic stance seems never to be labeled as sin—though its nearest biblical counterpart is perhaps the service of Baal or "greed, which is idolatry." American Christianity is often a *de facto* form of polytheism, where Yahweh and Christ are worshipped on Sunday but denied lordship on Monday. On Monday the gods of the marketplace rule. On the other hand, where Christians of various stripes have proclaimed the Bible's relevance and authority for all of life, including politics and public policy, we have too often seen a sad litany of unwise and sometimes downright wicked actions, including theories that merely hitched Jesus to this or that secular bandwagon. My point is simply that "Christians" in the past and present are often the worst enemies of the Bible as God's word for humans because of the panoply of misuse and misconstrual to which they have subjected the Bible and because of the domestication of Scripture to unbiblical modern agendas. Not every voice that says, "Lord, Lord," is recognized by the Master of the house. Too often we Christians have missed the part about being "as wise as serpents and as innocent as doves."

We also live in a time of unprecedented mass culture and institutions, fostered by means of mass persuasion and propaganda controlled by the wealthy and powerful few for the wealthy and powerful few. Our commercial culture is monolithic, a fact it conceals from itself by means of its myth of "multiculturalism"[13] in which cultural preferences, including faith, are reduced to competitive consumer choices in the all-encompassing market. Rather than being a system of wise and rational "free" choices in an age of the internet and television, our children are robbed of their innocence and independence before they know what seduction is. By the time they are 18, they have attended 11,000 hours of secular school and watched an estimated 15,000 hours of television.[14]

Given Paul's fundamental admonition that we glorify God in our bodies (1 Cor 6:20), it is not irrelevant to consider the massive *cultural* (i.e., *not* individual) phenomenon of obesity, especially child obesity in America. Both inactivity and the flight from healthy food and drink are not unrelated to TV and its values, whether covert or blatant. Nor is the general decline in reading competence among young Americans. The impoverishment of education, especially in high schools, is also a "Christian" problem, for without competent and willing readers in general there are no competent readers of Scripture in particular. Without readers Scripture cannot exercise its authority.

Among the great cultural myths that shape us in a post-Romantic world is the belief that meaning is constructed by humans who project inner "value" on an otherwise meaningless or, at best, neutral world.[15] That is, our culture has institutionalized the viewpoint of Adam and Eve that we humans define good and evil, since the Word of God is subject to human construals of reality (Eve saw that the tree was good . . .).[16] Again, it is not just that our hearts and "cognitive environments" are divided; our "ways" in the world are also conflicted. That is, the fundamental shape and praxis of our lives are structured by institutions and social patterns that rob us of the freedom to serve God without compromise. Consider something so omnipresent as our modes of transportation: millions of commuters spend an inordinate amount of time on "freeways" from Los Angeles to Philadelphia, polluting the air, consuming energy, and wasting precious human time and lives, often literally.[17] All this is considered "normal," even though it alienates humans from each other and creation and puts people in a place where the reality of God seems slightly absurd. On the freeway it seems implausible that the God of Israel actually structures the path of our lives and determines its meaning here and now. Such an existence seems to render only a gnostic Christian or other god credible, a god that will get us out of here someday.[18]

It is within such contexts, it seems to me, that we are discussing the authority of Scripture. It would seem laughable, if we did not have faith, hope, and love, if we did not walk by faith, rather than by sight, and if God had not spoken by the prophets and come to earth in the person of Jesus Christ. What do we do in the light of our circumstances and, frankly, the many past and present sins of us Christians, sins that shape the very institutions and patterns of existence we take for granted?

In the present paper I do not seek to answer that question—it is a question that only the people of God can answer. An adequate positive answer will only occur by the grace of God in the power of the Holy Spirit. On the human side, prayer, repentance, and obedience must take place. And yes, with prayer for the Holy Spirit must also come a renewed awareness of Scripture's authority and relevance for all of life. It is only to this last item that I wish to address the rest of this essay.

WHAT IS THE BIBLE FOR?

Second Timothy 3:15–17 is the most famous text on the Bible's authority. It recalls Timothy's early biography: "That from your youth you have known the holy writings, which are powerful to make you wise on the way of salvation through faith in Jesus Christ. All Scripture is God-breathed and useful for teaching, for reproof, for correction, and for cultural formation in righteousness, so that the 'man' of God might be capable, fully equipped for every good work" (2 Tim 3:15–17). If the church is to be renewed and revived on a biblical basis, we need to attend to these words and live them out in churches and lives that, in Lesslie Newbigin's great phrase, are a "hermeneutic of the gospel."[19]

With "Scripture" Paul refers here to what Christians today call the OT.[20] The "Bible" of Jesus, Paul, and the nascent church is simply the OT.[21] Through its lenses they learned to understand who Jesus was and is, and through Jesus they saw more deeply what the Hebrew Scriptures entailed. In what follows I speak of the Bible or Scripture, even when my reference may be to the OT, in keeping with the usage in 2 Timothy. I assume that what I have to say about the "Bible" of Paul applies with appropriate qualifications to the NT as well. The OT, then, forms the holy writings that Paul called God-breathed and useful. These useful things and the nature of the Bible are inseparable, for the Bible's use and purpose is inextricably rooted in what it actually *is*.[22] The focus of 2 Tim 3:15–17 is on the Bible's purpose, on what it is *useful and good for*. This already suggests that the Bible is not a magic book, utterly unlike other books and dropped from heaven to reveal mysterious things. Rather, it suggests that the Bible is a sort of tool kit, an *instrumentarium* to help us think about God, reality, and humanity (including ourselves), and to live rightly in relation to them all. Only when Scripture is used in this way can it be a *power* to convert and change hearts and lives; only so can it feed commitment and obedience by "the hearing of the word." To cite a Psalm, the Bible is not a light for us to stare at while we alternately meditate and stumble through life, but a light and lamp we carry and use to see clearly the world around us and our way through it (Ps 119:105). Paths and ways by their very nature are communal; it takes many feet to make a path. Scripture teaches that such cultural paths or traditions can be good or evil, wise or foolish, righteous or wicked (Ps 1; Proverbs 1–9; et al.). The language of 2 Tim 3:15–17 lays a great deal of emphasis on what *we* do with the Bible: become wise, have faith in Jesus, teach, rebuke, and straighten one another out when we go wrong—in sum, *use* the Bible as a tool for cultural formation (*paideia*) in righteousness.

We need to highlight some of the key terms of 2 Tim 3:15–17, for they are loaded with meaning often foreign to modern Christian conceptions. I begin with "to make wise" (*sophisai*), a verb related to *sophia* ("wisdom") and *sophos* ("wise").[23] Paul here says that the Bible *as a whole* is designed to make human beings *wise*. That is its purpose. "Wise" is not a word that appears much in Christian circles and writings today. It was not always so. The Church Fathers were deeply conscious that the Bible offered a wisdom for life in this world, a way of life that was radically opposed to the dominant ways of the Greco-Roman culture around them. For Augustine, as for Paul, the Bible was a *wisdom* book, and Christ was the revelatory Word and Wisdom of God.[24]

My sense is that Christians today look almost everywhere for wisdom—if indeed they consciously seek it—except to the Bible. Briefly stated, biblical wisdom is practical knowledge and skill in every human endeavor in every corner of creation, from building a house and rearing children to cooking, playing the violin, making a sermon, and running a government or business—all because the creation as a whole and everything in it was created and now exists by God's wisdom (Prov 3:19–20; 8:22–36; Ps 104:24; John 1). Biblical wisdom is thus characterized by "the fear of the Lord," by thought and action congruent with the basic patterns and norms of reality, and by individual, particular decisions and actions in terms of those basic patterns and norms in light of the specific situation before us. Such wisdom is traditional, an enculturated path or "way" through this world, laid down by others who have gone before.[25] The motive force that draws us toward the goal that is God and his wisdom is simply love, joy, and delight. Wisdom espouses love within limits, life within law, and freedom within form, all in ways that respect God's creation, foster human flourishing, and give glory to God. The Bible as a whole, and the wisdom literature in particular, are books designed to foster such wisdom for life in this world.[26] If this is correct, then the present Christian overemphasis on the world to come, especially in affluent countries like the United States, are an unbiblical flight from our responsibilities in this world. All of life matters because all of creation belongs to God and should express his glory and righteousness, also in so-called secular affairs.

The wisdom the Bible imparts is for *salvation*. But here too, much of contemporary Christianity seems to limit salvation to its future, ultimate sense, and has forgotten that the Bible, according to our text, focuses on the present lives of persons, families, and communities, and on Israel or the church as a whole (cf. Phil 2:12–13). Salvation in 2 Tim 3:15–17 does not refer to the world to come, for that life has no need of rebuke or correction. "Salvation" and "save" (Gk. *sōtēria/sōzō*; Heb. *yšʿ*),[27] like most of the words in 2 Tim 3:15–17, are OT words. They are "totality" concepts, as broad as reality, and cover a multitude of events and circumstances. Thus, when barren Hannah gets a baby boy, she sings a hymn and says, "I rejoice in your *salvation*" (1 Sam 2:1).[28] Apparently, giving birth can be an instance of God's *salvation*.

When evangelical readers understand "salvation" as referring to the life to come "in heaven," they assume incorrectly that such usage is the general biblical reference of these words. Unfortunately, recent translations of the Bible make it easier for English readers to exclude the here and now from salvation. For example, in Matt 9:21, the woman with perpetual menorrhea says, "If only I can touch his robe, *I will be saved*" (*sōthēsomai*).[29] With "I will be saved," the woman says much more than she realizes. Jesus turns and says, "Your faith *has saved* you" (*sesōken*). Then we are told, "from that moment (hour), the woman *was saved* (*esōthē*)." The woman's "healing" or being "made well" (as some translations have it) was a particular instance of God's comprehensive *salvation*. Concretely, the whole bodily person is saved. Yet, the scope of that salvation is more than she can imagine at this point. Ultimately, it is the forgiveness of sins and the removal of their consequences (cf. Mark 2:1–12), the resurrection of the body (complete healing!) and the life to come of God's people in a renewed creation.[30]

Biblical (including NT!) salvation means that *Whatever is wrong is made right*—no matter how "physical" or mundane the problem may be. The Christmas carol "Joy to the World" has it right: "He comes to make his blessings flow far as the curse is found" (cf. Rev 22:3). Again, "He breaks the power of canceled sin, he sets the prisoner free" already in this life. This all-encompassing righting of wrongs is the basic sense of biblical salvation. Only such an understanding can account for the word's amazingly wide and flexible use: the scope of salvation is as broad as creation itself (see Pss 96 and 98).

In our current translations the substitution of a variety of terms for a consistent use of basic biblical terms like "save/salvation" (or a consistent better word) contributes to obscuring of the verbal and conceptual coherence of the Bible. Many American evangelicals have no idea that the salvation that Jesus teaches and brings near in the Gospels is the "Kingdom of God." Nor do they generally know that "Christ" translates OT "messiah," which means "anointed" as Israel's prophets, priests, and kings were anointed.[31] In particular, Jewish kings were expected to "save" (Luke 23:35–39; cf. Isa 33:22; Jer 23:5–6). Consequently, the cosmic (John 3:16–17; 4:42; 12:47; cf. Col 1:15–20) and communal *political-social-economic* dimensions of the salvation that Jesus brings are quite lost in our individualistic society (cf. Luke 4:18–20 and its roots in Isa 61 and Lev 25). "Jesus saves" as an OT king *ought* to save, but he does so in a total cosmic-social way that OT kings never could (cf. 1 Sam 2:1, 10; 9:16; 10:1, 27; Ps 72:13 [LXX 71:13][32] et al.).

So the Bible as a whole is not intended as a manual for admittance into the world to come. If this were so, most of the Bible would be superfluous. Regrettably, many Christians behave as if most of the Bible is indeed superfluous, no doubt partly because of their view that salvation is something otherworldly, and the mechanism for salvation is quite simple or technological ("Four Spiritual Laws"), able to ignore the difficulty and complexity of life. Yet, the fundamental problem for Christians is not how to get into heaven or how to get others into heaven when they die. The fundamental problems for us all are how to live wisely and righteously *in this world here and now* (1 Cor 3:10–17) and how to train others, including our children (*paides*), to do so.[33]

Many Christians know that "training" (*paideia*, which I translate "cultural formation") stems from the Greek world for child, *pais*. It refers originally to the cultural formation of children, and we still use the loanword *pedagogy* to refer to teaching. The biblical word, however, is much richer than this. New Testament *paideia* (and related terms) is a word that carries a great deal of freight derived from two primary contexts, that of the Greek OT (translating the Hebrew original) and that of Hellenistic culture.[34]

In Hellenistic culture—the world of the New Testament's Jewish and Gentile audience—*paideia* had a long history as a term for cultural formation in the broadest sense: to form a child or adult into the ideal person or citizen of their culture according to the norms of reality. "In Plato, education [i.e., *paideia*] is the only possible way to overcome present injustice and to create a true, i.e., just, state." Plato's connection of *paideia* and *justice* would come as no surprise to an educated Gentile reader of 2 Timothy. For Plato, the highest goal of education was to enable humans to know reality, in his view the "archetypes of reality," the realm of the ideas.[35]

In the LXX and much of the NT *paideia* and related words overwhelmingly translate *mûsār* (root *YSR*), words which are especially at home in biblical wisdom, particularly Proverbs, the Bible's basic wisdom book (see 1:2–3). There the terms often refer to discipline of various sorts, including the self-limitation that leads to maturity. But in Scripture, *paideia* "can also . . . stand for 'culture,' in the sense of the possession of wisdom, knowledge, and discernment."[36] The Bible is designed to make us wise on the path of salvation and to form us communally to live according to the standard of righteousness. This is not to deny the hope of eternal life (which John rightly insists starts in *this* life), but to shift our focus from life after death to our human responsibilities in this life. (If you belong to Jesus, the world to come is already taken care of.) Of course, it is God who disciplines and forms his people corporately (Deut 4:36; 8:5; Hos 7:12; 10:10) and personally (Prov 3:11; 15:33; Sir 18:14). But discipline and cultural formation are human tasks and responsibilities which the Scriptures are designed to help us accomplish. Judging from the undergraduates and seminarians I have taught for over 20 years, the church in America is not doing well in teaching youth the Bible. The Bible cannot be authoritative for life unless it is known and understood.

A word on *righteousness* and *good works* is in order. From the Bible's beginning to its end, the standard and goal for human beings, especially God's covenant people, is righteousness. Abraham is to *command* his descendants to "keep the way of the Lord by doing righteousness and justice" (Gen 18:19). Israel is judged in Isaiah's parable of the vineyard simply for its failure to do justice and righteousness (Isa 5:1–7; see Matt 21:33–44). For Jeremiah, without the doing of righteousness and justice humans simply do not know the Lord (Jer 22:13–17). The *first* thing Jesus wants his followers to seek is "the kingdom of God and his righteousness" (Matt 6:33). Finally, Christians hope for "a new heaven and a new earth in which righteousness dwells" (2 Tim 3:13). In a world where "righteousness" has become a moralistic narrow human term (as in "self-righteousness"), we need to recover its biblical, cosmic scope, for "the heavens declare his righteousness" (Ps 97:6). Righteousness in Christ gives birth to good works here and now.

WHAT SORT OF BOOK IS THE BIBLE?

What sort of book then is the Bible that it can accomplish its purposes outlined in 2 Tim 3:15–17? Scripture is diverse: three languages, many centuries, different genres, with different views even on the same events. Still, there is a coherence to this universal, sprawling book of books, not unlike the tangled coherence of reality itself. Structurally we might look at the Bible as a great cathedral that has been centuries in the building, whose gargoyles and towers reveal clear historical differences, whose stones have blood stains. Yet what we now behold is *one* house of God, one world in which the many parts function together, a multi-faceted dwelling that demands exploration and interpretation. It is this entity before which we stand and into which we must enter. Its roof has no meaning or function without the walls, and its doors and windows—for all their shapes and colors—serve to give entrance and light to the worshipers who enter it. Some parts we no longer understand. Some byways have been subordinated to others. Bits here and there are somewhat ruined or damaged. Some parts seem to exist only as a witness to the wonder of reality, like Benaiah who fought a lion in a pit on a snowy day (2 Sam 23:20). For all that, perhaps because of it, the Bible is a cosmic house to dwell in.

More than 200 years of biblical scholarship have trained professors and preachers that they cannot read the Bible whole because it is comprised of many books, books that themselves have histories of composition. This is the fallacy of the cathedral which does not exist because it was built over time, and some parts appear to fit oddly together and offend our aesthetic or moral sense. It is the fallacy of those who say there is no story, because there are multiple accounts, not entirely susceptible to reconciliation at the bar of Enlightenment reason.[37] To change the metaphor, this is to miss the forest for the trees.

A good deal of the coherence and structure of Scripture arises from the universal story of reality it tells, from the beginning of all things to their consummation and new beginning.[38] This metanarrative claims to tell the truth about reality over against other universal narratives or accounts of reality. It does so using an astonishing variety of genres, including those that the modern period (including that very modern movement called Fundamentalism and its daughter Evangelicalism) finds unfit vehicles for truth, including apparently "fictional" materials that with reference to other cultures are disparaged as legend and myth.[39] Though the story focuses on Israel and Christ, its concern is finally the world and all they who dwell therein.

The biblical story presents one God who makes the world and creates humans as his servant-kings to rule in it.[40] They rebel against the divine king, submitting unwittingly and wittingly to the idea that they might themselves be ultimate kings like God. God calls Abram to father a people who will restore humanity to the proper service of God and the world to health. Israel and her kings fail in this task. Yet God is undeterred in his purposes and finally sends a Messiah-king who will free humans from slavery to all false kings and powers (sin, death, the Snake, Pharaoh, Rome, etc.). Christ is that king who takes Adam's place and restores humanity and the world by his death and resurrection. After he rose from the dead, the first fruits of a new creation, he sent his Spirit into the church to sanctify and renew it until he returns to finish the renewal of all things which began at his resurrection (2 Cor 4:6; 5:17–18; Rev 21:5).[41] Then the dwelling of God in glory and holiness among his people here on earth will be accomplished (Rev 21–22). Then the kingdom, for which we daily pray, will have come on earth (Matt 6:10).

Moreover, the parts of the OT that are not the primal story (Gen 1 to 2 Kgs 25) or retellings and extensions of it (Ezra, Nehemiah, 1 and 2 Chronicles, the NT) or prophetic commentaries on the story and its future are implicitly texts that inhabit that all-inclusive "metanarrative." They take place and function within the world YHWH created and, after the primal rebellion of humanity, is redeeming through Israel.[42] Thus, many Psalms of lament, hymns of praise, proverbial wisdom, the love song we call the "Song of Songs," the painful reflections of Job and Qoheleth—these too belong in the biblical world and its story.

All humans today, whether they know it or not, are characters in the one true metanarrative of reality which Scripture unfolds. We are included in the biblical story, for that story did not end with Christ's departure. The main lines of that story—past, present, and future—are clearly sketched in Scripture. But the details of our lives and of future world history have not been.[43] Nonetheless, the very possibilities of our lives and of history are defined and delimited by what is written and revealed.[44]

The Bible fosters wisdom and salvation and righteousness whenever humans find their place in that story in relation to God in Christ. For to find our place in the Bible's story is *to find our place and meaning in God's world as it wends its way through time.* The church accomplishes this only by entering into the world of the Bible and living in it through reading and rereading. We must so live *in the Bible* that when we turn our eyes to the concrete, specific social-cultural-natural world around us we see it through "biblical" eyes and recognize it in wise and saving ways that correct, reprove, instruct, and shape us and it in righteousness.[45] The Bible is meant to *change* us so we can do good works in the real world in ways that glorify God by showing forth his goodness (Matt 5:13–16).

Such an account of the Bible does not play well in the seemingly tolerant, pluralist ideologies of today. In the light of current epistemic confusion and rival truth claims, more modesty and less arrogance are required of Christians.[46] For the church historically has too often made claims to certainty about things that were not true and has done too many things in the name of God that were in fact false, reprehensible, and ungodly. But we should not confuse our feeble apprehension and obedience to the truth with Scripture and its truth claims about reality and righteousness. We humans are responsible for our response to those truth claims.[47] Whether we like it or not, this is the sort of book the Bible is. It has something to offend everyone. To be a Christian is to get over the offense and be saved by grace and hard work to do the works of Christ in the world (Phil 2:1–16, esp. 12–13).

But can such a diverse book generate such grand contextual meaning, both on the macro- and microlevel?[48] Can it tell one story and present fundamentally one view of reality in the midst of all its differences? Of primary importance here is the idea that the Bible (re)presents a "world" which sufficiently provides the context and cognitive environment for its own understanding, rather than expecting that the reader's prior knowledge alone will provide an adequate framework for understanding.[49] The Bible seeks to convert our paradigms and worldviews to its own. The Bible portrays the "real" world both as it *is* and as it *ought* to be and portrays the conflict of good and evil that pervades human history. It often speaks of the "real" world *directly*, as when it describes David's sin against Uriah (2 Sam 11:1–27). But it also often stands only in *mimetic*, indirect relation to the "real" world, as in Nathan's parable of the poor man and his sheep (2 Sam 12:1–15).[50] The parable *refers* to two men and a sheep that do not exist in the real world. Its *referentiality* is to a fictional world and its events. Yet, this *mimetic* parable is a *true* representation of reality, depicting David and his sin metaphorically. It is a *true fiction* whose mimetic, real world payoff is to make David *wise* about himself as the brute facts never could.

In a sense, my argument is a variation on the Reformation proverb "Scripture is its own interpreter." This saying is often misunderstood as if nothing but the Bible is needed—not tradition, not experience nor inference—all of which are inescapably present in all reading. It would also be a grave mistake to say that knowledge of the world—including ancient Near Eastern archaeology, languages, cultures, and history—is unnecessary.[51] The Reformation teaching of Scripture's clarity does not mean that there are no obscurities. Indeed, for *growth* in understanding, scholarship is a necessary gift to the church, since modern societies are increasingly removed from the realities and cultural world of the Bible. Instead, this Reformation interpretative motto is best understood as meaning that the Bible in its richly complex coherence provides enough data in itself so that *globally* it corrects misreading over time, through the repeated re-readings of individuals and communities over generations.[52] In a sense, this view links the Bible to all great writing, for great works of literature, from Homer to Tolkien's *Lord of the Rings*, create cognitive worlds in which readers can learn, for example, that adult Hobbits smoke "pipe-weed" and that trolls turn to stone in the light of day.[53] Boris Upensky describes the phenomenon this way:

> In a work of art . . . there is presented to us a special world, with its own space and time, its own ideological system, and its own standards of behavior. In relation to that world, we assume (at least in our first perceptions of it) the position of an alien spectator, which is necessarily external. Gradually, we enter into it, become more familiar with its standards, accustoming ourselves to it, until we begin to perceive this world as if from 'within.'[54]

For all its glorious diversity, the Bible is a book with a complex coherence. It exists together, and its collectors and editors have insisted that these documents belong together. This literary fact has been obscured by the narrow focus on diachronic analysis of the *process* of biblical composition. Yet, whatever this process may have been, readers have before them a synchronic whole, a complex work of art consciously brought together as canon.[55] This *product* of composition is now an entity in its own right; it has priority and is authoritative for the church and readers of all kinds. This is what we read. The context of meaning, now that the "building" is complete, is the entire Bible, existing in the world and history as God's abiding Word. The parts presuppose and interact with one another.[56] So it is with the Bible. As literature the Bible presents a system of "norms" which holds readers accountable for better and worse readings *worked out in the praxis of their lives*. According to Wellek and Warren: "the real poem [i.e., a literary work] must be conceived as a structure of norms, realized only partially in the actual experience of its many readers. Every single experience . . . is only an attempt—more or less successful and complete—to grasp this set of norms or standards."[57] The Bible is bigger and beyond any reader or generation of readers. In this sense, its reading and meaning is inexhaustible or *unfinalizable* (M. Bakhtin). Yet its basics are understandable to children.

Besides creating a universal metanarrative, the Bible develops its coherence through a complex consistency of concepts, metaphors, allusions, and symbols that is embodied in words, phrases, images, and (sometimes typological) patterns that are repeated again and again in Scripture—like musical themes and variations.[58] These words and phrases are not just decoration; they are essential to understanding the most fundamental aspects of the Bible's view of God and reality.

Finally, how does the Christian community *get* this larger story in which it lives? It is best gotten from the Scriptures themselves. Every Christian is called to be a hearer and doer of the Word (Jas 1:22). Tom Wright provides a parable that helps us think through the communal task of acquiring the biblical story and *living it out* in our times and situations. Wright suggests that "Since (a) stories are a key worldview indicator . . . and (b) a good part of the New Testament consists of stories, or narratives, it might be a good idea to consider how stories might carry, or be vehicles for, authority." Here is Wright's parable:

> Suppose there exists a Shakespeare play, most of whose fifth act has been lost. The first four acts provide, let us suppose, such a remarkable wealth of characterization, such a crescendo of excitement within the plot, that it is generally agreed that the play ought to be staged. Nevertheless, it is felt inappropriate actually to write a fifth act once and for all: it would freeze the play into one form, and commit Shakespeare as it were to being prospectively responsible for work not in fact his own. Better, it might be felt, to give the key parts to highly trained, sensitive and experienced Shakespearian actors, who would immerse themselves in the first four acts, and in the language and culture of

> Shakespeare and his time, *and would be told to work out a fifth act for themselves.*[59]

If Wright is correct, and in the main I believe he is, then we find ourselves in the somewhat daunting situation of playing out our mutual lives in a way that is faithful to the "rules" and purposes of the divine author of creation and history revealed in ancient, foreign writings. For our purposes I must repeat that the ability obediently to "play out" God's purposes in history requires that the people of God immerse themselves in God's great scriptural drama, with all its quirks, and strangeness, and that they get to know the biblical "world" and story so that their own *bodily* existence in the created world (Calvin's *theatrum mundi*) may play out to the glory of God (Eph 1:12, 14; 2:9; cf. 1 Cor 6:20). A fundamental dialectic in the biblical story is that the world is made to be filled with the glory of God, but that wicked humans everywhere lack that glory and obscure it (cf. Isa 6:3 and Rom 3:23 which, with Rom 14:23 and James 4:17, provide the most radical and comprehensive NT definitions of sin).[60] Human sin is the enemy of God's glory and holiness in creation. It may be that you or I have only a "bit" part in the drama and may not be able to study the world and writings of Shakespeare. Then especially, to play our little role rightly we need other players and teachers to help us see how our small part fits into the whole.

Practically, in many circumstances it is difficult for the majority of people to acquire a thorough knowledge of the entire Bible first hand—as translators and preachers around the world are well aware. Moreover, the acquisition of the story and its metaphors and symbols is an educational *process* which does not happen overnight. *If a hotel reader of a Gideon's NT is converted to Jesus by the Gospel of John, then where does she go to get the whole story and its fundamental symbols and metaphors for reality?* It can only be from the contextual stories, written or oral, told by preachers and more experienced Christians in ways that are congruent with the lives those Christians *live*. Yet all too often, even in nations with a rich Christian, biblical tradition, it is the stories of pagan cultures that subvert or domesticate the grand biblical story.[61] This is a fundamental problem for the Christian church today.

In other words, in addition to Bibles Christians and non-Christians alike need access to the larger biblical story in "reader's condensed versions." (I tremble to say this, for fear of inviting sloth on the part of educated Christians! One cannot become a Christian *leader* without a deep and broad reading and reflective knowledge of the Bible. Cf. Josh 1:6–9 and 2 Timothy above.) Indeed, even when cultures have the Bible entire, they are in constant need of summaries and explanations to help readers make larger sense of what is immediately before them. The Bible itself testifies to this need when it again and again retells the historical past in versions direct or parabolic to address the present and anticipate the future (Gen 45:4–11; 49:1–27 [future history in figurative form];

Deuteronomy *passim* [e.g. 8:1–20; 26:5–11]; Josh 24:2–18; 2 Kgs 17:7–23; Pss 78; 105–107; Isa 5:1–7; Neh 9:6–38; Mark 4:1–20//; Mark 12:1–12//; Acts 7; Rom 9–11; et al.). Such passages can easily be multiplied.[62] Jesus himself provided explanations of his own actions and teachings *because even the disciples were not able to make sense of them on their own.* They needed to be brought to a different cognitive place before they could understand. Initially, Peter, who recognizes Jesus as the Messiah/Christ, does not understand what the word means, though he thinks he knows the word very well indeed from his own biblical-Jewish cognitive environment. He cannot comprehend that the Messiah must suffer and die to achieve the glory of the kingdom (Mark 8:27–9:1). By his life and teaching and his death and resurrection Jesus changes the hearer's understanding of words and stories they thought they already knew. Reading the Bible (in the whole and in its parts) can do the same, but not without teachers, preachers, and other Christians who walk in the new "Way" (Acts 9:2 et al.).[63] Bible translation and reading are necessary but never enough. Again, we need to see "the congregation as hermeneutic of the Gospel."[64]

Without the whole Bible, finally, we do not know Jesus. To start with Jesus is to start at the decisive turning point of a long story. But to start there without the OT cosmic setting and development of the story makes it most difficult to recognize what the issues in that turning point are and who Jesus actually is. Among other things, he is God's Son Israel (Matt 2:15; Hos 11:1; cf. Exod 4:22–23),[65] Israel's Messiah (cf. 1 Sam 2:10 et al.), Israel's Passover Lamb (1 Cor 5:7; see Exod 12–13 also concerning the removal of leaven), cursed-one-hung-on-a-tree (Gal 3:13; cf. Deut 21:23 LXX), Son of Man/Adam (Mark 2:10; Dan 7:13–14 et al.), Son of David, *Seed* of Abraham (not "offspring," Gal 3:16–20; Gen 12:7), Second/Last/New Adam/*Anthrōpos* (Rom 5:12–21; 1 Cor 15:21–22, 45–49; Eph 4:22–24;[66] Col 3:9–10), Image of God,[67] Yahweh made visible in human flesh as the Tabernacle where God's glory dwells among humans (John 1:14–18; Exod 33:18; 34:6; 40:34 et al.), the Wisdom and Word of God (existing and active at creation), and the One in whom all things hold together (John 1:1–18; Col 1:15–20; Prov 8 et al.). As Irenaeus saw long ago, Jesus recapitulates in himself the history of Israel and of Adam and his descendants. Without knowledge of that larger story, the full significance of Jesus is inevitably missed. Also, it is even possible to substitute a false Jesus for the biblical Jesus. (In American evangelical circles, the imaginary internal "Jesus" who speaks to me "in my heart" is often clearly not the biblical Jesus—e.g., as when irresponsible, manipulative young men and women casually say to one another, "Jesus told me that we should be together," or, "The Lord told me that we should break up.") Without the whole Bible, we do not have Jesus.

NOTES

1. For example, fifty years ago, divorce was deemed unbiblical and contrary to God's will, something that might happen only to prevent severe abuse or evil. Today, divorce even among Christians seems a "lifestyle" choice and a taboo topic in virtually every American pulpit. The average effects on children appear negative and long lasting. See Sara McLanahan and Gary D. Sandefur, *Growing Up with a Single Parent: What Hurts, What Helps* (Cambridge, Mass.: Harvard University Press, 1994); Judith S. Wallerstein, Julia M. Lewis, and Sandra Blakeslee, *The Unexpected Legacy of Divorce: A Twenty-five-Year Landmark Study* (New York: Hyperion, 2000).

2. David Barret, ed., *World Christian Encyclopedia* (Oxford: Oxford University Press), 1:10.

3. The "heart" in the OT is not the agent of "feeling"as opposed to the "head" as the locus of reason. The heart is the deepest "I," the inner self behind thinking, feeling, and action.

4. It is not the burden of this paper to lay out this historical claim. For an accessible discussion of some of the problematic epistemological presuppositions and a proposal for a way forward, see N. Thomas Wright, *The New Testament and the People of God*, Christian Origins and the Question of God (Minneapolis: Fortress, 1992) and Lesslie Newbigin, *The Gospel in a Pluralist Society* (Grand Rapids and Geneva: Eerdmans and WCC, 1989/1994). More broadly on the modern period, see Stephen Toulmin, *Cosmopolis: The Hidden Agenda of Modernity* (New York: Macmillan, The Free Press, 1990).

5. By "scientism," I mean the inflation of science to become a worldview or religious myth. See Mary Midgley, *Science as Salvation: A Modern Myth and Its Meaning* (London and New York: Routledge, 1992).

6. George M. Marsden, *Fundamentalism and American Culture: The Shaping of Twentieth-Century Evangelicalism: 1870–1925* (Oxford: Oxford University Press, 1980).

7. In this paper I am not so concerned to address the real questions raised by the cultural and linguistic gaps between the ancient Bible and the modern world. But serious reflection on the variety of ways in which the Bible represents reality is an urgent desideratum for the church. See Othmar Keel, *The Symbolism of the Biblical World: Ancient Iconography and the Book of Psalms* (trans. Timothy J. Hallett; 1978; repr.; Winona Lake: Eisenbrauns, 1997).

8. See Stephan Toulmin, *Cosmopolis: The Hidden Agenda of Modernity* (New York: The Free Press, 1990) for the role wars of religion among Christians played in the move away from religion to reason and science as oracles of certainty in public affairs.

9. For the problem of Bible translation, see Raymond C. Van Leeuwen, "On Bible Translation and Hermeneutics," in *After Pentecost: Language and Biblical Interpretation* (eds. Craig Bartholomew, Colin Greene, and Karl Möller; Grand Rapids and Carlisle: Zondervan and Pater Noster, 2001), 284–311; and Ernst-August Gutt, *Translation and Relevance: Cognition and Context* (2nd ed.; Manchester: St. Jerome, 2000).

10. Contrast Arnold William's remarkable account of Scripture's role in public debate in sixteenth century England when the Bible and biblical commentaries were among the most read books. See his *The Common Expositor: An Account of the Commentaries on Genesis, 1527–1633* (Chapel Hill: University of North Carolina, 1948).

11. On the complexities of the issue see Eugene D. Genovese, "God Without Thunder," *The New Republic* (September 8, 2003). Concerning slavery and the Bible, Genovese, an expert on American slavery, provides a long, critical review of Mark A. Noll's magisterial, *America's God: From Jonathan Edwards to Abraham Lincoln* (Oxford: Oxford University Press, 2002).

12. Serious attention by Christians to the implications of Deut 15:12–15 and 22:15–16 alone might have undone the project of American slavery. Most American slaves were fellow Christians! Slavery in the Bible may be best approached, like divorce, as an accommodation to the

hardness and sin of human hearts, something that needed restraint but was never God's intention for his creatures. See Matt 19:1–14, where the passage on little children deliberately follows the condemnation of divorce.

13. Robert N. Bellah, "Is There a Common American Culture?" *Journal of the American Academy of Religion* 66 (1998): 613–625.

14. "Centurymarks," *The Christian Century* (December 13, 2003): 7. By contrast, Thomas Walters estimates that Roman Catholic children "spend 390 hours in parish religious education."

15. On projection see Charles Taylor, *Sources of the Self: The Making of the Modern Identity* (Cambridge, Mass.: Harvard University Press, 1989), 53–54. On Romanticism and its influence, see pp. 368–455.

16. Dietrich Bonhoeffer, *Ethics* (New York: Macmillan, 1965), 17–20, 88–109.

17. In 2000 there were 41,821 deaths and 5.3 million injuries on American highways. Statistics from the homepage of Roadwaysafety.org.

18. See Harold Bloom, *The American Religion: The Emergence of the Post-Christian Nation* (New York: Simon and Schuster, 1992) for an account of the gnostic character of much American religion, including Evangelicalism.

19. Newbigin, *The Gospel in a Pluralist Society* , 222–233.

20. I am aware of the misconstruals to which this name has given rise (i.e., old—and thus less important or significant, old and thus superseded by the new). Such Marcionite misreadings need to be addressed, not by name changes, but by education. The language "Old Testament" is best understood in a nonpejorative sense as the "Old Covenant" which failed *on the human side*, but was fulfilled and accomplished in the "New Covenant" wherein YHWH and the God-man Jesus Christ did what sinful humans themselves could not. In this I follow von Rad's profound reading of covenant failure and renewal in Jeremiah. Gerhard von Rad, *The Theology of Israel's Prophetic Traditions*, vol. 2 of *Old Testament Theology* (trans. D. M. G. Stalker; New York: Harper and Row, 1965), 191–219.

21. See Stephen Chapman's essay in this volume and his *The Law and the Prophets: A Study in Old Testament Canon Formation* (Tübingen: J. C. B. Mohr, 1999).

22. For this general biblical principle of the necessary connection/s among "kinds" of things and their "ends" or purposes, see Oliver O'Donovan, *Resurrection and Moral Order: An Outline for Evangelical Ethics* (repr. 1986; Grand Rapids: Eerdmans, 1994), 31–52.

23. The primary OT word for wisdom is *ḥokmāh*, root *ḤKM*.

24. See the superb article on the Western history of biblical Wisdom by David Lyle Jeffrey, "Wisdom," in *A Dictionary of Biblical Tradition in English Literature* (ed. David Lyle Jeffrey; Grand Rapids: Eerdmans, 1992), 831–837. The Fathers often referred to Christ as the "Word and Wisdom" of God. It is to be regretted that while many theologians and some pastors know Athanasius's "On the Incarnation," few know that it is only the second in a two-part work, being preceded by his "Against the Gentiles," where the role of the Word in creation is treated.

25. In NT terms, Jesus is the way, the truth, and the life. Thus Acts can simply call communal Christian existence and action in the world that adheres to Jesus "the way."

26. It is beyond the scope of this paper to attempt a fuller description of biblical wisdom. In a preliminary way, my understanding is expressed in Raymond C. Van Leeuwen, "Building God's House: An Exploration in Wisdom," in *The Way of Wisdom: Essays in Honor of Bruce K. Waltke* (eds. J. I. Packer and Sven K. Soderlund; Grand Rapids: Zondervan, 2000), 204–211; Raymond C. Van Leeuwen, "The Book of Proverbs," in *New Interpreter's Bible*, vol. 5 (ed. Leander Keck; Nashville: Abingdon, 1997), 17–264; and in "The Wisdom Literature," in Kevin J. Vanhoozer et al., eds., *Dictionary for Theological Interpretation of Scripture* (Grand Rapids: Baker, forthcoming).

27. My concern is not with *English* "salvation/save" as a translation of these terms per se, but with *a wise consistency* in rendering key biblical words and phrases, so that the English Bible

comes to aid Christians in discovering basic biblical concepts in ways that *change* their preconceptions. One might employ other English terms. My point is that we need an English expression that can carry the comprehensive sense of *sōzō*, and we need to use it as consistently as possible in ways that shape the reader's understanding of salvation in terms of related biblical words, concepts, metaphors, and images.

28. Hebrew, *yšw ʿh*; Greek, *sōtēria*, the same word used in 2 Tim 3:15.

29. NIV has "I will be healed." Even the ESV (which is based on the RSV and claims to be more "literal") has "I will be made well" (cf. Luke 8:36, variously "saved," cured," "made well"). At first glance, the matter is trivial. Yet something crucial has been lost.

30. See Oscar Cullmann et al., *Immortality and Resurrection: Death in the Western World: Two Conflicting Currents of Thought* (ed. Krister Stendahl; New York: Macmillan, 1965); O'Donovan, *Resurrection and Moral Order*; N. Thomas Wright, *The Resurrection of the Son of God*, Christian Origins and the People of God (Minneapolis: Fortress, 2003). The last mentioned work offers some important distinctions concerning concepts of immortality ignored by some earlier works.

31. For more than 20 years I have been asking mostly reformed or evangelical college students what the biblical world "Christ" means. Most of them do not know. It follows that they do not know why they are called "Christian." Compare the Reformation creed, "The Heidelberg Catechism" Q. & A. 31–32.

32. *Psuchas penētōn sōzei,* "He will save the lives of the poor." Cf. Mark 3:4; 8:35. Such passages show how misleading the evangelical expression "to save souls" can be. The Messiah saves whole *persons* or *lives*. Note the evangelical translations of the difficult Prov 11:20b, "he who wins souls is wise" (NIV), "he who captures souls is wise" (ESV).

33. On this whole paragraph, see Lesslie Newbigin, *Signs Amid the Rubble: The Purposes of God in Human History* (ed. Geoffrey Wainwright; Grand Rapids: Eerdmans, 2003), 71–75.

34. The great classicist Werner Jaeger actually called his three volume history of Greek culture *Paideia: The Ideals of Greek Culture*, followed by his *Early Christianity and Greek Paideia*.

35. For the quotation and this description see D. Fürst, "Teach, Instruct, Tradition, Education, Discipline," *NIDNTT* 3:775–776.

36. G. Bertram, *TDNT* 5;604. See also Fürst, *NIDNTT* 3:777: "In the LXX the vb. *paideuō* remains nearer in meaning to the OT 'chasten'; the noun *paideia* tends more in the direction of the Hellenistic idea of culture, instruction." Biblical knowledge is a form of cultural knowledge, including theology, but not limited to it. The "*paideia* of the Lord" in Eph 6:4 appears to allude to Deut 11:2. This suggests that Christian training includes the history of YHWH's acts as recorded in the Scriptures. Again, Bible knowledge—*OT knowledge*—is basic cultural knowledge for Christians.

37. For instance, the diverse law codes of the Pentateuch, the contrary accounts of the Conquest in Joshua and Judges, or of kings in Kings and Chronicles. In general, biblical art is the art of parallels and juxtaposition, in which the reader is required to infer the significance of parallel or contrasting, juxtaposed parts. This places great responsibility on readers, but also yields great rewards. Reality is presented complexly.

38. Some postmodern arguments say such a story is *de facto* illegitimate since no human has a global, transtemporal viewpoint. If the biblical story were not revelation, a mode of God speaking in and through the words of humans, such arguments would be correct. Postmodern repudiations of all metanarratives are, however, self-stultifying because they themselves take a metastance which implicitly claims to see, as it were, that there are many roads up the mountain to whatever. Such a position implicitly claims to float, like a god, above all things and see them whole.

39. The positivist, quasi-"scientific" epistemology of most Evangelicalism continues to

do tremendous damage to the church's attempt to read the Bible as God's word given in ancient cultural forms. In particular, the widespread notion of a one-to-one correspondence of narrative and event sadly ignores the constraints of the artistic representation of reality whether in word or picture. Fundamental confusions and insoluble conundrums result when the *representation* of reality is confused with "factual" reality that is represented. Evangelicalism needs more adequate theories of epistemology and aesthetics. The question is, can God use a variety of genres to teach us the truth about reality? Some evangelicals think that novels are "untrue" and should not be read because they are "fictions." See the essay by Walhout on the important distinction between mimetic and other modes of representation of reality in Roger Lundin, Anthony C. Thiselton, and Clarence Walhout, *The Responsibility of Hermeneutics* (Grand Rapids: Eerdmans, 1985).

40. Gen 1:26–28; Ps 8; cf. 1 Kings 12:7; Mark 10:45. A king's power and authority exist only in service of God, the great king, and of all that is properly entrusted to the king's care (his "kingdom").

41. 2 Cor 5:17–18: "Therefore if anyone is in Christ, *there is a new creation*; old things have passed away, in fact [*idou*], they have become new. *All things are from God*, who is reconciling us to himself through Christ. . . ." For this general interpretation see V. P. Furnish, *II Corinthians* (AB; Garden City: Doubleday, 1984), 314–320. Cf. Isa 42:9; 43:18–21; 48:6–7; 65:17 LXX; and for 2 Cor 5:18a, cf. Rom 11:36.

42. The pervasive reference to "the Fall" owes much to neo-Platonic metaphysics via Augustine. In terms of Scripture's basic metaphorical system, it seems to me less misleading to label the sin of humanity as "rebellion" or "usurpation" of the divine king's prerogatives. This is most clearly seen in parallels to Gen 3 such as Isa 14:4–21 and Ezek 28.

43. Wright, *People of God*, 132, cf. pp. 87–98 which usefully provide several summaries of the biblical metanarrative.

44. I do not mean this in the sense of a dispensationalist reading which thinks it can spell out the details of current history in (literalistic) biblical terms, as in the *Left Behind* series of fiction.

45. I trust readers are clear I am not arguing for "theonomy" in the line of Rushdooney! Such attempts to make the Bible "relevant" and authoritative deny the reality of historical and cultural change and the consequent need for hermeneutical reflection.

46. N. T. Wright's "critical realism" and Lesslie Newbigin's approach in his *Gospel in a Pluralist Society* are helpful, properly humble correctives to the "quest for certainty" that has characterized modernity and the evangelical churches as well. Christian faith does not rest in epistemic certainty, but in Christ. Faith is a form of knowledge based on trust in YHWH and his Messiah, even when we cannot give an adequate epistemic account of our experience. This is not an irrationalist move, for reason proceeds always on the basis of one's ultimate trust or faith in the way things are, even when reason cannot fully explain them. It is rational to believe that Almighty God can raise the dead, even if we can not explain it.

47. Erich Auerbach, *Mimesis: The Representation of Reality in Western Literature* (trans. Willard Trask; Garden City: Doubleday, 1957). See chapter 1 on Gen 22.

48. I am very aware that the coherence of the Bible is contested, so much so that disunity is an unquestioned assumption in some quarters. In this context I will only say that surface contradictions and differences do not affect its fundamental, underlying coherence of worldview—in spite of important shifts like the move to an explicit belief in the resurrection of bodies in Second Temple Judaism and Christianity. On worldview coherence with diversity as illustrated by the Middle Ages, see N. Max Wildiers, *The Theologian and His Universe: Theology and Cosmology from the Middle Ages to the Present* (trans. Paul Dunphy; New York: Seabury, 1982).

49. It goes without saying that all learning is an interactive process of the "unknown" being understood in terms of the "known" and the "known" being adjusted—sometimes radically—to accommodate the "unknown." For this general principle, see O'Donovan,

Resurrection and Moral Order, 76–97. For language learning, see A. Goatly, *The Language of Metaphors* (London and New York: Routledge, 1997), 28–29. A crucial difficulty is that sometimes learning is of a sort that requires a "paradigm shift," a change in worldview that entails a reorientation of one's most fundamental, "taken for granted" presuppositions. In biblical terms, this is *metanoia*, conversion, a "circumcision of the heart." Conversion is simply an act of grace that simultaneously requires a willingness to lose one's life (and ideas) to gain it. The Bible is designed to "convert or "turn"our "heart" and "way"over lifetimes and generations. For example, the massacres in Rwanda happened in a "Christian" nation that had not been converted on the level of worldview *including praxis* (so Jim Engel, veteran missiologist, in private conversation).

50. For the important distinction between referential and mimetic relations of literary texts to reality, see Walhout in Lundin, Thiselton, and Walhout, *The Responsibility of Hermeneutics*, 71–84.

51. Just one helpful example from a vast literature: Philip J. King and Lawrence E. Stager, *Life in Biblical Israel* (Louisville: Westminster/John Knox, 2002).

52. Meir Sternberg, *The Poetics of Biblical Narrative: Ideological Literature and the Drama of Reading*, Indiana Literary Biblical Series (Bloomington: Indiana University Press, 1985). Sternberg's great work on the Hebrew Bible speaks of "fool-proof reading" which the text fosters. A key factor in the Bible's ability to correct misreading is the literary use of *repetition* of all sorts, which Sternberg and many other scholars abundantly illustrate. See especially "The Structure of Repetition: Strategies of Informational Redundancy," pp. 365–440. Of course, gains in biblical understanding are also lost over time for a variety of reasons. Each generation must reread the sources and appropriate past readings—a huge communal task.

53. The Bible is of course unique in that it is the one true, God-given portrait and description of reality.

54. Boris Upensky, *A Poetics of Composition* (trans. V. Zavarin and S. Wittig; Berkeley: University of California, 1973), 137.

55. I am aware of the problem of the canon's disputed boundaries. But what is significant is that there is no argument among the churches on the core canon as normative. Again, on the complexities, see S. Chapman's essay in this volume and his *The Law and the Prophets.*

56. This interdependence of meaning in the Bible and in reality itself is characteristic of worldview as a religiously informed view of the whole in which all things hang together (cf. Col 1:15–20). O'Donovan puts it this way, "If we know the value of the family, and do not know its relation to individual freedom, then we have misunderstood even the family. If we grasp the importance of compassion, but cannot relate it to justice, then even our compassion has become a vice rather than a virtue. Knowledge of the moral order is a grasp of the total shape in which, if anything is lacking, everything is lacking" (*Resurrection and Moral Order*, 89). Knowledge of God's world ("general revelation," cf. Rom 1:18–20; 2:14–15) informs our reading of Scripture, and reading of Scripture informs, corrects, and shapes our (sinful, partial) reading or experience of the creation—sometimes radically.

57. René Wellek and Austin Warren, *Theory of Literature* (3d ed.; New York: Harcourt, Brace and World, Harvest, 1957), 150.

58. For example, in Luke, John the Baptist is to Christ as Samuel is to David, a point underscored by Mary's borrowing from Hannah's song in 1 Sam 2. On typology see "*Figura*" in Erich Auerbach, *Scenes from the Drama of European Literature: Six Essays* (New York: Meridian, 1959); Leonhard Goppelt, *Typos: The Typological Interpretation of the Old Testament in the New* (trans. Donald H. Madvig; Grand Rapids: Eerdmans, 1982).

59. For both quotations see Wright, *The New Testament and the People of God*, 140 (italics his).

60. That humans were made to embody God's glory on earth is evident from many passages, from the glory of Aaron's priestly robes to Paul's talk of transformation into imaging the *doxa* of Christ (2 Cor 3:7–4:18; esp. 3:18; 4:17).

61. In spite of all the beneficial remnants of Christianity still active in our midst, I include European and North American nations among "pagan cultures."

62. Wright provides a fine account of the Parable of the Wicked Tenants as the story of Israel in which Jesus retells for his time the story Isaiah told 700 years earlier (Isa 5:1–7). Wright, *The New Testament and the People of God*, 74–77. "The Parable, like most of Jesus' parables, tells the story of Israel—that is, it sets out the Jewish worldview in the regular appropriate manner—but gives it a startling new twist." At stake in the retelling of the old story was "a controversy about *different tellings of the story of Israel's god, his people, and the world*" (both quotations p. 76, italics his). See also 215–243.

63. It is good to reflect that the "Way" in Acts is actually the old way of God's people, made new and revealed in Jesus Christ so that we may walk in it. Root metaphors like "way" and "walk" are universal in human cultures and understood by all. In the Bible they are used pervasively to map reality in rich and variegated ways. They are essential to the biblical understanding of existence. A word like "walk" (*peripateō*) should not be casually translated with "live" or some other colorless substitute (cf. Gal 5:16 in NIV; NRSV). We would never do that to Shakespeare. "Walk" and "live" are not equivalent because "walk" conceptualizes life and the world in ways that Christians need to learn.

64. Newbigin, *The Gospel in a Pluralist Society*, 222–233.

65. David E. Holwerda, *Jesus and Israel: One Covenant or Two?* (Grand Rapids and Leicester: Eerdmans and Apollo, 1995), 27–58. Holwerda's book is illuminating on a number of topics in my list of descriptions of Jesus.

66. Cf. Eph 2:15 and Gal 3:27–28 (with the masculine *heis*, not neuter *hen)* which make clear that this "new man" in Christ is conceived of collectively, i.e., as the "body of Christ."

67. See Seyoon Kim, *The Origin of Paul's Gospel* (repr. 1981; Grand Rapids: Eerdmans, 1982) on this phrase in Paul.

SCRIPTURE, TRADITION, AND THE FORMATION OF CHRISTIAN CULTURE: THE THEOLOGICAL AND PASTORAL FUNCTION OF THE HISTORY OF INTERPRETATION

JOHN L. THOMPSON

Let me begin by attempting to locate myself in relationship to the theme of our symposium, the authority and function of Scripture in the contemporary world. There are two aspects of my background that may aid in understanding the historical-theological perspectives that I will bring to bear in the body of this paper.

First: *vocationally*, I have been trained as a historical theologian. Although I specialize in John Calvin more than any other single figure, my teaching and research interests embrace virtually the whole of Christian history, and especially the swath that runs from the church fathers through the Reformation. My special interest is in the history of the interpretation of Scripture, and I spend more time reading old Bible commentaries than works of systematic or polemical theology. For the past twenty years, I have focused on the books of Genesis and Judges and the writings of Paul, tracking texts that bear on gender issues, including gender roles and the abuse of women. I have recently begun to study other texts that Christians today generally do not like to read, such as the imprecatory psalms. I like to look at texts that make readers uncomfortable because they tend not only to disclose the interests and predispositions of commentators, but also to show how a commentator will bridge the gulf between biblical narrative and contemporary culture. With respect to our symposium, this means that I am very interested in how Scripture functioned for Christian writers of the Reformation and before—whether these writers meant it to function in a particular way or not.

Second: *ecclesiastically*, my own interests and predispositions have been shaped by the culture and controversies of American evangelicalism. I was a seminary student at Fuller Seminary in the mid 1970s, when the so-called "battle for the Bible" broke out. This was a time when evangelicals and fundamentalists drew lines of division over whether the Bible is inerrant. Many of my teachers were branded as doctrinally deficient for eschewing this term as a helpful descriptor for Scripture. Distressing as it truly was, this feud over inerrancy was also highly illuminating for me, and in a way that again bears on our symposium. Although there can be no doubt that those who affirmed the *inerrancy* of Scripture meant also to affirm the *authority* of Scripture in the highest possible terms, I have always been impressed with how little this affirmation effected. That is to say, one could (and can) find among inerrantists those who affirm the ordination of women and others who oppose it. There were (and are) inerrantists who manifest the so-called "charismatic" gifts and others who believe such gifts have ceased. Ethical positions among inerrantists are diverse: there are pacifists and just warriors; some who are prolife, while others may be (at least moderately) prochoice. Moreover, all of these positions and practices can be found also among noninerrantists.

The doctrinal divisions among inerrantists and noninerrantists made it clear to me, even when I was a seminarian, that there was a disturbing disconnection between proclamations about the authority of Scripture and the way Scripture was actually used, interpreted, or proclaimed. Theories or doctrines about the status or authority of Scripture often had little to do with the way Scripture functioned for conservative American Christians. Rather than leaving me cynical, however, this disconnection between theory and practice has fruitfully informed my own reading of ancient, medieval, and early modern Christian sources. Accordingly, my work could be characterized as an attempt to correlate Christian *theories* about the authority of Scripture both with *the way Scripture actually functioned* in the Christian past and with the *reading strategies* that Christians have traditionally used in order to make sense of Scripture and themselves.

Let me now introduce my topic. However interesting it may be to *describe* the function (or dysfunction) of Scripture in our own contemporary world, it is my assumption that a greater concern is to establish and implement a *normative* function for Scripture in our contemporary world. Whatever the Bible *can* be used for, there are surely some uses of the Bible that are better or more appropriate than others—a sort of "best practices" approach. I propose to argue that our own quest for the "best practices" of Scripture can be aided by a consideration of the practices of our exegetical forebears. But "aided" is really too weak a verb here. I would further propose that our reading of the Bible, our exegesis of the Bible—and, consequently, our *use* of the Bible—will be *anemic* if it ignores the history of interpretation. We may learn something about the Bible (and even about specific Bible passages) from the *history* of exegesis that we do not learn from exegesis alone.

The balance of this essay will do three things. The first part will recap the approach to Scripture inherited by the Reformers and comment on what they sought to change or preserve. A second section will offer two case studies in the history of interpretation: one that I regard as an inspiring example, another that seems less so. The essay will conclude with reflections on the role that the history of interpretation can play in the formation of Christian practices and Christian culture.

THE PRACTICE OF SCRIPTURE FROM THE FATHERS TO THE REFORMATION

The impact of the Reformation is often caricatured. The Protestant slogan of *sola scriptura*—"Scripture alone"—is frequently taken to suggest that Protestants rejected all human authority and tradition, turning only to the Bible and to no other book or source of wisdom or authority. After all (the caricature runs), late medieval Catholicism had replaced the Bible's authority with that of Mother Church. The actual function of Scripture was to serve, at best, as a distant source of inspiration for anecdotes and allegorical inventions.

There are some grains of truth in that caricature. But there is also much distortion—so much so, that if we were really to believe that the Reformers were all "men of one book" in just this way, we would find it impossible to imitate them or even understand them. After all, they not only read many other books besides the Bible, they often appealed to these noncanonical (often Christian) writings; and they themselves found it meaningful to add to this body of literature by way of sermons, commentaries, polemics, letters, tracts, and treatises. In order to understand our Protestant heritage, we need to refine the picture by describing—with more sympathy and less caricature—the practice of exegesis in medieval Catholicism and the changes sought (or not sought) by the Reformers.

Medieval exegesis is often supposed to follow the "fourfold rule" or *quadriga*, according to which every passage or story in the Bible has four levels of meaning: the *literal or historical* sense, which describes what happened; the *moral or tropological* sense, which looks for what the story teaches us about moral conduct or what it might symbolize about moral conduct; the *allegorical* sense, according to which the story reveals something about Jesus Christ and/or his church; and the *anagogical* sense, which usually designates something about the eternal life to come. In practice, the fourfold rule often looked more like a twofold rule, consisting of the literal sense and a spiritual reading composed of any or all of the three "spiritual" senses. While some passages were fully treated to a fourfold exposition, not every exegete seems to have been either so clever, so industrious, or so obsessive. You can find confirmation in the various OT commentaries of Hugh of St. Cher in the thirteenth century, Nicholas of Lyra in the fourteenth, or Denis the Carthusian in the fifteenth—all of whom default to a twofold scheme: either literal and moral or literal and mystical. (The word choice here is not significant.)

One question to address, then, is how the pervasive interest of medievals in nonliteral exegesis functioned and whether it *served* the authority of Scripture or whether, instead, it *subverted* it. Any attempt at an answer must bear in mind how the church fathers justified their spiritual exegesis. Origen offered two explanations for these "extra" senses of Scripture. On the one hand, there were some passages in the Bible that he felt simply could not be literally true, either because they were *absurd* (such as the picture of God, who is spirit, walking about in the garden in Gen 2) or because they were *embarrassing or morally offensive* (such as the suggestion in Gen 16 that Abraham committed polygamy with Hagar). On the other hand, Origen had discerned in his own teaching ministry that biblical narratives seemed to accommodate levels of Christian maturity by offering lessons suited for diverse hearers: for the *immature*, there was the basic story of salvation history; for the *mature*, there were lessons of morality implied in this story; for the truly *wise*, there were hidden hints about Christ and his eternal kingdom. (Even today, most pastors and teachers would recognize that both they and those whom they teach continually find new insights—sometimes deeper, sometimes spurious—when they return to familiar passages.) Virtually the same point is made by Augustine, who adds that since the goal of the whole of Scripture is to cultivate the love of God and the love of one's neighbor, the interpretation of seemingly offensive or obscure passages should always be directed to this goal of love.[1]

Both Origen and Augustine illustrate how the "spiritual" reading of the Bible, in all its variations (three or otherwise), was impelled by a pastoral practice—by the imperative to unlock the authoritative and inspired letter of Scripture and set it loose to function as an agent for transformation in the contemporary world. Indeed, the *three spiritual senses* of allegory, anagogy, and morality were sometimes linked to the *three theological virtues* of faith, hope, and love. In this way, even the most remote and unadorned narrative might be unlocked to serve as a means of teaching Christians *credenda*, *speranda*, and *agenda*: what to believe, what to hope for, and what to love and do. It would be hard to imagine that we have outgrown these pastoral goals today.

The exegesis of the Reformation saw Origen in particular as a villain. Both Luther and Calvin regularly treated him as the supreme example of how allegory subverts the true message of Scripture. For Luther, Calvin, and all the Reformers, the recovery of the "evangelical" or authentic character of Christianity was linked above all to the recovery of an "evangelical" or authentic reading of the Bible. For them, the greatest threat to the authority and function of Scripture was the *false* authority attributed to various traditions and teachings of the medieval church—traditions and teachings that claimed to be apostolic but that had no demonstrable root in the apostolic writings. Significantly, neither Origen nor the allegorical reading of Scripture was necessarily implicated in the Reformers' rejection of human traditions that went against the Word of God. Luther and

Calvin vilified Origen more because they regarded his allegories as capricious and a waste of time. In Calvin's case Origen was guilty of leading his readers away from what Calvin considered to be the true meaning of Scripture and the true task of the interpreter, namely, what is the *intention* of the biblical writer (regardless of whether the "writer" was understood as Moses, Paul, or the Holy Spirit)? One should add, however, that Calvin's interest in the intention of the writer inclined not to psychology but to the sort of rhetorical analysis favored by many humanists and Reformers in his day. So when Calvin sorted out the meaning of sentences and paragraphs by appealing to what the apostle intended, he often stressed less what the apostle intended to *say* than what he intended his words to *effect* in the life of the church at Rome. For Calvin, rhetoric is about *practice*. For Calvin, St. Paul was an inspired rhetor. So is God.

It would also be quite wrong to suppose that Calvin (or any other Reformer) did away with all allegory. It is true that he is not prone to speak overmuch in defense of "allegory," yet even in contexts where Origen is criticized, Calvin can go on to assert that there are crucial allegories to be discovered in Scripture—chief of which are the various allegories or analogies between the people of God in the OT and the church of Christ in the New. For Calvin and many of his colleagues, rhetorical criticism offered a simpler way to explain how old Scriptures could continue to address a new audience. The spiritual senses no longer needed to be mystical or obscure; they could simply be the practical effects intended equally by the Bible's human and divine authors. (Not surprisingly, Calvin usually preferred the more mundane term *analogy* over *allegory*.) Whatever else took place regarding Scripture in the Reformation, interest in the practical and pastoral function of the Bible was amplified, not diminished.

Nor did Calvin do away with tradition. It is true that he refused to regard the extracanonical traditions of the church as on a par with Scripture. But his commitment to *sola scriptura* actually pushed him toward a greater interest in postapostolic Christian writings, not away from it. In 1539, right after Calvin had completed the first revision of the 1536 *Institutes* and his *Commentary on the Epistle to the Romans*, Calvin also wrote a prospectus for a project that he never completed. This was his plan to translate the homilies of John Chrysostom into French.[2] There, Calvin reiterated his criticisms of Origen, but he had much to say in praise of Chrysostom and in defense of the fathers. His comments reveal how he related patristic literature to the authority and function of Scripture. The writings of the church fathers are aids for the reading of Scripture, he says. Indeed, they are resources *provided by the Lord* to serve in tandem with the inward, illuminating work of the Holy Spirit. Such writings are not to be accepted uncritically, of course, but to spurn them would be an act of gross ingratitude. In other words, these writings have been passed down to us by providence for our benefit. Here, Calvin seems to have practiced what he preached. The humanist scholarship of the sixteenth century was constantly producing new editions of ancient sources, including most of the church fathers. Like so many other Reformers, Calvin bought as many of these editions as he could afford. In his later argument with Cardinal Sadoleto, it will be important to Calvin that he can claim the church fathers as Protestant allies—not because the fathers are authorities equal to Scripture, but because they testify that Calvin and the other Reformers were not innovators. In his polemics, the fathers are *allies* for Calvin. In his commentaries, they are also *tutors and colleagues*, part of the process of good exegesis.

To sum up: while the fourfold method of exegesis fell into disrepute among Protestant Reformers and the practice of allegory was certainly transformed, the traditional agenda by no means passed away. Although the terminology that described the practical use of Scripture changed, as did the rationale by which the pastoral and doctrinal functions of Scripture were justified, the medieval quest for an understanding of Scripture that prized its spiritual and practical application was not abandoned. Similarly, while the Reformers denied that the church could claim binding authority for traditions and doctrines seemingly unknown to the apostles or church fathers, their rejection of tradition was not wholesale. The fathers and even some medievals were held in esteem by the Reformers and were regularly consulted in the course of formulating their own theology and exegesis—not as a hobby, but as a matter of principle.

RELATING TRADITIONAL EXEGESIS TO THE CONTEMPORARY WORLD—CASE STUDY ONE: JEPHTHAH'S DAUGHTER

The preceding bit of revisionist history has aimed to raise your opinion of medieval interpreters, most of whom set out not to subvert Scripture but rather to fathom and apply its riches. Both Augustine and Aquinas insisted that while doctrines could be *illustrated* by figurative or allegorical readings, no doctrine could be *established* by anything but the literal sense of a text.[3] Also to be contested is the notion that the Reformers' pursuit of the "literal" sense of Scripture represented the dawning of modern, "objective" historical criticism. It did not. The Reformers' interest in critical history was always tethered to a profound awareness that they were not archaeologists, detached from these curious textual "artifacts," but that they were part of the one and continuous people of God to whom the text of the Bible was and is addressed.

What remains to ask, however, is whether *we* ought to treat Calvin's exegesis as Calvin treated the exegesis of the church fathers: not as having the same authority as the apostles, but as offering us guidance—maybe even providential guidance. By "Calvin's exegesis," of course, I do not mean to single him out. I really mean, should we consult Calvin and the entire tradition of Christian exegesis, particularly the huge body of exegetical writing that we pejoratively call *precritical* exegesis? Can these precritical commentators relate to our contemporary world? Can they somehow augment Scripture? Indeed, do we really need them for anything at all? My answer is yes. But let me speak more boldly than that. Precritical commentators are not just a fine hobby for scholars or pastors, not just an extra decoration for a sermon (although only if we finish our "real" exegesis and have time to spare). Calvin claimed quite a lot when he said such writings were divinely provided for us, and I would like to make a similar claim. Namely, I think there are instances where we learn something from the history of exegesis that we cannot learn from technical exegesis or historical criticism alone. In other words, I think that our exegesis should be shaped not only by the Holy Spirit working in and through the text, not only by the Holy Spirit working in and through our hearts and minds, but also by the Holy Spirit working in and through the history of the church—in and through the history of interpretation. To illustrate this point, I want to offer two case studies: one that I find extremely persuasive and one that gives me some problems.

The first case study derives from my work on the stories of certain OT women, all of whom were marginalized and abused in some way, if not killed. My selection was guided by Phyllis Trible's pioneering lectures, published as *Texts of Terror*—a title that communicates much of the lectures' content. Here, I want to examine the history of the interpretation of Jephthah's daughter. This text interests us for two reasons. On the one hand, her story has been of great interest to feminist readers, many of whom find the message of Judg 11 to be sinister and patriarchal. The intense interest of feminists raises the question of how *this* part of the Bible does or does not carry authority in the contemporary world, and how it does or does not function for *these* contemporaries. On the other hand, her story is as notorious for what it does *not* say as for what it does say. Here, even the cleverest of preachers and the most expert of historical-critical exegetes will be driven to argue many things from silence. Not surprisingly, it is also a story that the lectionaries skip.

The story can be easily outlined. Jephthah was exiled by his brethren, then later sought out to deliver Israel from the Ammonites. The "spirit of the Lord" falls on Jephthah, who then vows that, if victorious, he will offer in sacrifice whatever first greets him on his return. That turns out to be his only child, a daughter, but at her insistence Jephthah fulfills his awful vow. Both the puzzling silences of this story and the interests of feminists are epitomized in the questions routinely raised.[4] One set comes from *traditional interpreters*, for whom the story has raised questions such as these:

(1) How does Jephthah's anointing with the spirit of the Lord relate to his vow? Did one lead to the other? Did God therefore approve of Jephthah's vow? Or was his vow misguided?

(2) What did Jephthah intend to sacrifice? What or whom was he expecting to meet, a sheep? Surely he did not intend a human sacrifice—or did he?
(3) Might Jephthah have been influenced by Abraham's near sacrifice of his only son, Isaac, as a precedent? Might he have expected God to intervene for him as he did for Abraham?

There are additional questions raised by *feminist critics*. Consider these:

(1) Why was Jephthah's daughter killed, when two other sons slated for sacrifice were freed? Isaac is one example, saved when an angel intervened, but there is another story like his. In 1 Sam 14:24–46, King Saul rashly vowed that no one should eat until the Philistines were defeated. Unaware of his father's oath, Jonathan ate some honey and would have been killed had the people of Israel not intervened to ransom him. So why are two *sons* rescued from human sacrifice, but this *daughter* is not? Indeed, why did she not resist or run away?
(2) Why is it that, although it is Jephthah who makes the rash vow, it is his daughter whom he blames? "Alas, my daughter! You have brought me very low; you have become the cause of great trouble to me." This looks suspiciously like "blaming the victim," as if it were the daughter's fault for greeting her father.
(3) How is it fair that Jephthah should be listed among the heroes of faith in Heb 11, despite his cruel and foolish deed, while his faithful and obedient daughter is not listed there and no one even remembers her name?

All interpreters of Judg 11 have to grapple with the silences in this text, but our feminist contemporaries have raised particularly acute questions. For some feminist readers, the story of Jephthah's daughter exemplifies so much indifference to women—on the part of Jephthah, on the part of the biblical narrator, and on the part of a church that ignores this story and others like it—that they would prefer to abandon such a church that clings to such a Bible. The problem of the authority and function of Scripture among *these* contemporaries, who are often among our own parishioners, could scarcely be more seriously registered.

As noted, Judg 11 raises these questions but provides mostly silence. God does not intervene, and there is not even a word to censure Jephthah. The Bible, alas, is virtually silent in the face of the story's obviously distressing—if not patriarchal—developments. It should be all the more surprising, then, to find that the supposedly patriarchal commentators of the distant past were *not* at all silent but were, instead, as distressed as some of our contemporaries. Accordingly, one feminist concern is quickly resolved: the story of Jephthah's daughter was by no means ignored or neglected by precritical commentators. Despite the relatively small number of commentaries on the book of Judges that survive from these sixteen centuries or so, Jephthah's daughter appears with a fair degree of frequency. For this first case study, I will offer three vignettes from the history of interpretation.[5]

Origen: Jephthah's daughter as martyr. The low opinion of Origen held by Luther and Calvin has already been noted, so it seems fair to give equal time to Origen for rebuttal. We do not have Origen's homily on Judg 11, but we do have a passing remark in his comments on the Fourth Gospel. At John 1:29, where the Baptist proclaims that Jesus is "the lamb of God," Origen labors to explain the significance of the symbol and of sacrifices in general. Old Testament sacrifices were like the deaths of martyrs today, he writes, in that both prefigure the death of the Lamb of God. Though it seems cruel of God to demand martyrdom, Origen insists that these deaths do contribute somehow to the defeat of evil. It is here that he comments on Jephthah's daughter. She too was a martyr, for it was by her willing death that Jephthah triumphed over the Ammonites.

I will confess that the first time I read Origen's account, it made me angry. It struck me as artificial, as forcing Jephthah's daughter to recruit Christian martyrs for Origen's own purposes. But as I continued to read, my conscience began to bother me about dismissing him. No one can accuse Origen of being naive about martyrdom. His own father was martyred when Origen was but a teenager. We are told that the young Origen was stopped from following his father only because his mother had hidden all the boy's clothes. When Origen was fifty, persecution resumed, and he responded by composing *An Exhortation to Martyrdom*, perhaps the best-known treatise on martyrdom ever written. And you may know that Origen, too, practiced what he preached: his own life was ended some twenty years later, as an effect of the torture he suffered under Emperor Decius.

What is most remarkable about Origen, however, is his clear denial that martyrdom is a visible triumph of any kind! Martyrs do contribute to the defeat of evil, but this is not something we see. It is something we believe. Indeed, were we to believe what we *see*, we would have to conclude that God enjoys it when Christians suffer cruel and senseless deaths. No, the martyr's crown is visible only to faith: the true significance of these cruel deaths remains, for now, a secret known only to God.

Consequently, when Origen admits that the death of Jephthah's daughter looks and feels senseless, he's not treating her as just a problem to be solved. No: he is filling in the silences, extrapolating from Israel's defeat of the Ammonites and the selfless virtue of the daughter in order to make sense of the story. Amazingly, Origen (himself a would-be martyr) admits that martyrdom—all martyrdom—looks senseless. And God, too, seems heartless and cruel. But where sight fails, faith thrives. The martyr's crown may be visible only to faith, but it *is* visible to faith.

What we see in Origen, then, is his clear recognition of the problematic silences in this text—a problem that the text itself does not resolve. Origen draws on his best theological instincts to find some sense, asserting that this daughter did not die in vain—even though that *is* the way it seems. Whatever you think of Origen's exegesis, he has not neglected Jephthah's daughter. Neither has he failed to praise her virtue, weigh her death, or mourn her passing—even as he commends her as a saint beloved by God and somehow also connected to Christ.

Denis the Carthusian: The climax of the typological reading. Origen's account is remarkably nonallegorical. Even though he wandered into his detour on Jephthah's daughter as a way to explain the *symbolism* of Christian martyrdom, he ended by dealing fairly directly with the literal daughter and her literal, if puzzling, martyrdom. Jephthah's daughter enters the realm of nonliteral exegesis only insofar as she serves as an example or type of devotion to God against evil.

However, as you might expect, other interpretations of Jephthah's daughter were more properly allegorical and typological. The longest and most influential of these was the huge treatise offered by Augustine on Jephthah in his *Questions on the Heptateuch*, many aspects of which passed into Isidore of Seville and on into the *Ordinary Gloss*—the twelfth century compilation that was the basic Bible commentary for preachers in the Middle Ages. Nonetheless, we must bypass the extensive remarks of Augustine, whose typological interpretation was neatly interwoven with a rigorous ethical analysis of the text and the problem of rash vows. Instead, for a second vignette, I want to recount the views of a Carthusian monk named Denis, who wrote in the middle of the fifteenth century, virtually at the close of the Middle Ages.

It is typical for Denis to offer two full expositions of any given chapter of the Bible: one will comment on the literal or historical sense of the text, while the other will comment on the "mystical" or spiritual meaning. Both are usually of interest. When he expounds *the literal meaning* of the story, Denis displays not only a good deal of sympathy for Jephthah's daughter, but also a remarkable sensitivity to the daughter's suffering and virtue. Three points may be noted. First, he seems to understand the value to the daughter of being surrounded by her companions—the value, that is, of the companionship of women with other women. Second, Denis sees and dislikes the way the father blames his daughter for "deceiving" him, and he defends her from such blame. Third, he does not hesitate to compare the daughter's goodness and obedience to that of Isaac and again underscores her innocent suffering.

Denis's *mystical exposition* is also rich. He is clearly aware of a traditional typology, popularized by Augustine, according to which Jephthah represented Christ and his daughter represented the flesh or humanity that Christ offered as a sacrifice. But he also likes an alternative, whereby the daughter represents not merely the flesh of Christ but Christ himself. What is striking about Denis's adaptation of the latter typology, however, is the way he illustrates it with five biblical references to the sufferings of the Messiah. Among the texts that he applies equally to Jephthah's daughter and the Messiah are, first of all, Rom 8:32: "God did not spare his own Son, but gave him up for us all." He then moves on to quote Isa 53 as it might have been spoken by God the Father to the suffering servant: "I have stricken him for the transgression of my people." There are also references to two messianic psalms, Pss 69 and 88, as well as to Acts 3:18.

Not everyone will like or embrace Denis's typological reading of Jephthah's daughter as a figure of the sacrifice and suffering of Jesus Christ. However, the relevance of the history of interpretation for the contemporary reading of this text is not to get readers to adopt this particular typological reading. What is rather to be appreciated is Denis's sympathy for Jephthah's daughter and her sufferings, as well as the instinct by which he tries to relate her sufferings and sacrifice to what happens on the cross. Clearly, he is not afraid to confront the ironies or continuities between Jephthah's daughter and Jesus Christ. Is there something to learn from Denis's example?

For an answer, let us confer with our feminist contemporaries. The most striking feature of *Texts of Terror* is the way each chapter is prefaced by an illustration—a pen-and-ink tombstone for each woman, bearing an epitaph from Scripture. These epitaphs are all christological or messianic, and the verse Trible chose for Hagar is from Isa 53—the exact text Denis applied to Jephthah's daughter. Whatever Trible intended by these gravestones and epitaphs, many other feminists have wondered why the church has cared so much about the sufferings of Jesus Christ yet neglected the similar sufferings of many biblical women. The question begs for a reply. The good news is that Denis offers one. When the Bible's silence is juxtaposed with the trenchant questions of feminist readers, it surely makes a difference to know how the instincts of the Christian tradition—here, in the person of Denis—have also lingered compassionately over what Jephthah's daughter endured and have drawn a similar connection between her suffering and our only comfort in life and death. One might be so bold as to say that the if the silence of Scripture seems dysfunctional, taken on its own, the history of interpretation may offer a silence-dispelling supplement, if not a corrective.

Jephthah's daughter among the Reformers. A final vignette may be conflated from three insights from a variety of Reformers. Although they are all more concerned with the ethics of Jephthah than with the text's symbolism, their interpretations are neither cold nor detached.

The first insight comes from *Martin Luther*, who marveled at this tragedy of errors, wondering how Jephthah could have been so ill-informed. Equally marvelous to him, however, is the fact that the sacrifice was actually carried out. If Jonathan escaped his father's vow unharmed, Luther argued, Jephthah's daughter deserved no less. The same argument is raised by feminist writers.

A second insight derives from a chorus of Reformers, including the Lutheran *Johann Brenz* and the Reformed writers *Conrad Pellican* and *Peter Martyr Vermigli*. All three condemned Jephthah's vow. While they praised the daughter for her obedience and piety, all three also underscored that no daughter is ever obliged to submit to such a vow—again, a concern of contemporary feminists. In other words, Jephthah's daughter could have said no or run away.

Finally, it is worth looking to the early seventeenth century and a sermon preached by the Puritan *Richard Rogers* sometime before 1615. He had only the highest possible words of praise for the courage, obedience, and grace of Jephthah's daughter. But what makes his remarks even more striking is his unexpected allusion to Heb 11. Earlier I noted the irony, registered by many recent critics, that Jephthah should be praised in Heb 11:32 while his daughter is forgotten. Rogers, however, looked forward to Heb 11:34 and proclaimed that its praise for those "who by faith grew strong" surely applies to Jephthah's daughter. In effect, this Puritan preacher gave to Jephthah's daughter that place on the roll of heroes that she had previously been denied.

We will return to the implications of this case study later on, but the most important observation needs to be underscored before moving on. In my opinion, the case of Jephthah's daughter successfully illustrates how the authority and pastoral function of Scripture may be enhanced precisely in the face of contemporary needs and challenges by bringing to light the history of how the Bible has been received and interpreted.

RELATING TRADITIONAL EXEGESIS TO THE CONTEMPORARY WORLD—CASE STUDY TWO: THE IMPRECATIONS IN THE PSALMS

We may turn now to a more problematic case study. For most of this year, I have been working on a project to make accessible the history of exegesis of a number of neglected texts. As mentioned earlier, I prefer passages that are difficult or offensive because they force commentators to disclose something about their relationship to exegetical tradition, about how they make their exegetical judgments, or about how they relate Scripture to their own culture and context. All these reasons led me to look at how commentators have addressed the imprecations (the curses) in the Psalms. I quickly discovered that it would be hard to research this question and survey this huge body of literature in a single lifetime. So I have limited my examination to a few well-known writers and a few of the better known imprecatory psalms. Let me sketch the problem, then turn to my findings.

Anyone who has read the Psalms knows these jarring outbursts. The ending of Ps 137 is notorious: "Happy shall they be" who take the children of Babylon and "dash them against the rock." Maybe you also recall the picturesque but brutal rant of Ps 58: "O God, . . . let them be like the snail that dissolves into slime; like the untimely birth that never sees the sun. . . . The righteous will rejoice when they see vengeance done; they will bathe their feet in the blood of the wicked." The problem may seem obvious but there are complications. First, it is easy to see why lectionaries just skip these verses as too harsh for the ears of worshipers. Yet other factors drive us back to these verses, particularly when the NT puts many psalms of lament on the lips of Jesus—including the vehement Ps 109, which appears in Acts as a prophecy of Judas's betrayal and his eventual replacement by Matthias. And yet the same Messiah whose kingship and sufferings are foreseen in these psalms also preached that we should love our enemies and pray for our persecutors (Matt 5:44). Obviously, there is quite a discrepancy between the footwashing Jesus commands in John 13 and the one called for in Ps 58! Finally, we have been called by our contemporaries—including some well-known commentators on the Psalms, but also feminists and voices from the third world—to recognize that the psalms of lament, which harbor many of the imprecations, are implicitly pleas for justice and equity.[6] As such, are they not timely for our own day? The Psalter today is like the rope in one of those circular tug-of-war games, pulled in many directions at once.

Is there any wisdom to be found among past readers of the Psalms? As you might expect, my answer is yes—but a *qualified* yes. In fact, precritical commentators offer some commendably balanced approaches to the curses in the Psalms, and they are troubled and torn by the same issues that perplex us. In order to keep my remarks brief, I will offer a synoptic account of what the church fathers say, then take a quick look at Calvin.

Imprecations in the Church Fathers: three approaches. I described earlier how the allegorical method was propelled in part by Christian worries over texts that were embarrassing or unedifying. The curses in the Psalms were certainly in this category, but the fathers were as aware as we are of the tension between the psalmists' example of cursing one's enemies and Jesus' command to love them. Consequently, all of the fathers found some way to ameliorate these curses, regardless of whether they favored allegory, typology, or literal exegesis. Let me illustrate their approaches.

Origen often employed a moralistic, allegorical approach, and he was widely copied. Accordingly, the captivity spoken of in Ps 137 represents *our* captivity by sin and Satan. The "little ones" of Babylon are our own sinful desires, depicted while they are still small. Happy then, is the Christian who dashes these desires to death before they grow much larger. Augustine develops this a step further, suggesting that we ourselves cannot kill these vices, but they will die if we dash them against the rock. And, as he knew from 1 Cor 10:4, "this rock was Christ." We may be inclined to think that none of this was in the mind of the psalmist, but the moral that Origen and Augustine found here was true just the same. In effect, they gave their hearers permission to use the curses, but to do so exclusively against the only unambiguous enemies anyone can ever know:

namely, against one's own sin. It might be added that C. S. Lewis was attracted to this reading strategy.

Origen's approach was typical of a whole school of allegorical interpreters that hailed from the great city of Alexandria. These allegorists, however, had many rivals to the north in another great city—Antioch in Asia Minor. The commentators of Antioch who wrote on the Psalms included Diodore of Tarsus, Theodore of Mopsuestia, John Chrysostom, and Theodoret of Cyrus. For them, the historical, original, or intended meaning of Scripture was paramount; allegory was an unwanted fabrication. Accordingly, their list of messianic psalms was governed strictly by what the NT authorized, and their homiletical applications could be rather spare. Both Chrysostom and Theodoret approached the curses so as to minimize the offense; one suspects they were also concerned to minimize the likelihood that their congregations would imitate the psalmist. In any case, the psalmists' words are not to be taken as curses, but as prophecies or as timeless wisdom. For Chrysostom, the curses are really predictions, couched as curses for rhetorical effect. Indeed, they signal how "God's unspeakable rage" always hangs over "such people," who bring this end on themselves.[7] For Theodoret, Ps 137 requires neither a moral nor an allegory but only a historical explanation of the psalmist's outburst as an anticipation of how Babylonian atrocities would be repaid against their own children when the Persian king Cyrus defeated Babylon and freed the Jewish exiles from their captors (in 539 B.C.).[8]

If we survey the fathers who took a more typological approach, we see some of the same moves recur. Augustine will serve as an example here. His exegesis of the Psalms was usually typological or christological, for he felt that Christ was the subject of the entire psalter. Nonetheless, Christ fulfilled diverse roles in the Psalms.[9] Sometimes Christ is spoken to or about, while in other texts Christ speaks in his own voice, either as the suffering, crucified one or as the triumphant and resurrected Lord. As the "second Adam," Christ could also speak in the psalms both to or in the name of fallen or redeemed humanity—that is, Christ can speak to or as his body, the church.

The flexibility of Augustine's reading enabled him to deal with the psalmists' curses in diverse ways. We have already seen how he could turn these curses against the "interior" enemies of the Christian. But Christ has other enemies worthy of cursing as well, including heretics, schismatics, and persecutors. Against such declared enemies of Christ, one would think, there is no reason not to utter psalm-like curses, but Augustine insists that what look like prayers or curses against an enemy are really prophecies or predictions of divine judgment. Nonetheless, there *is* a way Christians can wish for vengeance. In Ps 139:22, the psalmist (speaking as the body of Christ) declares his "perfect hatred" for the enemies of God. Mindful of the words of Jesus, Augustine reminds his hearers of what is a commonplace even today, that we should hate the sin but love the sinner. The sort of vengeance Christians are supposed to seek, then, consists in their enemies' *conversion*, not destruction. To be sure, these prayers for "conversion-vengeance" also warn of the just judgments of God, whether they come sooner or later. However, "our enemy is to be loved in such a way that we are not dissatisfied with the divine justice that punishes him; yet our satisfaction in that punitive justice must derive not from the bad consequences for the offender but from the goodness of the judge."[10] In theory, then, Augustine seems temperate: Christ's church, like Christ himself, does have real enemies. But *our* laments and grief should lead to prayers for our enemies, not their execration.

These patristic approaches have three things in common. First, these readings of the imprecatory psalms are held in check by the words of Jesus, which restrain our anger, call for us to love our enemies, and urge us to examine ourselves. Second, they are all aware that God has enemies, Jesus had and has enemies, and these enemies—spiritual and fleshly—have savaged the church and earned divine wrath (whether or not wrath takes the form of cursing). Third, there is reason to wonder if the meekness of patristic theory fails in practice. Athanasius's exegesis of the Psalms often mirrored Origen's in turning the imprecations inward. But if you read the controversial writings or letters of Athanasius, it is clear that he knows who God's other enemies are: they are Arius and his heretical allies, and Athanasius is quite capable of using the Psalms to heighten his own attack on them. Augustine scarcely differs. In his exegesis of the Psalms, it is the Donatists who take the fall as the enemies of God. And if Augustine restrains himself from cursing them, he did more than *pray* for their conversion: he eventually ratified the use of force to *compel* their conversion. The fathers furnish other examples, too. One would be remiss not to mention the common refrains against not only Judas as the enemy of Christ but against all the Jews, then and now.

Calvin and the imprecations. I will return in a moment to what one could call the problem of over-contexualizing or over-contemporizing the curses, but we should take at least a quick look at the Reformation exegesis of the Psalms. I will mention here only Calvin, who introduces a helpful distinction under an unlikely guise. Owing to his avoidance of allegory, Calvin will probably prove more attractive to many readers today. But Calvin is quite capable of recognizing christological references, usually those cited in the NT, and he is also inclined to characterize David in many instances as acting or speaking as a representative of Christ—both in his kingship and in his laments and sufferings. Calvin's exposition of the imprecations relies heavily on this link between David and Christ to maintain both its theological and its historical character.[11]

Calvin does not hesitate to admit that the imprecations are harsh. Prayers such as Ps 79:6 ("Pour out thy fury upon the heathen") seem "inconsistent with the rule of charity."[12] The faithful ought to seek unbelievers' salvation, not their destruction. How, then, can such prayers for revenge stand in the Scriptures? For Calvin, the solution lies in the office, character, and discernment of the psalmist—usually, David. As for *office*, Calvin claims (in Ps 41:10, "raise me up, that I may repay them") that David acted lawfully not only as king and judge, and thus not as a private person, but also as representative of Christ. As for David's *character*, Calvin is sure that, again as representing the person of Christ, David "cherished in his heart pure and holy affections," neither indulging "his own angry spirit" nor speaking "from an impulse of the flesh."[13] As for the psalmist's *discernment*, Calvin frequently imputes to David the ability to distinguish which of his or God's enemies are beyond repentance. Only those who are incapable of repentance—in other words, those truly numbered among the eternally reprobate—are liable to the kinds of curses we find in the psalms. Calvin does not mind working backwards here: wherever he finds such vehement curses, there he assumes the psalmist has discerned, and now declares, the outcome of divine judgment. Thus Calvin reads Ps 137 as simply a further indication of the punishments against Edom promised in Ezekiel, Jeremiah, and Obadiah.[14]

Calvin often reformulated his threefold characterization of David for congregational use (so to speak) in Geneva. The point to be taken was that if anyone wishes to echo David's curses against his enemies, one should also possess David's calling and piety. In other words, prayers of cursing are not to be employed by private persons for personal vengeance. Such prayers are to be offered only on behalf of the whole church, usually by those who are called by office to offer prayers. In addition, one must be free from angry passion and possess the wisdom of the Holy Spirit. Calvin often cited Luke 9:54, where Jesus rebuked James and John for wishing to call down fire from heaven upon the Samaritans. Christians should pray for their enemies, avoiding misplaced zeal,[15] for today's enemies may repent tomorrow. Unless you know that your enemies are reprobate and beyond hope, you may not pray for their destruction.[16] (Of course, as anyone who knows much about Calvin's teaching on predestination will recall, while the elect may be assured of their own election, *no one* can know the reprobation of another—not even of oneself.)

Nonetheless, even if we are all but disqualified from mimicking the curses in the Bible, they remain good for us to read and they hold forth benefits for us.

> By proclaiming *vengeance against the ungodly*, he subdues and restrains our perverse inclinations, which might lead us to injure a fellow-creature. By imparting *comfort to us*, he mitigates and moderates our sorrow, so that we patiently endure the ills which they inflict upon us. . . . And as *we* cannot distinguish between the elect and the reprobate, it is our duty to pray for *all* who trouble us; to desire the salvation of all; and even to care for the welfare of every individual. At the same time, if our hearts are pure and peaceful, this will not prevent us from freely appealing to God's judgment, that he may cut off the finally impenitent.[17]

There are plenty of Christians, even in churches with Calvinist roots, for whom predestination is a strange and threatening notion. Here is a fine opportunity to see it used as Calvin intended: to remind Christians of their need for faith, humility, and neighbor-love, even when one's neighbor is unjust; but to remind them even more that their heavenly Father reigns, and injustice is doomed.

Space will not allow me to add further details on the history of the interpretation of the imprecatory psalms. Let me skip to the key question: *What do we learn from the history of exegesis here that we might not learn from exegesis alone?* I would focus on two things in particular. First, precritical commentators overwhelmingly ratify some of the most significant trends in grappling with the imprecatory psalms today—in particular, the belief that these parts of the Bible should be an active part of the church's teaching and worship resources rather than neglected or censured, as the lectionary has done. However, precritical commentators also corroborate the instincts of contemporary interpreters that these parts of the Psalter in particular are to be read with one's other eye on the words of Jesus about loving our enemies. (Calvin's implication, that only Jesus Christ is truly qualified to pray the imprecations, is explicitly echoed by William Holladay.) In other words, no one I have read wants to trust or encourage Christians at random to emulate the sort of anger and vindictiveness that we read in the Psalms. There is comfort to be found here, but one might argue that the imprecations are best used defensively, not offensively.

This remark leads to a second observation—one that continues to make me uncomfortable with some of these precritical commentators. Despite all their warnings about praying for one's enemies rather than seeking retribution, and despite the common emphasis on using these curses as an occasion for confronting one's own internal enemies, there is still a worrisome tendency among Christian writers not to practice what they preach. I noted earlier how Athanasius and Augustine found living counterparts of the enemies of Christ among the Arians and Donatists of their own day. There were few precritical commentators, Reformers included, who did not identify contemporary Jews as the enemies of Christ. And one could add details about how the psalm-loving Huguenots were quite successful in terrorizing their Roman Catholic opponents precisely in the way they used some of these psalms to rally the troops on the battlefield itself.[18] I would not imagine for an instant that any contemporary society is likely to do better on this score, particularly when the line between biblical Christianity and civil religion is so easily and frequently crossed. But once we have noticed the speck in the eye of precritical commentators, we ought to attend more seriously to the log in our own. That, too, is a benefit of reading these old commentaries.

CONCLUDING REFLECTIONS

This essay has argued that contemporary efforts to articulate the authority of Scripture and to restore or enhance its function among the churchgoers of our day will do better to attend to past readings of Scripture than to ignore them. To this end, I have offered two case studies in the history of interpretation—Jephthah's daughter and the imprecatory psalms. To be sure, there are many other cases that could be accessed without too much effort, even as there are multiple projects underway to translate patristic, medieval, and Reformation exegetical writings. There has never been a better time (in the English-speaking world, at least) to be a lay reader of Christian tradition. Let me conclude with just a few summary theses.

First, we can learn something from the history of exegesis that we do not learn from exegesis alone. When I say this, I do *not* mean to commend the writings of centuries past as a sort of undiscovered "biblical illustrator," a trove of sound bites to spice up sermons. What I mean, rather, is that the history of interpretation reminds us that the most problematic passages of the Bible *have always been* problematic. In the case of some passages, such as the story of Jephthah's daughter, the Bible is simply silent where readers yearn for an editorial comment. The history of interpretation—that is to say, the church—speaks to this silence in ways we can admire, perhaps even emulate. In John 16:13 Jesus told his disciples that the Holy Spirit would guide them into all truth. It is refreshing to find instances in post-biblical Christian history where that really seems to have happened!

Second, some of the sharpest contemporary challenges to the authority of Scripture are themselves challenged by the history of interpretation. My own expertise on this point pertains to challenges that come from some recent feminist critics, particularly claims that the church has always neglected women and perpetuated patriarchy in its use of Scripture. I am not suggesting that the ancient or medieval church was full of closeted feminists. Nor would I deny that there are texts and issues that traditional commentators fumbled badly. But there are also texts and issues that cast precritical commentators in a remarkably good light, as paying closer attention to issues of gender and justice than we would ever have supposed. We can learn from their exegetical findings, but we can and should do more. These writers are our ancestors, our brothers and sisters in Christ. Christian culture today—Christian identity and practice—is formed, in part, by embracing and owning our kin.

Third, bringing the history of a text's exegesis into the pulpit is a way to ground one's own exegesis in the whole church, as well as a way to reconnect congregations with the larger household of faith. It strikes me as very American to want to figure out every text on your own, to claim no help from the commentaries. But why do we want to do that? Post-moderns can easily suffer from the malaise of rootlessness, from a quest for identity that is adolescently obsessed with individuality and newness. Hebrews 12 tells us that we are surrounded by a great cloud of witnesses—in other words, by the community of faithful pilgrims who have preceded us. Newness we may need, and change in our practices of witness and worship, but it is precipitous to change the way we have always done things until we understand *how* we came to always do them this way. I am not arguing against change here. What I am saying, instead, is that an informed appreciation for the *diversity* of past readings and "practices" of Scripture can actually help us see how the authority of Scripture can function in and through a diversity of perspective.

Fourth, even where the exegetical findings and practices of the past cannot be appropriated, there are other lessons to learn from precritical exegesis. It requires little reflection to realize that the history of exegesis is often also the history of the misuse of Scripture. The use of the Bible to undergird slavery is an easy example, recently recounted by Stephen Haynes's book on *Noah's Curse*.[19] But I would rather leave you with a positive example. In Paul Wilson's recent work on preaching, he commends a cautious and thoughtful retrieval of the fourfold pattern of exegesis as a tool for the preparation of sermons.[20] The foundation of his recommendation is his recognition that *allegory* really is just an extended metaphor, and preachers and readers are always in search of metaphors and analogies to connect them to the text. I would like to make a point that is complementary, but different. Origen explicitly said that he looked for allegorical readings as a way to avoid offenses found in the literal reading of a text. That might look like a dysfunctional way to approach Scripture, but from a historical perspective, it may prove functional for us. That is to say, having read lots and lots of these allegories, I have come to think that even when they are forced or inappropriate, they may still be useful to us at a secondary level, insofar as they signal what could be called "exegetical distress." Typologies and allegories are sometimes an interpreter's way of signaling disturbances in the text: stunning silences, perhaps, or a moral problem desperately in need of damage control. Interpreters today often stumble over the same problems, whether uncovered by historical criticism or by the more "readerly" approaches. However much we properly worry about the hermeneutical legitimacy of allegory, an appreciation for its varied functions can help us understand the history of exegesis, the common cause we share with even our precritical forebears, and, indirectly, the text itself and the theological formation that the text should serve.

NOTES

1. Origen makes his point in *On First Principles* 4.2–3; Augustine addresses the issue in *On Christian Doctrine* 3.

2. See W. Ian P. Hazlett, "Calvin's Latin Preface to His Proposed French Edition of Chrysostom's Homilies: Translation and Commentary," in *Humanism and Reform: The Church in Europe, England, and Scotland* (ed. James Kirk; Oxford: Blackwell, 1991), 129–150. For a fuller discussion of Calvin, see my chapter, "Calvin as a Biblical Interpreter," in *The Cambridge Companion to John Calvin* (ed. Donald K. McKim; Cambridge: Cambridge University Press, 2004).

3. Aquinas makes this point in *Summa Theologiæ* I.1.10 *ad* 1, explicitly crediting Augustine (e.g., Epistle 93.8.24).

4. Some of the material in this section is drawn from my essay, "Preaching Texts of Terror in the Book of Judges: How Does the History of Interpretation Help?" *Calvin Theological Journal* 37 (2002): 49–61.

5. Full bibliographic details for the following discussion of Origen, Denis, and my sampling of Reformers can be found in *Writing the Wrongs: Women of the Old Testament among Biblical Commentators from Philo through the Reformation* (New York: Oxford University Press, 2001), pp. 113–114, 152–163, and 169–171.

6. See, for example, William L. Holladay, *The Psalms through Three Thousand Years: Prayerbook of a Cloud of Witnesses* (Minneapolis: Fortress, 1993), 293–300, and the sources noted there.

7. Chrysostom, *Commentary on the Psalms* 139 (2 vols.; Brookline, Mass.: Holy Cross Orthodox Press, 1998), 2:261, italics original.

8. Theodoret, *Commentary on the Psalms* 137.6 (Fathers of the Church 102:324).

9. I am indebted here to Michael Fiedrowicz's introduction to Maria Boulding's ongoing translation of Augustine's commentary for *The Works of Saint Augustine* (Hyde Park, N.Y.: New City Press, 2000–), esp. *Works of Saint Augustine* 15:43–65.

10. Augustine, Exposition of Psalm 79:10 (*Works of St. Augustine* 18:137); see also his remarks on Ps 140:10.

11. In my discussion of Calvin, I have been helped by the recent work of Paul Mbunga Mpindi, "Calvin's Hermeneutics of the Imprecations of the Psalms," (Ph.D. dissertation, Calvin Theological Seminary, 2003).

12. Calvin, *Commentary on Psalms* 79:6 (CTS edition 3:287).

13. Calvin, *Commentary on Psalms* 41:10 (CTS edition 2:123–124).

14. Calvin, *Commentary on Psalms* 137:7 (CTS edition 5:196).

15. Calvin, *Commentary on Psalms* 69:22 (CTS edition 3:67).

16. Calvin, *Commentary on Psalms* 79:10 (CTS edition 3:292–293), 109:6 (CTS edition 4:276).

17. Calvin, *Commentary on Psalms* 109:16 (CTS edition 4:283, altered).

18. See W. Stanford Reid, "The Battle Hymns of the Lord: Calvinist Psalmody of the Sixteenth Century," in *Sixteenth Century Essays and Studies* (ed. Carl S. Meyer; St. Louis: Foundation for Reformation Research, 1971), 36–54.

19. Stephen R. Haynes, *Noah's Curse: The Biblical Justification of American Slavery* (New York: Oxford University Press, 2002).

20. Paul Scott Wilson, *God Sense: Reading the Bible for Preaching* (Nashville: Abingdon, 2001).

RESPONSE TO THOMPSON

MICHAEL PASQUARELLO III

I want to express my deep appreciation to Professor Thompson for a stimulating and enjoyable paper. It will be obvious that I share a number of his vocational interests since I too was trained as a historical theologian in addition to serving in pastoral ministry for 18 years prior to teaching. My field of study is homiletic history, in particular, the preaching tradition from the Fathers to the Reformers. In my work I look for ways that preachers from our Christian past might guide us to see how the biblical narrative engages the contemporary church, and through the life and mission of the church engages the world.

To begin, I want to call attention to the paper's concluding reflections, and for the sake of our discussion I will gloss Thompson's conclusions in the form of questions.

(1) We can learn something from the history of exegesis that we do not learn from exegesis alone. *Is it sufficient, or even acceptable, to limit the scope of our reflection and consideration to contemporary exegetes and exegetical work?*

(2) Some of the sharpest contemporary challenges to the authority of Scripture are themselves challenged by the history of interpretation. *How willing are we to expose our assumptions to the challenge and wisdom of the past?*

(3) Bringing the history of a text's exegesis into the pulpit is a way to ground one's own exegesis in the whole church, as well as a way to reconnect congregations with the larger household of faith. *Is the thinness of much contemporary preaching and church life related to our ignorance of, or even deep prejudice against, the exegetical tradition?*

(4) Even when the exegetical findings and practices of the past cannot be appropriated, there are other lessons to learn from precritical exegesis. *Have we been too hasty in our dismissal of the history of interpretation because it does not always accommodate our most pressing problems or interests?*

I would like to push these reflections further in our discussion by asking you to consider if it is even possible to arrive at a contemporary understanding or understandings of the authority and function of Scripture without seriously engaging our Christian past. For example, John Henry Newman, writing in *A Grammar of Assent*, asserts the importance of imitating the character and practical wisdom demonstrated by wise predecessors:

> Instead of trusting logical science, we must trust persons, namely those who by long acquaintance with their subject have a right to judge. And if we wish ourselves to share in their convictions and the grounds of them, we must follow their history, and learn as they have learned. We must . . . depend on practice and experience more than on reasoning . . . by following this we may . . . rightly lean upon ourselves, directing ourselves by our own moral and intellectual judgment, not by our skill in argumentation.[1]

In response to Thompson's paper, I want to suggest that without a strong sense of vocation that we have been called to an ecclesial practice situated within a particular tradition which gives it life and purpose, and which is embodied by salutary exemplars, we are simply left homeless.

In a recent work, *Theology and Action: After Theory in Christian Ethics*, Charles Pinches has discussed at length such homeless behavior as those words or actions of which it is meaningful to ask, "What on earth could that person be saying or doing?" Pinches argues that for an action or activity, let us say exegesis and preaching or notions such as the authority and function of Scripture, to be intelligible, that is, a deliberative, moral activity, it requires a home; it must find its place in a whole way of life or a "narrative" in which it makes sense.[2] I believe this is what Thompson has so admirably done in his paper. He has helped us to see that we are simply at a loss to make any meaningful sense of human activities such as exegesis and preaching that do not fit into any recognizable human narratives, which I fear is the case for many Christians, congregations, and their pastors. Moreover, finding a home for our practices of Scripture cannot simply amount to locating them in the characteristics of a particular personality according to his or her own preferences or decisions, which, however, has become standard practice in liberal cultures that privilege individual choice and consumption, a prevalent view throughout the contemporary church.

Thompson has invited us to remember by means of his brief case studies and accompanying commentary that the church is a particular community that describes interpretation, speech, and action within the tradition of a people whose life is constituted by Scripture and therefore constitutive of what we mean by Holy Scripture. It is an ecclesial culture characterized by a peculiar language, wisdom, and way of life in which certain patterns of activity are faithfully and meaningfully performed. We see this exemplified in his descriptions of patristic, medieval, and Reformation practices. As Tom Long comments in *The Witness of Preaching:*

> When the preacher goes to the Scripture, new ground is not being broken. The church has been to this text before—many times—and a theological tradition, is, in part, the church's memory of past encounters with this and other biblical texts. A theologically informed interpreter of Scripture enters the text guided by a map drawn and refined by those who have come to this place before. Coming to a text from a theological tradition, the interpreter arrives not as a disoriented stranger but as a pilgrim returning to familiar land, recognizing old landmarks and thereby alert for new and previously unseen wonders.[3]

It is precisely at this point that I am most appreciative of Thompson's emphasis on both the theological and pastoral function of the history of interpretation, which in my view is the practice which must be recovered in order to find our way forward. For despite moral imperfections and confession differences displayed by the figures discussed in this paper, they saw themselves and their work as situated within a larger world of Trinitarian faith and practice, a living tradition that provided their vocabulary, shaped their imaginations, and formed their life. Despite changing circumstances and conditions, this ecclesial world remained the natural habitat for interpreting, speaking, and obeying Scripture. The Bible was the book of the church, and the church was a people of the book. The use of the Bible shaped and was shaped by Christian doctrine, worship, and life. The authority and function of Scripture was constituted within a larger theological world that we must inhabit if we hope to share in its wisdom.

NOTES

1. John Henry Newman, *An Essay in Aid of a Grammar of Assent* (ed. Ian T. Ker; Oxford: Clarendon, 1985), 220–221.

2. Charles R. Pinches, *Theology and Action: After Theory in Christian Ethics* (Grand Rapids: Eerdmans, 2002), 158–159.

3. Thomas G. Long, *The Witness of Preaching* (Louisville: Westminster/John Knox, 1989), 53.

THE AUTHORITY OF THE BIBLE: A NEW TESTAMENT PERSPECTIVE

MORNA D. HOOKER

A snippet of conversation on the radio, overheard by chance one day recently, focused my mind on the problem of the authority of the Bible. A man who firmly believed that the sun moved round the earth was being interviewed. Why did he hold this view, he was asked? The answer was that he based his whole life and philosophy on the Bible. So for an explanation of the universe, he turned first of all to Gen 1. Blithely ignoring the statement that God's first action had been to create light, and that light had been separated from darkness, night from day, on the very first day of creation, he observed that the earth had been created on the second day, and that it was not until the fourth day that (somewhat belatedly!) God had created sun, moon and stars, and had placed the sun in the dome of heaven to provide light to the earth. In this scheme, the sun clearly goes round the earth.

As far as this man was concerned, that was the end of the discussion. For him, everything was based on the Bible, so that it dictated even his understanding of science. Reminded that the Roman Catholic Church had recently, centuries after the event, apologized to Galileo for condemning his views, he remarked that the church had been right at the time, and that the apology had been a mistake.

Written centuries before modern scientific discoveries, the Bible reflects the views of a different age. In order to take its teaching seriously, this man clearly feels it necessary to deny the discoveries and views of the modern world. For him, the Bible is locked into a time capsule, and he is in effect imprisoned in it. Ironically, his very devotion to the teaching of the Bible makes it irrelevant to the world of today.

How does the Bible itself assist us with the problem of "the authority of Scripture"? If the biblical books have any kind of authority for Christians today, then the attitude of our NT writers to their Scriptures is relevant to our quest. Since they rarely referred directly to the question of authority, however,[1] we need to look at the way in which they handled Scripture. If we are to understand their approach, we need to remember that their worldview too was shaped by biblical teaching—which in their case meant, of course, the Jewish Scriptures. Their starting point was the faith in God and in his promises set out in what we call the OT. For the early Christians it was axiomatic that God was the creator of the universe, that he had entered into a covenant relationship with his people Israel, and that one day the world would be restored to peace and harmony and God's rule would be obeyed by everyone. The authority of Scripture was self-evident. What they needed to understand and explain was how their new experience of what God had done in the life, death, and resurrection of Jesus Christ fitted into these beliefs.

Some might have argued—and indeed they did!—that the new experience and the old beliefs were irreconcilable. In that case, they must either reject the Christian gospel, as did many of the Jews, or abandon the writings of the OT, as did Marcion and his followers in the second century. But our NT writers all insist that there is no conflict between old and new. In their various ways, the four evangelists all show how the "good news" about Jesus is the continuation of God's purposes for Israel and for the world. For our purposes, however, it is perhaps best to concentrate on the teaching of Paul, who approaches the problem by using theological argument. Even in Paul, however, the question of "the authority of Scripture" is approached obliquely, rather than head-on, since for him, as for all Jews, the authority of Scripture is axiomatic and does not need to be discussed. Like all Jews his faith and understanding of the world were shaped by the Scriptures. Writing primarily to *Gentile* Christians in Rome, he reminds them that "The Scriptures written long ago were all written for our instruction" (Rom 15:4). The gospel that he proclaims was "announced beforehand in sacred Scriptures through the prophets" (Rom 1:2), and it is to those Scriptures and the words of the prophets that he turns in order to expound it. If we want to understand how Paul understands the authority of Scripture, then we must see how he *uses* it; in particular, we must look at how he relates the teaching of what we call "the law" with the new life that has come to him through Christ. I shall concentrate on three passages where the issue of old and new demonstrates the kind of "authority" that Paul gave to Scripture.

Before we examine these passages, however, it may be helpful to make some introductory comments. First, in what follows I shall normally render the Greek word *nomos* as "law." Although *nomos* is used in the LXX to translate the Hebrew term *Torah*, meaning "teaching," and so has a wider range of meaning than our word "law," that teaching certainly included the commandments set out in the Pentateuch. It is with those commandments that Paul is concerned in the passages that we are to examine. The term should not be understood to imply that Judaism was of necessity a legalistic religion.[2]

Second, Paul's methods of exegesis are those of his own day. They may well make preachers in the twenty-first century uneasy, for he tears passages out of context, uses allegory or typology to give new meanings to old stories, abandons the "original" meanings of texts, and turns them on their heads. We may well shy away from his methods, but the important issue for us is the authority that he ascribes to Scripture, rather than his ways of interpreting it. The different ways in which he finds meaning in "what is written" underlines its importance.

Third, Paul's explicit quotations of Scripture occur in Romans, 1 and 2 Corinthians, and Galatians. In Romans and Galatians he is involved in arguing specifically about the relation between God's self-revelation in the past (as recorded in Scripture) and his self-revelation in Christ. In these two epistles Paul appeals to Scripture in order to argue against what he regards as a false understanding of Scripture. In 1 and 2 Corinthians he is concerned to uphold the truth of the gospel and the genuineness of his own ministry over against the arrogant views of the Corinthians, who, influenced by the values prevalent in their city, boasted in their own wisdom, knowledge, and status. In both contexts—the "Jewish" one in Romans and Galatians, and the "pagan" one of 1 and 2 Corinthians—he appeals to Jewish Scripture, in order to justify his gospel and its implications for his manner of life (and the manner of life appropriate for Christians).

We turn, then, to the three passages I have chosen as the focus for our thinking.

SECOND CORINTHIANS 3–4

Second Corinthians 3:1–4:6 is a complex passage, about which many monographs have been written.[3] This is not the place to discuss the many exegetical difficulties found there. We are concerned only to consider the light the passage throws on Paul's use of Scripture. Its relevance to our concern is, however, inevitably oblique, since here, as elsewhere, Paul is not concerned to discuss the authority of Scripture, which for him is axiomatic. Nevertheless, the way in which he handles it is illuminating.

Paul's purpose in this passage is to defend his own ministry against those who have been attempting to undermine it. Hints of the accusations that have been brought against him are seen in the final verse of the previous chapter. He begins his defense by contrasting himself with those who come bearing letters of introduction, setting out their credentials. He has no need to commend himself, or to provide any kind of letter, since the Corinthians themselves are all the evidence he needs of his apostolic calling; the existence of the Christian community in Corinth is itself a "letter," written on Paul's[4] heart, and this letter speaks for itself (3:1–2). The letter is from Christ himself, but it has been *delivered* by Paul. The verb Paul uses here (*diakoneō*) is, of course, related to the noun *diakonia*, meaning "service" or "ministry," a theme that Paul takes up a few verses later. This letter is written, not with ink, but with the Spirit of the living God. With a sudden change of metaphor, Paul now contrasts a letter written on tablets of stone with one written on tablets consisting of human hearts (v. 3). Letters written with ink and tablets of stone both stand over against what God himself effects.

Linda Belleville has rightly argued that the shift of metaphor from letters written with ink to tablets of stone is not accidental; the rest of the chapter, which focuses on the story in Exod 34, is not a mere diversion.[5] Paul's ministry is of a piece with his gospel, and both are about the work of the living God, whose Spirit is at work in human hearts. It is the Spirit who authenticates the truth of the gospel, over against reliance on carrying out the commandments of the law (Gal 3:1–5). Fearing that what he claims may sound like boasting, Paul insists that his confidence is based, through Christ, on God, and that any competence he has comes from God (vv. 4–5), who has empowered the apostles "as ministers of a new covenant." Now Paul is using the language of Jer 31:33. Jeremiah's vision was of a time when the covenant would be written on human hearts and so observed, in contrast to the covenant made by God with his people on Mt. Sinai—a covenant which they then broke. But Jeremiah was not alone in his hope for the future. Compare, e.g., this passage from Ezek 36:26–28:

> A new heart I will give you, and a new spirit I will put within you; and I will remove from your body the heart of stone and give you a heart of flesh. I will put my Spirit within you, and make you follow my statutes and be careful to observe my ordinances. Then you shall live in the land that I gave to your ancestors: and you shall be my people, and I will be your God.

The condemnation of Israel for failing to observe God's commandments, and the belief that God would not only punish her for her sins, but renew her through his Spirit, are constant themes in the prophets. The new covenant, Paul tells us, is characterised by Spirit (*pneuma*), not letter (*gramma*), for the letter kills, but the Spirit gives life (v. 6).

The ministry of Paul and his co-workers is now contrasted with the ministry of death—a ministry that was engraved in letters on stone. Yet that ministry was inaugurated with overwhelming glory, such that the Israelites could not bear to look at the face of Moses (v. 7). How much greater then is the glory that accompanies the ministry of the Spirit (v. 8). Paul now repeats this same idea in several different ways. If glory accompanied the ministry that brought condemnation, how much more will the ministry that brings righteousness abound in glory (v. 9). Indeed, what had once been glorified has not been glorified at all in comparison with what is a far greater glory (v. 10). For if what was being abolished (i.e., Moses' ministry, which was concerned with an "old" covenant[6]) was accompanied by glory, how much more is what endures accompanied by glory (v. 11).

The background of Paul's imagery is clear. He is thinking of the giving of the law to Moses on Mt. Sinai; such was the glory that accompanied this event, that Moses' face reflected it when he descended from the mountain, and the Israelites were afraid to look at him.[7] It is extraordinary that in a passage where Paul is defending himself against accusations of being arrogant and commending himself, he should not only compare his own ministry with that of Moses, but claim that it is superior! He is surely asking for trouble. The only explanation is that his whole ministry depends on what he here describes as the "new covenant" in contrast to the old. This new covenant is written in Spirit, not letter, and the implication is that the reverse was true of the "old covenant." The superior glory of the new ministry depends on the glory that is seen and reflected, and since "glory" is nothing less than the self-revelation of God, what is being claimed is that God is more clearly revealed in the new dispensation, of which Paul is a minister, than in the old. The reason that he is called to be an apostle, and so proclaims the gospel with such boldness, is that what was "promised beforehand in the holy Scriptures and through the prophets" has been fulfilled (Rom 1:2).

The climax of Paul's argument comes in vv. 12–18. With extraordinary boldness, he now makes a direct contrast between his own ministry and that of Moses himself! No wonder he begins by explaining that it is on the basis of this hope (of enduring glory) that he is acting so boldly (v. 12). He now picks up another detail from the story in Exod 34: having passed on the words of the Lord to the Israelites, Moses covered his face with a veil, removing it only when he spoke to the Lord and passed on God's commandments to the people; when he was not communicating with the Lord or with the people, he kept his face covered (Exod 34:33–35). In the Exodus narrative the explanation is that the people were afraid to look at Moses' face, which continued to reflect the glory of God: they needed to be protected from this ethereal light. Paul has already referred to this explanation in v. 7. Now, however, he gives another explanation for the veil: it was intended to prevent the Israelites from gazing at the end of what was in the process of fading away (v. 13). But, he adds in v. 14, their hearts were hardened.

What does Paul mean? That they did not realize that Moses was concealing anything from them? What does he mean by "end" in v. 13? And what was it that was fading away? The word *katargoumenon* has been repeated from v. 11, and presumably refers to the ministry of Moses, for Paul is still contrasting his own ministry with that of Moses: it is Moses' ministry—that of the old covenant—that has what we would today describe as "built-in obsolescence." The word *telos* can mean "end" both in the sense of "termination" and "goal." Does Paul mean that the Jews failed to recognize that Moses' ministry was only temporary?[8] Or does he mean that they failed to recognize its true goal?[9] This, as we shall see, may well be the meaning of the word in Rom 10:4, where Christ is said to be the *telos* of the law. If this is what he intends here, then he is suggesting that what was hidden from the Jews was the fact that Christ was the fulfillment of Moses' ministry. Whatever meaning we give to the word, however, it would seem that Paul is maintaining that the ministry of Moses, in passing on the law to Israel, was temporary, and that the Jews had failed to recognize this.

At this point in Paul's argument the veil shifts from Moses' face to the "old covenant" itself, from which it is taken away only by Christ (v. 14). Indeed, whenever Moses is read (for the old covenant is, of course, "of letter, not of Spirit," v. 6), the veil lies over the hearts of those who hear his words (v. 15). It would seem that they failed to see that the "old covenant" pointed to a "new covenant," and that the true significance of the old covenant is revealed only in Christ. But (and here Paul quotes loosely from Exod 34:34) "whenever he turns to the Lord, the veil is removed" (v. 16). The original passage refers to Moses going in to speak to the Lord. But who is now doing the turning? Is it still Moses? If so, then "Moses" must stand for any Jew of Paul's own time. More difficult, perhaps, is the question "Who is the Lord?" After the reference to Christ in v. 14 we might perhaps think that Paul is thinking of Jews turning to Christ, but the passage in Exodus was clearly referring to God himself: Moses was understood to be going into the tabernacle to speak to God. But there is more to be said on the matter. Paul's next words are probably a comment on the Exodus story. "Now the Lord is the Spirit," he explains, "and where the Spirit of the Lord is, there is freedom." When one "turns to the Lord" and speaks with him directly, one is confronted by the Spirit of God. Paul has neatly taken his argument back to the beginning and to his claim that the letter that certifies his ministry is written by the Spirit of the living God. That is why he wears no veil over his face but reflects openly the glory of the Lord. The claim to direct communication with God over against the "hidden" revelation of the law reminds us of what Paul says in Gal 3:19 about the law having been administered through angels at the hand of an intermediary. The result is that the Lord who is Spirit is changing "us" into his own likeness, so that the glory we reflect is increasing, not diminishing (v. 18). Men and women are being restored to what God created them to be.

Since God in his mercy has entrusted this ministry to Paul, he does not lose heart (4:1); there is nothing shameful or deceitful in what he does, neither does he distort the word of God. By declaring the truth of God openly, he commends himself to others in the sight of God (4:2). His gospel (in contrast to the law, 3:14) is not veiled—except, that is, to those who are on the way to destruction (4:3), whose unbelieving minds have been blinded by the god of this world. They are unable to see the light of the gospel of the glory of Christ, who is the image of God (4:4). In what is probably a refutation of an accusation brought by his critics, Paul declares: "We do not preach ourselves; we preach Christ Jesus as Lord, and ourselves as your servants for Jesus' sake, because the God who said 'Let light shine out of darkness' has shone in our hearts to give the light of the knowledge of the glory of God in the face of Jesus Christ" (4:5–6). The glory seen in the face of Christ is reflected from the face of his ministers (3:18), and since Christ is the image of God, this glory is the glory of God himself, a glory that was revealed when God created the world (Gen 1:3).

It is important to recognize what Paul is doing in this passage. His purpose is to defend his own ministry. He has perhaps been accused of lacking the necessary credentials, but his authority is not from any human source, but from God (3:1–3; cf. Gal 1:1). For Paul, the commission to proclaim God's Son among the Gentiles went hand-in-hand with his acceptance of the gospel (Gal 1:15–16), and the gospel, too, is a direct revelation from God of his glory, seen in the face of Christ (4:6; cf. Gal 1:12). The revelation of God's Son was made both to him and through him.[10] The real source of Paul's confidence regarding his ministry is found in the nature of the gospel itself. For proof of the superiority of "the Spirit" to "the letter," Paul turns, paradoxically, to what is written—not, of course, to letters of commendation, but to Scripture. Just as in Rom 3:21, he maintains that the law and prophets witness to the fact that God's righteousness has been revealed "apart from the law," so here in 2 Corinthians he uses Scripture to argue that it points to something greater than itself.

"Paradoxically," and yet inevitably, Paul turns to Scripture since "what is written" is also God-given. Paul nowhere denies that Moses saw God's glory: indeed, he stresses the fact that Moses' face reflected the glory that he had seen. But Moses' ministry was temporary, and the glory was therefore fading. Moses is said to have concealed this fact from the Jews, and this is matched by their inability to understand the "old covenant" when it is read. The problem was that this ministry, engraved in letters on tablets of stone, brought death. The result was that the full glory of God was hidden. That glory is now revealed on the face of Jesus Christ (4:6). It was of course the same God who had called light out of darkness and who had spoken to Moses on Sinai who had now revealed his righteousness in his Son. Of course the Scriptures were "holy," and of course the ministry of Moses reflected the glory of God; but God had spoken more clearly and more directly in the person of his Son and had revealed his lasting glory in him.

What Paul expresses in 2 Cor 3–4 in his exposition of Exod 34 has parallels elsewhere. We see similar ideas in the opening verses of Hebrews, where we are told that whereas in the past God spoke to our forefathers in many ways through the prophets, he has now spoken to us in this final age in the person of his Son. The author goes on to contrast the Son not only with angels but with Moses, who was not a son but God's faithful servant, and whose glory is therefore less than that of the Son (Heb 3:1–6). Once again, the authority for all these statements is Scripture itself.

A similar assumption appears to be reflected in the so-called "Antitheses" in Matt 5:21–48. Six times we have a quotation from a commandment of Moses. The passage is introduced by the statement in 5:17–18:

> Do not suppose that I have come to abolish the law or the prophets; I have not come to abolish but to fulfill. Truly I tell you, that until heaven and earth pass away, not the smallest letter or stroke of a letter shall pass away from the law, until everything is fulfilled.

It is clear that unless Matthew is totally unaware of the significance of what he is writing, the Antitheses cannot be understood as contradicting the meaning of the original commandments. What they do is point behind the purpose of the command and widen its scope. One should not simply avoid murder, one should not hate; one should not simply refrain from adultery, but from lust also; one should not simply spare a woman from disgrace by giving her a legal document of divorce, but refrain from divorcing her; one should not simply be true to oaths sworn before God, but be true to one's word in every circumstance; one should not merely limit revenge to the equivalent punishment—"an eye for an eye"—but refrain from revenge altogether; one should not merely love one's neighbour, but one's enemy as well. Matthew, who appeals constantly to what is written, shows himself aware of the limitations of "the letter of the law." Law points *beyond* itself to the will of God.

Perhaps the most interesting parallel to 2 Cor 3–4, however, is found in the Fourth Gospel. The Prologue of John's Gospel, which provides the key to understanding what follows, is, like 2 Cor 3:1–4:6, an exposition of Gen 1 and Exod 34. Through his Word God created the world and revealed himself to men and women, but they failed to comprehend his self-revelation. He gave his people the law through Moses, but an even greater gift—"grace and truth"—came in the person of his only Son: in other words, "the Word made flesh" is the full revelation of God's nature, the embodiment of what he is. Not even Moses was able to see God, but God's only Son, who is closest to God's heart, has made him fully known. Because we have seen the glory of the only son, we have seen the glory of God himself. This passage does not deny the validity of the revelation to Moses; the law was "given" (John 1:17), and in the following narrative Jesus appeals to what was written by Moses. But the reason that he does so is because the Scriptures bear witness to him (John 5:37–40, 45–46).[11]

Even more illuminating is the discourse on the theme of bread in John 6. This is linked to the miracle of the feeding of the five thousand in 6:1–14, which is interpreted as a "sign" (v. 14). The story is expounded in terms of the gift of manna to the Israelites in the wilderness. Comparisons are drawn between Moses and Jesus, who is seen as "the prophet who is to come into the world" (v. 14), since the prophet was expected to repeat what Moses had done. But the manna eaten in the wilderness, like the bread shared in the miracle of the loaves and fishes, is in fact a symbol pointing to something greater. The manna was not itself the bread that comes down from heaven, since the bread from heaven which is given by God—the bread of life—is Jesus himself (vv. 32–35, 48–51). Those who ate the manna in the wilderness died, but those who eat the "living" bread will live (vv. 48–51, 58).

Although the miracle of the feeding is ostensibly set against the story of the giving of the manna, there is clearly another OT scene in John's mind, and that is the giving of the law on Mt. Sinai. In Jewish exegesis manna was seen as a symbol of the Torah, the word of God that feeds and nourishes his people.[12] What is being claimed here then is that the true source of nourishment is not the law, but Jesus himself; it is his words, not the words of Torah, that give life because they are also spirit (v. 63). He has come down from heaven to do God's will (vv. 37–40), and those who come to him and who believe in him will have eternal life (vv. 44–47). What is written in the prophets (Isa 54:13) has been fulfilled, for the people are now "all taught by God," for they are taught by his Son, who has seen him face to face (vv. 45–46). The law was said to offer life, but those who ate the manna all died, whereas those who eat the living bread will live (vv. 48–51). The Jews strive to "do the works of God" (v. 28), but the true "work of God" is to believe in the one whom God has sent (v. 29). The chapter ends with a scene in which the disciples are faced with a choice: others reject Jesus' teaching, but they confess that he is the Holy One of God and has the words of eternal life (vv. 68–69).

Many of the ideas used in 2 Cor 3–4 reappear here. We find the same contrast between Moses and Jesus, between faith and works, between death and life, between something that was clearly transient and something that is eternal, because it is "spirit and life." The links are so close as to suggest that early Christians had to rethink their understanding of the story of the law-giving on Sinai. The question of the authority of the law and the prophets was clearly an important issue.

In Paul, John, Matthew, and the author to the Hebrews, then, we have four very different writers, all of whom appeal constantly to Scripture as their authority, nevertheless all maintaining that Scripture points beyond itself to a superior revelation in Christ.

ROMANS 2:12–16, 25–29

My second passage, like my first, is not specifically about Scripture. Its purpose is very different from 2 Cor 3–4, since in Rom 2 Paul is arguing that Jews have dishonoured God because of their transgression of the law; like the Gentiles, they do not give God the glory that is due to him and so fail to reflect his glory (Rom 1:23; 3:23). Once again, however (v. 29), Paul uses the contrast between *pneuma* (spirit) and *gramma* (letter). No one, he says, will be accounted righteous before God simply by hearing the law; it is necessary to *do* it (2:13). Gentiles who have what the law requires written on their hearts will put to shame Jews who fail to observe it (vv. 14–15). So, too, with circumcision: neither "written code"[13] nor physical circumcision is of value if one transgresses against the law (vv. 25–27); the mark of the true Jew is "circumcision of the heart" and is a matter of spirit not letter (v. 29).

The images of law written on human hearts and circumcision of the heart both suggest once again Jeremiah's vision of the new covenant, which Paul has already used in 2 Cor 3. Remarkably, Paul is talking here about Gentiles, who are described as "not having the law" (v. 14) and as "uncircumcised" (v. 27). There is considerable disagreement as to whether Paul is thinking of pagan Gentiles who instinctively do what the law requires or of Christians who do not by birth have the law but nevertheless fulfill it. Is Paul underlining his argument regarding the Jews' failure by suggesting that Gentiles are capable of natural goodness? Or is he already pointing forward to the fact that those who did not belong to Israel are, through Christ, included in the new dispensation (Rom 9:30)?[14] Whichever he means, he is pointing to a righteousness before God which does not depend on the law, even though it is witnessed to by the law and prophets (Rom 3:21), a righteousness which will be disclosed when God judges human hearts through Christ Jesus (2:16).

Between these two paragraphs in Rom 2, in vv. 17–24 Paul makes a most extraordinary attack on his fellow Jews, and specifically on those who rely on their observance of the law. "You who teach others," he asks, "why do you not teach yourself?" Four accusations follow, though it is not clear whether we should understand these as statements of what certainly is the case or questions about what may be true:

> While preaching "do not steal," do you steal?
> While preaching "do not commit adultery," do you commit adultery?
> While abhorring idols, do you commit sacrilege?[15]
> You boast in the law, but through transgression of the law you dishonour God.[16]

The proof that these charges are justified is to be seen in the words of Scripture: "The name of God is blamed because of you among the Gentiles" (Isa 52:5).

Many OT passages have been suggested as parallels to Paul's extraordinary accusations. They are indeed in the tradition of the prophets. The most interesting is found in Jer 7:9–10: "Will you steal, murder, commit adultery, swear falsely, burn incense to Baal, and go after other gods and then come and stand before me in this house which is called by my name, and say, 'We are delivered'—only to go on doing all these abominations?"

Jeremiah's accusations include those listed by Paul when he writes "do you steal, commit adultery, and commit sacrilege?" But instead of his summary statement that those who boast in the *law* dishonour God, Jeremiah's accusations are addressed to those who trusted in the *temple*, saying: "this is the temple of the Lord, the temple of the Lord, the temple of the Lord" (Jer 7:4). Both Jeremiah and

Paul, however, have the same concern. Those they condemned were boasting in God, but failing to obey his will. Their worship was external only, not a matter of the heart.

Those whom Paul attacks here regarded themselves as devout Jews, and believed that they were following exactly what the law—Scripture—decreed. While scrupulously following the letter of the law, however, they were, he maintains, failing to do what in reality it demanded.

The contrast in 2:29 between "letter" and "Spirit" is picked up later in Rom 7 where Paul deals specifically with the inadequacy of the law. Although the law is holy and its commandments are holy, righteous, and good (7:12), it is unable to prevent sin because of human weakness. Although it is "spiritual," the law operates in the sphere of "flesh," not "Spirit" (7:14). Christians, however, have been released from its demands and so are able to serve God in the new life of the Spirit instead of under the old written code (*gramma*, 7:6). This has come about because God himself has done what the law could not do, by sending his Son to share our human condition, and in doing so has not only condemned sin but, paradoxically, enabled the demands of the law to be fulfilled in those who live according to the Spirit instead of the flesh (Rom 8:3–4).

The idea that the law is fulfilled in those who are "in Christ" (Rom 8:1) is reflected in various other passages in Paul. In Rom 13:8 Paul declares that those who love others have fulfilled the law; he then quotes four of the ten commandments and says that all the commandments are summed up in the command to love one's neighbour, since love is the fulfillment of the law. Out of context we might suppose that Paul is simply insisting on obedience to the law's commands, but of course he is appealing to the principle *behind* the law, which is the law of love. He understands the commandments to be spelling out some of the implications of what it means to love one's neighbour. Paul is not, of course, alone. Jesus himself appeals to the same principle,[17] as do contemporary Jewish rabbis.[18] Once again, Paul is loyal to Jewish tradition and to the demand to see the implication of the commands.

We have to remember, however, that for Paul this "new" commandment depends on the "Therefore" of Rom 12:1. What Christians now do they do because they are enabled, in Christ, to offer themselves to God "as a living holy sacrifice," and it is in him that their attitudes have been transformed (12:2). Moreover, Paul's argument in Rom 13:8–10 shows that he thinks there is a danger that in concentrating on each and every commandment Christians may miss their point. What is important is not avoiding this or that action, but loving others. One must not limit the principle of loving others to particular examples.

The same idea is expressed in Gal 5:14. The whole law, says Paul, is summed up in the commandment to love one's neighbour as oneself. Once again, we need to read this in context, for in this chapter Paul is insisting that Gentile Christians must not accept circumcision and so put themselves under the law

(5:2–6). Christians have been set free (v. 13) and must be guided by the Spirit (v. 16). Those who are guided by the Spirit must express their love for others by bearing one another's burdens; in doing so they will fulfill "the law of Christ" (6:1–2). What the law commands is good and true, but men and women are unable to "do" what the law commands until they are in Christ and the Holy Spirit takes over their lives. "The law" finds its "fulfillment," its true significance, in the law of Christ: what is written points beyond itself to the purpose of God.

ROMANS 9:30–10:10

In Rom 9–11 Paul is endeavouring to explain God's dealings with Israel. He insists that Israel's failure to respond to the gospel does not mean that God's word has failed; on the contrary, the promises made to Abraham have been fulfilled. God's purposes have been worked out in extraordinary ways, but the result has been that he has made known "the riches of his glory" for those whom he has called, including Gentiles as well as Jews (9:23). He concludes (9:30–32):

> What, then, are we to say? Gentiles, who did not strive after righteousness have obtained righteousness—that is, righteousness on the basis of faith (that is, trust in God)—whereas Israel, who strove after the law of righteousness, did not attain that law. Why not? Because she strove after it as though it could be fulfilled on the basis of works, not faith.

Paul does not say here quite what we expect him to say! In particular, what he says about Israel surprises us. Contrary to the translators, he does *not* say that Israel "did not succeed in *fulfilling* [the] law,"[19] nor does he say that Israel was striving "for the righteousness that is based on the law"[20] or that she "did not attain *righteousness*."[21] He says that she did not attain *the law*. Why? The answer becomes clear when we turn back to the previous sentence. We might well have expected Paul to make a clear contrast with what he said in v. 30 and to write: "Gentiles, who do not strive after righteousness. . . . Israel, who *does* strive after righteousness. . . ." In fact, however, he spoke of Israel striving after a *law* of righteousness: it is this "law of righteousness" that Israel has failed to attain. But is this law of righteousness simply the equivalent of the righteousness of the law he refers to in 10:4? I suggest not. For what we have here is the idea of two contrasted goals. The goal for which Gentiles were *not* striving, but which they nevertheless reached, was *righteousness*. The goal for which *Israel* was striving was *the law itself*, the law whose own goal was, indeed, righteousness. In striving to fulfill it, however, Israel lost sight of the law's purpose. She treated it as an end in itself instead of pursuing its goal—righteousness. Since she did not attain the law, there is no need to explain that she did not attain righteousness either. Her mistake was to pursue the law as though it could be achieved on the principle of works and not through faith (v. 32). Paul's accusation, then, is not simply that Israel did not attain righteousness, but that she pursued the wrong goal because she had misunderstood the role of the law.

Paul backs up his argument with a quotation from Scripture—here a mixed quotation from Isa 28:16 and 8:14 about a stone that leads to stumbling. In Isa 8 the stone is God himself, who nevertheless becomes a rock that causes Israel to stumble. In Isa 28 the rock is laid by God in Zion as a cornerstone and sure foundation. Its significance is unclear, although here too it may symbolize the presence of Yahweh himself on whom the new spiritual temple—the new society of God's people—depends. The targum of Isa 28, however, understands the stone as referring to the Messiah. In Romans the stone which is laid by God, and over which Israel has stumbled, is assumed by almost all commentators to refer to Christ.[22]

Is Paul affirming here that Israel's problem is simply that she has failed to believe in Christ? The majority of commentators accept this interpretation, but the possibility supported by some scholars that the stumbling-block is the law[23] should not be too easily dismissed. It should be noted after all that Christ has not been mentioned since 9:1–5 and that the two subjects under discussion in Rom 9:30–31 are the law and righteousness. Moreover, what Paul has just stated is that Israel has misunderstood the function of the law. Perhaps then the stumbling-block over which Israel has fallen is the law.[24]

But the reason that a stone causes one to stumble is normally that it is hidden from view—hardly true of the law. The metaphor suggests something obscure, which appears here to be the "hidden" meaning of Scripture. What was hidden from Israel seems to be the fact that the law could not be attained by works and that the righteousness promised in the law came only through faith—i.e., trust in God. It was this, says Paul, that Israel had failed to grasp even though it is set out in the law itself (3:19–22). In other words, Israel has tripped up because she has misunderstood the law and been unaware of its true significance. Scripture promises that those who have faith will not be ashamed (9:33). But in whom or what should they believe? The ambiguity in the quotation in v. 33 reminds us that the answer is still hidden from Israel. It will be spelled out in the next paragraph, where Christ is revealed as the "purpose" or "goal" of the law, and where the promise that those who believe on him clearly refers to him. The "hidden" meaning of Scripture is then Christ himself and the righteousness that is found in him. Those who maintain that the "stumbling-block" is Christ are also right!

The chiastic structure of vv. 30–33 supports the suggestion that what has caused Israel to stumble is their understanding—or rather, their misunderstanding—of the role of the law. This misunderstanding led her to regard the law as though the righteousness it demanded were based on works. In fact, this righteousness was based on God's faithfulness and on faith in him.

a) Gentiles, who did not pursue *righteousness*, nevertheless attained it on the basis of faith (v. 30).
b) Israel, who pursued the *law* of righteousness, did not attain the law because she did so "as though" its basis was works, not faith (vv. 30–31).
b) She tripped over the stone of stumbling, as Scripture itself testifies.
a) Scripture also affirms that those who have faith in it/him will not be ashamed.

So far, Christ has not been specifically mentioned in the argument that began at 9:6. Nevertheless, no one who has read Paul's argument in Rom 1–8 can doubt that the references to "faith" and "righteousness" are pointing towards him. What Paul says here is consistent with what he said in Rom 7, where he described the law as holy and spiritual (7:12, 14) and the commandment as holy, righteous, and good. The law is God's law (7:22, 25), but it is unable to do what it promised because of the weakness of the flesh (8:3) which has come under the power of sin and death (7:23; 8:2). But for the contrast between the principles of "works" and "faith" we have to go back to 3:19–4:6. The law itself, we are told there, supports Paul's assertion that "no one will be accounted righteous in God's sight *by the works of the law*," while both the law and prophets witness to the fact that in the gospel "God's righteousness has been revealed to all who believe" (3:19–22). The law which is "of works" leads to boasting, but the law which is "of faith" excludes it (v. 27). Paul appears to be opposing two interpretations of the written law, one of which sees it as demanding works, the other as witnessing to faith. When the law is understood in terms of works, it leads to boasting, not to righteousness, which comes only by faith, or trust, in God (v. 28). We have here the same contrast that we find in 9:30–33. That contrast is between seeing the law as a means to achieving righteousness and understanding it as witnessing to what is offered to those who have faith.

In 10:1 Paul speaks of the zeal that his fellow countrymen have for God—a zeal which according to Phil 3:6 he himself shared. This zeal is misinformed, however, because they are "ignorant of God's righteousness." "Seeking to establish their own righteousness, they have not submitted to the righteousness of God" (v. 3). The same contrast reappears in Phil 3:9.[25] We know from earlier statements in the epistle that the "righteousness of God" is revealed in the gospel (1:17), that it is attested to by the law and prophets (3:21), and that it is effective for all who believe "through the faith of Jesus Christ" (3:22), though the meaning of this last phrase is, of course, disputed. Now Paul tells us that because Christ himself is the goal of the law he brings righteousness to all who believe (v. 4). Christ is the goal of the law because he *is* righteousness (cf. 1 Cor 1:30) and because he realizes righteousness for every believer. This is the righteousness which has been granted to Gentiles (9:30). What Paul's fellow Jews lost sight of in seeking their own righteousness was the righteousness of God. Like climbers toiling up a mountain, they had set their sights on a ridge, mistaking it for the top, and had not noticed their *real* goal—the peak hidden behind it.

The context of Paul's statement in Rom 10:4 demands that we understand *telos* to mean "goal" rather than "termination."[26] The role of the law is affirmed, but it is temporary. When we set out on a journey, we do so in order to reach our destination; when we take a college course and sit for an examination, it is in order to obtain a certain qualification. The fact that we arrive at our destination is not a denial of the interest of our journey. Neither is the degree certificate we receive a denial of the value of the work we have undertaken, but it is no longer necessary for us to sit on a train or to attend lectures. Similarly, the role of the law, in terms of discipline, belongs to what is past.

Once again, Paul appeals to Scripture to back his argument—this time to Moses himself—and draws a contrast between the righteousness which is based on law and that which is based on faith. Even without the parallel in Phil 3:9, it is clear that the former is the righteousness that the Jews have sought to establish—their own righteousness—while the latter comes to those who trust in God. Since Paul clearly assumes that both of the passages he quotes[27] were written by Moses, he is appealing to the law itself as the witness to these two kinds of righteousness. The law, then, speaks of a righteousness based on works (v. 5)—a righteousness which, however, has already been described in 9:32 and in 10:3 in disparaging terms.[28] But the law *also* speaks of a righteousness that is based on faith (vv. 6–10) and witnesses to the fact that all that is necessary for salvation is the confession that Christ is Lord and faith that he has been raised from the dead. In a remarkable piece of hijacking, Deut 30:12–14 is discovered to refer, not to the law and to obedience to it, but to the gospel and to faith in Christ. The law itself thus points beyond itself to its goal, namely Christ.

The implication of Paul's argument is clear. If God's promises have been fulfilled and his purpose—set out in the law—is achieved in Christ, that purpose must be *prior* to the law. Although he comes *after* the Law, Christ is certainly no "afterthought," but represents God's purpose from the beginning of time. This is well summed up in Rom 16:25 (whether or not this passage was written by Paul himself): the proclamation of the gospel means the revelation of the secret which has been hidden for long ages but which is now made manifest, and has been made known through the prophetic writings—or rather (though this is not spelled out), through Christian exegesis of the prophets. If Christ is the "end of the law," the *goal* of the law rather than simply its ending, then he must also have been there at its beginning. The law is seen as witnessing to Christ and finding its fulfillment in him.

Paul's understanding of the relationship between Christ and the law in this passage is in keeping with his argument in the rest of Romans. Throughout, Paul emphasizes that the gospel was the fulfillment of God's promises, set out in

Scripture,[29] that his people would experience his righteousness, promises which are now revealed to include Gentiles as well as Israel. By sending his own Son God has enabled the requirements of the law to be fulfilled (8:3–4), and the goal of the law—righteousness—has been reached (10:4). Since Christ is the fulfillment of the law, the obedience required by the covenant is achieved in him. So it is that the proclamation of the gospel leads to the obedience of faith (1:5; cf. 15:18; 16:26). The law is not abrogated, but *fulfilled.*

THE ROLE OF SCRIPTURE

Arguments about Paul's ministry, about the place of Jew and Gentile in God's design, and about the contrast between "works" and "faith," may seem to have little to do with the authority of Scripture. Yet all these passages throw interesting light on the question, not only because Paul appeals in all of them to Scripture itself, but because behind his discussion of all these issues lies the question of his understanding of the *role* of Scripture. For in talking about "the law," Paul is talking about the five books of Moses. Indeed, as we have already noted, the term is sometimes used in a way that includes other books of the Hebrew Scriptures as well. The law is what is written, it is *gramma*, "letter," and what is written has authority. How, then, can Paul oppose what the law says?

The answer, of course, is that he does not. Rather, he points *beyond* the law to the purpose of God. The giving of the law to Moses was accompanied by great glory, but Moses was unable to look on the face of God, and the glory that he glimpsed was hidden since he was able to see only Yahweh's back (Exod 33:18–23). Although what is written is itself holy, it is only a witness to the far greater holiness of God. When Paul contrasts *gramma* and *pneuma*, he is not comparing different ways of interpreting Scripture—what we might call "literal" and "spiritual"—since he uses various methods in his own interpretation—sometimes what we might term literal, sometimes allegorical. *Gramma* refers rather to the *function* of Scripture. Scripture is what is written, and its purpose is to witness to what God is and does. But what God himself does is the work of *pneuma*. What is written cannot in itself give life; it can only witness to the life that God desires to give us.

In pointing to the meaning behind Scripture, Paul stands within the tradition of OT prophets, who had condemned their people for worshipping God with their lips but not their hearts and for keeping the letter of the law while ignoring its fundamental demands. He stands too in the tradition of Jesus himself, who is reported to have come into conflict with those who were scrupulous in their observance of the sabbath, while failing to see that to save life was to do God's will, and to take life was to deny it.[30] Other NT writers, as we have seen, continued that tradition.

Does any of this help us in considering the authority of Scripture for us today? It is perhaps because so much of the discussion is couched in terms of the role of "the law" that we fail to see its relevance. But "the law" is "that which is written." "The law and the prophets," together with the writings, made up the Jewish Scriptures. The contrast Paul was making was between what had become static (that which was written) and that which was alive and which gave life (the Spirit).

Because "law" has been understood so often as standing over against Christ, Christian tradition has tended to oppose OT and NT. But for Paul the contrast between the "old covenant" and the "new" was between *gramma* and *pneuma*, between what was written with ink and what is written by the Spirit. "Gospel" for our NT writers did not mean a written account but good news that is proclaimed by word of mouth. When John declared that "the Word had become flesh," he was referring to the living Word of God, who revealed the nature of God in a way that the Pentateuch given through Moses was unable to do. The church, however, has frequently *identified* the words of Scripture with the Word of God. As a child, I remember singing the hymn "O Word of God incarnate" and assuming that I was singing a hymn addressed to the Bible; the hymn was, after all, in the section of hymns concerned with "the Holy Scriptures"! Only later did I discover that it was Christ who was the incarnate Word. How many others, I wonder, have made the same mistake? And how many in effect make that mistake by thinking of the Bible as "the Word of God"? If our exegesis of various passages teaches us anything, it is that the Bible is the *witness* to God's self-revelation—to his Word—and not that Word itself. We need to distinguish between the Word of God and the words of Scripture.

Because the self-revelation of God witnessed to in the Bible is found above all else in Christ, the incarnation is in fact the best model for understanding the Bible's authority. In the incarnation God chose to accept the limitations of time and space and culture and to become vulnerable to misunderstanding and rejection. The image of the helpless child reminds us of the risk which is involved in the incarnation, of the vulnerability of God's self-revelation. In Christ, God makes himself known to men and women, but his Word is always heard in a particular time and space and culture and is always open to misunderstanding and rejection. When God spoke to prophets and evangelists and apostles, he ran the risk of being misunderstood, for to speak is to risk the danger of being misunderstood, rejected, or simply ignored. When the record of what men and women thought they heard God say to them became part of the canon, the danger was multiplied. When God speaks to us today through the pages of the Bible, he makes himself vulnerable again.

Scripture, then, is meant to be a witness to the truth; it is not a substitute for the truth. "What the law could not do," writes Paul, God has done (Rom 8:3). God acts apart from law, but the law and prophets witness to what he does (Rom

3:21). The danger is to treat what is written as a binding code rather than a witness to the reality beyond. The choice is expressed well in the lines of George Herbert's hymn:

> A man that looks on glass
> On it may stay his eye,
> Or if he pleaseth, through it pass,
> And then the heaven espy.

Although the formation of the Christian canon in the early centuries A.D. was a necessary and inevitable step for the church to take, there were obvious dangers inherent in adopting a closed canon. It was now all too easy for Christians to treat all Scripture as *gramma* and to behave as though God's Spirit were no longer at work in the world. It was all too easy to assume that our biblical writers had encapsulated the whole truth, and so to confine Christ himself to the pages of Scripture, forgetting that those who claim to follow the Risen Christ must be prepared to recognize that he continues to lead his people into a fuller understanding of the truth. If we today are to hear the Word of God, then we must remember that the written word is only a witness to that Word. The church must seek to interpret the Word of God—the will of God—*behind* the written word by listening to the Spirit who gives life. If we persevere, we shall find that God speaks to us *through* the Bible and that behind its words we can begin to discern the Word, the self-revelation of God.

NOTES

1. 2 Tim 3:14–17 is exceptional.

2. Paul sometimes uses *nomos* to refer to the Pentateuch and even to all the Jewish Scriptures (e.g., Rom 3:19).

3. See, e.g., Linda L. Belleville, *Reflections of Glory: Paul's Polemical Use of the Moses-Doxa Tradition in 2 Corinthians 3.1–18* (JSNTSup Series 52; Sheffield: JSOT Press, 1991). I have discussed the passage myself in "Beyond the Things That are Written? St. Paul's Use of Scripture," *NTS* 27 (1981): 295–309, reprinted in *From Adam to Christ: Essays on Paul* (Cambridge: Cambridge University Press, 1990), 139–154.

4. There is a textual problem here: both *hēmōn* ("our") and *humōn* ("your") are well attested, and each makes sense in the context. If we read the former, the word presumably embraces Paul's fellow workers, who would share his lifestyle and so be criticized together with him.

5. Belleville, 146–149.

6. Paul describes himself and his co-workers as ministers of a "new covenant" in v. 6. In v. 14 he uses the contrasting phrase "old covenant."

7. Exod 34:29–30.

8. So, e.g., Victor Paul Furnish, *II Corinthians* (AB 32A; Garden City, N.Y.: Doubleday, 1984), 207; Margaret Thrall, *The Second Epistle to the Corinthians* (ICC; Edinburgh: T. & T. Clark, 1994), I:256–258. She argues that Moses concealed what was negative, not what was positive.

9. So, e.g., Jean Héring, *The Second Epistle of Saint Paul to the Corinthians* (London: Epworth, 1967), 25.

10. Gal 1:15–16. The Greek phrase *en emoi*, though normally translated "to me," should perhaps be rendered literally as "in me." See Morna D. Hooker, *Paul: A Short Introduction* (Oxford: One World, 2003), 107.

11. For a more detailed exposition of this passage, see Morna D. Hooker, "The Johannine Prologue and the Messianic Secret," *NTS* 21 (1974): 40–58.

12. For examples, see Peder Borgen, *Bread from Heaven* (NovTSup X; Leiden: Brill, 1965), 147–192.

13. REB. Paul's word is *gramma*, literally "letter."

14. The matter largely depends on whether the word *phusei* ("by nature") is taken with the words that precede it or with those that follow. In favour of the former interpretation is the order of words; in favour of the latter is the use of the term in v. 27, where it clearly means "by descent." Those who support the former view include C. K. Barrett, *The Epistle to the Romans* (London: A. & C. Black, 1991), in loc., and James D. G. Dunn, *Romans 1–8* (WBC; Dallas, Tex.: Word, 1988), in loc. Among those who support the latter is C. E. B. Cranfield, *The Epistle to the Romans* (ICC; Edinburgh: T. &T. Clark, 1975), in loc.

15. Literally, "rob temples."

16. The slight change in construction (to a relative pronoun with the indicative) suggests that this last accusation is a statement rather than a question.

17. See Matt 22:34–40//Mark 12:28–31//Luke 10:25–28.

18. Similar sayings are attributed to R. Hillel (first century; see *b. Šabb.* 31a) and to R. Akiba (second century; see *Sipra* 89b, and are also found in *Testament of Issachar* 5:2; 7:6; and *Testament of Dan* 5:3).

19. NRSV; cf. NJB.

20. RSV; cf. JB.

21. F. F. Bruce, *Romans* (2d ed.; New Century Bible Commentary; Grand Rapids: Eerdmans, 1989) 138. P. W. Schmiedel's suggested emendation of the text is noted in the margin of Nestle-Aland's text.

22. This interpretation is supported by the christological interpretation of the two Isaiah texts in 1 Pet 2:4–8. The words that follow, referring to "trusting in him/it" are normally understood to refer to Christ also. Certainly the phrase has this meaning when the words are repeated in Rom 10:11: "the Lord" of vv. 12–13 must be "the Lord" of v. 9.

23. So C. K. Barrett, "Romans 9.30–10.21: Fall and Responsibility of Israel," in *Die Israelfrage nach Röm 9–11* (ed. Lorenzo De Lorenzi; Rome: Abbey of St. Paul Without the Wall, 1977), 99–130; also *The Epistle to the Romans* (2d ed.; London: A. & C. Black, 1991), in loc. Cf. Paul W. Meyer, "Romans 10:4 and the End of the Law," in *The Divine Helmsman: Studies on God's Control of Human Events* (ed. James L. Crenshaw and Samuel Sandmel; New York: Ktav, 1980), 59–78.

24. This interpretation of the "rock" as symbolizing the law finds some support in the structure of the mixed quotation from Isaiah, which inserts a phrase from Isa 8:14 into a framework drawn from Isa 28:16. Paul's quotation ignores the positive descriptions of the stone found in both LXX passages and so places the emphasis on the stone as a cause of stumbling. His quotation of Isa 8:14 is much closer to the Hebrew than to the LXX which expands the text, emphasizing that to those who are faithful to him God is a sanctuary rather than a stumbling-block. The words from Isa 28:16, on the other hand, appear to be drawn from the LXX text, but omit the positive description of the stone as a cornerstone that has been tested and is sure.

25. Paul's own righteousness is there said to be based on the law, while God's is based on trust.

26. For a discussion of this passage and a defense of understanding *telos* as "purpose" rather than "abrogation," see Robert Badenas, *Christ the End of the Law* (JSNTSup 10; Sheffield: JSOT Press, 1985). Cf. also Morna D. Hooker, "Christ: the 'End' of the Law," in *Neotestamentica et Philonica: Studies in Honor of Peder Borgen* (ed. David E. Aune, Torrey Seland, and Jarl Henning Ulrichsen; NovTSup CVI; Leiden and Boston: Brill, 2002), 226–246.

27. Lev 18:5 and Deut 30:12–14.

28. Paul described there how Israel had pursued the law of righteousness *as though* it could be attained by works and how her people had *ignorantly* sought to establish their own righteousness.

29. This idea is set out in his opening sentence: the gospel of God was promised beforehand through his prophets in the holy Scriptures (1:2).

30. Matt 12:9–14//Mark 3:1–6//Luke 6:6–11 and 14:1–6.

FAITH, ASSURANCE, AND CONVICTION: AN EPISTEMOLOGICAL COMMENTARY ON HEBREWS 11:1

WILLIAM J. ABRAHAM

"NOW FAITH IS THE ASSURANCE OF THINGS HOPED FOR, THE CONVICTION OF THINGS UNSEEN."

The standard Western way of thinking of the role of Scripture in relation to epistemology is to think of Scripture as canon and to think of canon as a criterion. On this analysis Scripture is pivotal in the epistemology of theology, that is, in theories that think through the nature of rationality, justification, and knowledge as these relate to theology. To express the matter succinctly, Scripture operates as foundation for theological reflection, providing secure warrant for the material claims on offer. I say "foundation" rather than "a foundation" because I want to signal that this move leaves much unfinished business on hand. Most especially it leaves open whether Scripture operates as the sole foundation for theology, or whether one may also appeal to tradition, reason, and experience. At this level one can be an inclusivist or an exclusivist, with all sorts of mediating positions in between. Thus the exclusivist takes a hard line allowing nothing but Scripture to operate as securing positive epistemic status in theology; the inclusivist allows a variety of ways of appealing to tradition, reason, and experience.

Provided one can resolve the disputes between inclusivists and exclusivists, three sorts of difficulty present themselves immediately. First, how is the foundation of Scripture itself to be secured? Does Scripture itself show itself to be the relevant foundation for theology? If it does not, are not our claims patently inconsistent? If it does, are we not begging the question by securing our position by appeal to the very premise under scrutiny? Second, what actual material claims can we secure from Scripture? The history of Western theology from the Reformation onwards shows how maddeningly difficult it is to secure consensus on this matter. The appeal to Scripture has turned out to be the source of endless conflict and division rather than consensus and unity. Third, what do we do if we do not secure consensus on material theological claims? Does this mean that the original foundation was deeply flawed and we should now look for a better foundation? Again, the history of Western theology, including its modern and now its postmodern or ultramodern phase, can legitimately be read as a series of efforts to find the proper foundations of theology, especially so when the foundation of Scripture, and the substitutes sought out to replace it, become discredited by the failure to secure consensus on proper belief.

I have argued elsewhere that the difficulties that have piled up in and around these three questions have brought us to the end of the line in Western theology.[1] We have simply become exhausted and hopelessly divided searching for adequate foundations of theology. More importantly, we have lost the canonical faith of the church and are now suffering extensively from cognitive depression and spiritual starvation. On the other side of the line, I have argued that we need to abandon the standard conception of canon as a criterion, that we should welcome Scripture as one element in the rich canonical heritage of the early church, that we should receive all of this heritage as indispensable means of grace in the church, and that we need a new subdiscipline identified as the epistemology of theology that will engage in a rigorous and comprehensive way with the nature of rationality, warrant, justification, and knowledge in theology.

Not the least of the merits of this radical change in direction is that it allows us to visit the extraordinary network of epistemic hints, suggestions, and proto-proposals on the epistemology of theology that show up in Scripture itself. We are all aware of the rather arid debate between Barth and Brunner on the exegesis of Rom 1 as to whether Paul does or does not sanction natural theology. James Barr's Gifford lectures are a brilliant attempt to clean up this arena and shed some badly needed light on the terrain.[2] However, there is much more to explore than that given in the classical discussions of Rom 1. Indeed, we have not begun to look at the host of materials that show up all over the place. Consider the claim about perception of the divine to be found in Matt 5:8: "Blessed are the pure in heart, for they will see God." Or ruminate on 1 Cor 12:3: "No one can say 'Jesus is Lord' except by the Holy Spirit." Or cast a close eye on one of John Wesley's favorite texts, Rom 8:15–16: "When we cry, 'Abba! Father!' it is that very Spirit bearing witness with our spirits that we are children of God." These texts are laden with fascinating epistemological overtones that deserve the most careful reflection.

In this paper I want to look at another text that was extremely important to John Wesley in his ruminations in the epistemology of theology, namely, Heb 11:1: "Now faith is the assurance of things hoped for, the conviction of things unseen." For Wesley, this text was at the heart of his vision of perceptible grace.[3] He took faith to be a supernatural work of God in the eyes and inner understanding of the believer that enabled him or her to see the truth about God with assurance and conviction. Thus faith was a form of perception of the divine, a direct encounter or experience with God, which, at one level, operated as the foundation of his knowledge of God. As best he could, Wesley combined this with a stout Protestant vision of *sola scriptura* that sought the warrant for this epistemological move partly in Scripture itself. Thus in his terms he sought for a deeper warrant for his appeal to religious experience in divine revelation. While at times he makes perception (including perception of the divine) a bedrock epistemic practice, at other times he was deeply uneasy with this, looking in Scripture for warrant for this appeal to experience of God. This creates enormous problems for Wesley and his successors, but this is not the time or place to chase that hare.[4] What interests me is whether we can find a better way to think about the epistemic overtones of this fascinating claim in Hebrews.

Consider the puzzle that emerges as we look at the content of this text. Faith, we are told, is the assurance of things hoped for, the conviction of things unseen. Normally we do not think of either assurance or conviction along the lines suggested here. Assurance and conviction are characteristically tied to evidence, not faith. Thus suppose I am assured of the truth of proposition *p*, or suppose I am convinced of the truth of proposition *p*; one immediately assumes that the relevant belief is backed up by good evidence. As we proceed, I shall take the terms 'assurance' and 'conviction' as rough, verbal equivalents. Thus, if I have *assurance* that the weather in Belfast is good, then we can usually assume that there is solid evidence on which I am resting. So I am actually in Belfast on the relevant date and can see for myself that the weather is good, or I have reliable testimony from my wife who knows firsthand how things are in Belfast, or I have checked with the meteorological office or with the quality press. It is in circumstances like these that I can claim to have assurance. Likewise, if I am *convinced* that I still have money in the bank, then I have just phoned through on the eight hundred line and checked my current balance, or I have tallied up all my inputs and outputs, or I have just made a withdrawal from the wall machine and gotten a receipt with the remaining balance. Assurance and conviction normally rest on evidence derived from an epistemically reliable source; it is not merely that I believe *p*; I go way beyond merely believing *p* and have assurance of *p* and am convinced of *p*; this mode of belief is characteristically tied to relevant, reliable evidence. I am not claiming here that I have to have thought through the issues self-reflexibly and ascertained that the pertinent evidence is really reliable evidence. All I am claiming is that I do have the evidence to hand and could cite it if challenged.

Moreover, this applies to believing states of affairs that are future oriented or that have the invisible as their cognitive content. Thus I can have assurance that I will be traveling out of town next month and be convinced of so doing; but again it will be pertinent to look for relevant, reliable evidence. Thus I have agreed to speak at a conference and have already bought the tickets, and I have no good reason to think that the airlines will be on strike, that the weather will prevent my flying, that the conference will be cancelled, and the like. Equally, I can be convinced that there is a life beyond this life provided, for example, that I had a near-death experience, or that I had good testimony to that effect from others, or I have a good *a priori* argument to the same conclusion. In all these cases, assurance and conviction are linked to evidence. It always makes sense to ask the believing agent why they believe as they do, and it is right and proper to expect a reply in terms of relevant evidence.

Yet this is not at all how the writer to the Hebrews proceeds. It is faith rather than evidence that is the assurance of things hoped for and the conviction of things not seen. There is not a word here about evidence; it is faith that is the source of assurance and conviction. Not surprisingly, critics of Christianity have fastened on this switch of concepts and readily ridiculed believers for their credulity, stupidity, superstition, wishful thinking, emotionalism, and the like.[5] In popular parlance faith is a form of believing what you know ain't so, that is, it is believing without evidence, when evidence is relevant and essential, but clearly lacking.

In the last generation the most searching and original attempt to turn the tide of this criticism has been provided in the extraordinary and original work of Alvin Plantinga. In a series of marvelous papers culminating in his magisterial *magnum opus*, *Warranted Christian Belief*,[6] Plantinga took the standard critics head-on. Here let me highlight three elements in Plantinga's counterattack.

First, Plantinga concedes that Christian belief is not a matter of evidence. However, this is not a matter for either ridicule or criticism because many of our beliefs are held without evidence. Many of our most important beliefs, say, about the existence of ourselves, the world, the past, and the like, are properly basic; all these beliefs are rightly held without evidence. The effort to rule out religious belief from this coveted position rests on classical foundationalism, the view that only certain very restricted kinds of claims can be held without evidence. Thus we are only allowed to count self-evident beliefs, or beliefs evident to the senses, or incorrigible beliefs, without evidence. These strict requirements clearly rule out religious beliefs. However, as Plantinga shows with great skill and dexterity, classical foundationalism is deeply flawed, so there is no good reason to be intimidated by this kind of stricture at all.[7] Hence, religious beliefs may indeed be held without evidence. Second, while properly basic beliefs may be held without evidence, this does not mean that they are groundless. They are rightly formed under certain circumstances. Thus I form the belief that I had toast for breakfast when my memory evokes this belief, or I form the belief that two plus two equals four by introspection, or I form the belief that my roses are red through perception, and so on. Provided my faculties are properly functioning, the default position is that I am entitled to believe a wide variety of propositions as they arise in pertinent circumstances. Third, the great truths of the Christian religion are warranted in similar fashion. Christians come to believe through the work of the

Holy Spirit, who brings it about that we believe, as various beliefs are triggered within our *sensus divinitatis* in relevant circumstances. Assurance and conviction are not then tied in these circumstances to propositional evidence but to the work of the Holy Spirit, the strength of our belief, and the depth of our conviction registering the level of the Spirit's operation. So just as we form beliefs through memory, or perception, or testimony, or introspection, we also form beliefs through the proper working of our *sensus divinitatis*. That is why it is entirely appropriate to speak of being assured or convinced as a matter of faith, for faith is simply shorthand for the work of the Holy Spirit operating in, with, and through our *sensus divinitatis*. In these circumstances faith is not opposed to reason but constitutes a fully legitimate form of knowledge.

Contrary to initial appearances, Plantinga's position is in the neighborhood of the strategy deployed by John Wesley in his exposition of our text from Hebrews. Thus both make much of the work of the Holy Spirit in the genesis of faith, and both go on to deploy the witness of the Holy Spirit in their epistemology of theology. Equally, both skillfully tie the work of the Holy Spirit to assurance, conviction, and knowledge of God. The divergences at this point are illuminating. Wesley's doctrine veers off in the direction of an appeal to religious experience or perception of the divine, a feature of his work that makes it relatively easy for his later followers to be radically open to the epistemic labors of Frederick Schleiermacher. Plantinga's proposals veer off in the direction of a full-scale epistemology that works out with exquisite philosophical care a vision of knowledge that makes much of the concept of proper functioning.[8]

For our purposes the critical difference that surfaces is that of the place of Scripture and divine revelation in their respective views. For Wesley even his appeal to the inner witness of the Holy Spirit has to be brought back and grounded in Scripture as construed in a very strict sense as divine revelation. For Plantinga, the place of Scripture and revelation turns out to be entirely contingent and even superfluous. What is critical is that the Holy Spirit operates as a belief-forming mechanism or agent; the medium used as the occasion for the work of the Holy Spirit appears to be entirely contingent. What is pivotal is that the Holy Spirit triggers the relevant beliefs, say, about the future or about the unseen world, with the pertinent degree of assurance and conviction. This may or may not be on the occasion of the believer hearing Scripture. Perhaps the believer was listening to a diatribe by a radical critic of the gospel, or perhaps the believer was overhearing a child reciting mindlessly this or that passage of Scripture. All that really matters is that on listening to the material cited the believer forms the belief that various propositions are true due to the inner witness of the Holy Spirit. The intention and beliefs of the original speaker and the first origination of the text are entirely secondary.

The contingent place of divine revelation in Plantinga's vision of faith strikes me as extremely odd. It is odd because it locates virtually the whole of epistemology of theology in the inner witness of the Holy Spirit and because it has no real place for a robust vision of divine revelation. Such oddity suggests that we look for an entirely different way of thinking about the nature of faith and how faith operates to provide assurance and conviction. The clue to an alternative reading is surely to be found in the simple notion of trust in the promises of God, that is, of faith as the entirely appropriate response to divine revelation or to the Word of God. It is an extraordinary development, one that we leave to the historians of contemporary Christian thought, as to how this idea has simply disappeared off the contemporary theological landscape.[9] I shall be content if I can unfold its distinctive grammar and indicate how faith can indeed operate as relevant evidence. The core ideas are manifold.

First, God really has spoken to us, making precious promises of future blessing through his Son. Second, the appropriate response to God's Word to us is one of faith, that is, one of obedience and trust in God to keep his Word over time. Third, this trust is marked by assurance and conviction because God's character and power are such that we can rely on him to be faithful through thick and thin. Fourth, there is within this faith an implicit appeal to relevant evidence, that is, to the evidence provided by divine revelation. Thus the general grounding of assurance and conviction in evidence is not set aside but satisfied; it is epistemically right and proper to rest on God's Word with assurance and conviction. Fifth, the authenticity of the identification of God's revelation in Christ is accompanied by divine testimony in direct declaration and in accompanying signs, wonders, and miracles. Sixth, such faith requires tenacity in believing, so that we pit ourselves against temptation to turn aside and rightfully draw on the life stories of the saints to encourage and cheer us on in the midst of suffering. Seventh, this faith is defeasible. It can be lost, not just because of the cost of obedience, and not just because it can be eroded by sin and by the refusal to face suffering and persecution; it can also be undercut by finding fresh evidence that undermines the original data on which it was based. Thus it is not some covert form of infallibility, or of spurious certainty, or of arbitrary appeal to authority.

Let me now explore these different elements in the logic of faith by relating them schematically to the argument laid out in various elements in the epistle to the Hebrews as a whole. It is surely no accident that the little gem on faith in Hebrews 11 comes as it does well into the more general development of ideas in this work. It crops up only after the writer has already laid out a network of interrelated claims. Thus the book begins with a ringing declaration of God's having spoken definitely in a Son whose status surpasses all previous expressions of God's work in creation and redemption. This Son is higher than the angels; he shares fully in our humanity; he is worthy of more glory than Moses; he is a high priest able to sympathize with our infirmities who matches the order of Melchizedek; he is superior to Abraham; he is the guarantee of a better and more permanent covenant than that mediated by the Levitical priests; through his death he offers eternal redemption; through his ongoing priestly office he offers intercession on our behalf in heaven; and in the future he will appear again to save those who are eagerly awaiting him.

Given this vision of Christ's person as Son of God and his work as revealer, sacrifice for sin, mediator of the promised new covenant, and future savior from sin, then the only fitting response is obedient trust. The writer brilliantly lays this out both positively and negatively, moving back and forth between the positive and the negative with exquisite rhetorical skill. Positively speaking, through the Son the believer approaches God "with a true heart and in full assurance of faith" (10:22). Negatively speaking, it is clearly disastrous to neglect such great salvation, for this salvation has been declared by the Lord and accompanied by fitting divine testimony expressed "in signs, wonders, and various miracles, and by gifts of the Holy Spirit, distributed according to his will" (2:4). Turning away from such a salvation reflects an "evil, unbelieving heart" (3:12) and being "hardened by the deceitfulness of sin" (2:13). Every effort must now be made to enter the promised rest, for we will give an account to a God whose word is "living and active, sharper than any two-edged sword" and before whom "no creature is hidden but all are naked and laid bare to his eyes" (4:12, 13). The appropriate response is one of steadfast "confession" (4:14), and one of boldness in approaching "the throne of grace" (4:16). Believers are exhorted to avoid becoming "dull in understanding" (5:11), and the mature are identified as those "whose faculties have been trained to distinguish good from evil" (5:14). To come to faith in the Son is to have been enlightened and to "have tasted the heavenly gift, and have shared in the Holy Spirit, and have tasted the goodness of the Word of God and the powers of the age to come" (6:4–5). Thus the potential risks of turning away after conversion and repentance are catastrophic. To avoid this it is pivotal to "realize the full assurance of hope to the very end" (6:11), and this is assisted by becoming "imitators of those who through faith with patience inherit the promises" (6:12). If believers do this, the end result is epistemically magnificent, for they will receive the promises of the new covenant. In that covenant God "will put [his] laws in their minds, and write them on their hearts. . . . They shall not teach one another or say to each other, 'Know the Lord,' for they shall all know me, from the least of them to the greatest" (8:10–11).

This kind of faith is to be sustained corporately and socially rather than just individually, thus they must avoid neglecting to meet together but should encourage one another, and all the more so as they see the Day approaching (10:25). Yet, there is a deep personal element in that their helping each other occurred in the midst of persecution. Loss of property and imprisonment led them to show compassion and to accept the plundering of their possessions, "knowing that [they] possessed something better and more lasting" (10:34).

It is this theme, the personal persistence in obedience and faith that is initially pursued in Heb 11. Essentially the writer works through a litany of heroes and heroines of faith. There is Abel whose faith brought divine approval, Enoch who pleased God, Noah who heeded God's warning, and then Abraham who obeyed and journeyed by faith, received powers of procreation, and offered up Isaac. There is Jacob who blessed the sons of Joseph, and Joseph who looked ahead to the exodus. There is the great Moses who spurned the wealth of Egypt, left Egypt unafraid, and kept the Passover. There are the people who passed through the Red Sea and who saw the wall of Jericho crumble. There is Rahab who received the spies in peace and last of all the magnificent "tail enders" (11:32–38) whose batting included extraordinary blessing and excruciating suffering. In turn, these heroes and heroines of faith are transfigured in chapter 12 into a cloud of witnesses who now stand in the wings to cheer on those tempted to fall back and falter. They are incorporated as "the firstborn who are enrolled in heaven . . . and the spirits of the righteous made perfect" (12:23) into an assembly that has the angels, the living God, and the risen Jesus as constitutive of its membership.

What I have tried to do in the preceding section is to draw attention to the wealth of epistemic concepts and the variety of modes of argument employed by the writer to the Hebrews as he seeks to persuade the hearer to remain steadfast in faith in the midst of abuse and opposition. Thus we have an appeal to a definitive and unsurpassed Word of God in history in his Son, to divine testimony expressed in original and ongoing signs, wonders, and miracles, to inward enlightenment, to tasting of the goodness of the Word of God and of the powers of the age to come, and to the infusion of the divine law in mind and heart. In terms of traditional epistemology we have an appeal to revelation, to miracle, and to religious experience. Interestingly, the epistemic goods on offer are expressed in terms, not of probability or opinion, but of confession, assurance, conviction, and knowledge. Furthermore, it is assumed that human agents have cognitive faculties that can be trained to distinguish good from evil, that they have hearts that can be hardened and deceived by rebellion, evil, and sin, and that their capacities to see the truth about God are linked in profound ways to trust, obedience, the quest for virtue, and the like. All these factors are pursued in contemporary epistemology in terms of properly functioning or reliable belief-producing mechanisms and in terms of virtue epistemologies. Equally important, social considerations represented by meeting together, by compassion for the persecuted, and by great historical memories and recitals of heroic faith, steadfastness, and suffering are vital in sustaining properly formed belief. In traditional epistemic categories these features are currently pursued in terms of the inescapable social dimensions of epistemology. Yet the social dimensions in no way override the personal nature of faith as the proper cognitive response to the promises of God now given with such lavish richness and generosity in Jesus and confirmed in experience by the work of the Holy Spirit. Moreover, faith is construed as an ongoing disposition to obey and believe that must be sustained, guarded from erosion by rebellion and sin, expressed by personal identification with the people of God, inspired by the model of Christ's passion and victory over evil, and manifested in corporate worship with the saints and angels in heaven. Clearly faith is seen here as a form of belief that involves trust and growth on the one hand and participation in knowledge of God on the other. Thus faith rises above mere belief, goes far beyond mere opinion, and is marked by full assurance and conviction.

My aim in the aforementioned section has been simple; I have set out to capture something of the complexity of faith as enshrined in a host of epistemic material that shines through the epistle as a whole. This complexity has been expressed in three ways: by an initial summary of critical elements of faith; by drawing attention to a network of epistemic concepts and varied arguments; and by a delineating of the epistemological territory occupied by the writer. It remains to conclude by drawing attention to the contrast furnished in this analysis to that currently available in much work in the epistemology of theology. The challenge posed to the theologian and philosopher at this point is surely startling. I shall make seven general points and then draw a couple of concluding lessons for future work.

First, the writer is interested in a very robust version of theism that readily and even enthusiastically embraces a rich vision of divine engagement in the Son and the Holy Spirit for the healing of the world. There is here no cutting back to some mere theism beloved by so much contemporary philosophy of religion.

Second, the writer to the Hebrews is not afraid to employ a host of epistemological materials and moves. The tendency in most epistemologies of theology is to look for a monothematic and formal vision of rationality, justification, warrant, knowledge, and the like. Here the tendency is to make use of a host of epistemic themes accompanied by a readiness to employ them tacitly and informally.

Third, the arguments deployed here are person, tradition, and community relative, but that in no way means that they are lacking in cognitive content or persuasive effect. The mere fact that our concept acquisition is tradition dependent, or that the argument relies on earlier consensus, in no way inhibits confidence in the claims advanced or the conclusions drawn.

Fourth, the writer works not just synchronically but diachronically. Thus the prevailing picture is not that of a set of single propositions that are to be inspected once and for all and given their relevant epistemic status but of a believing agent who is embarked on a journey of faith that yields its epistemic treasures over time. Thus the full force of the argument is not given once for all but is developed over time and thus allows for retrospective accumulation of evidence from different sources.

Fifth, the writer clearly sees divine revelation as indispensable to the grounds of the theology embraced and expounded, and he clearly thinks that signs, wonders, and miracles constitute divine testimony pertinent to the proper identification of divine revelation. Thus against Karl Barth, there is no question of shunting aside the problem of rival claims to divine revelation; against the New Yale School, faith is not seen as secured by the persuasive exposition of the internal grammar or coherence of belief; and against the general trend within analytical philosophy inspired by David Hume, miracles are seen both as genuinely historical events and as epistemically valuable.

Sixth, faith is not some generic mode or structure of belief but a very particular form of trust and obedience directed to the God now made manifest in Christ. Thus faith is not some generic will-of-the wisp, standing as a placeholder for our ultimate concern, but a very particular confession accompanied by repentance, baptism, and participation in the people of God.

Seventh, such faith yields knowledge, and en route to knowledge it is marked by assurance and conviction. This is not the more-probable-than-not prize offered at the end of Richard Swinburne's cumulative case argument.[10] Yet neither is it the mere person-relative assurance that is product of our properly functioning faculties arising from the work of the Holy Spirit and delivering properly basic beliefs, as offered by Alvin Plantinga. Against the former we have assurance, conviction, and knowledge; against the latter we have an assurance that is tied quite specifically rather than contingently to divine revelation and relevant evidence.

Where do these disparate observations leave us? I think that they are extremely significant at two levels. On the one hand, they dispel any idea that casting aside canon as a criterion leaves us defenseless in articulating the epistemic status of our theological beliefs. On the contrary, these comments show that at least one biblical writer is adept at deploying a host of epistemic measures and strategies to persuade believers and sustain them in their convictions. One can readily understand the intellectual panic that can set in when a venerable but failed vision of epistemology in theology collapses, but the response to this kind of crisis is not to abandon epistemology, or to look for quick and easy fixes, but to find better options in epistemology that will do justice to the robust claims that really matter in theology.

On the other hand, these disparate comments on Heb 11 make it all too clear that we have not resolved longstanding challenges on how best to think through the whole gamut of issues that crop up in the epistemology of theology. Certainly, we have seen extraordinary and even revolutionary developments over the last thirty years in epistemology generally and in the epistemology of religious belief in particular, developments that barely show up on the radar screen of most contemporary Christian theology.[11] What we now need is for theologians to come to terms with the fresh insights that have emerged in epistemology and for philosophers to pay much greater attention to the insights that lie below the surface in the canonical heritage of the church. We can surely profit in this endeavor by looking carefully at the material that crops up from time to time in the canon of Holy Scripture. Hebrews 11:1 is as good a site as any to pursue this enterprise. Central to that text is this epistemological insight: faith is grounded in a divine revelation that is worthy of assent, that is discerned by spiritually sensitive faculties, that is authenticated by signs, wonders, miracles, and the work of the Spirit, that is confirmed by cross-generational testimony and by deliverance from sin, and that is nourished and sustained in a community of worship and praise. Such faith rightly provides a basis for full assurance and lasting conviction. Faith is indeed "the assurance for things hoped for, the conviction of things unseen."

NOTES

1. *Canon and Criterion in Christian Theology: From the Fathers to Feminism* (Oxford: Clarendon, 1998).

2. James Barr, *Biblical Faith and Natural Theology* (Oxford: Clarendon, 1993).

3. Wesley took up this theme in two sermons on Heb 11:1. See "On the Discoveries of Faith" and "On Faith," which are sermons 117 and 132 in *The Works of John Wesley* (ed. Albert C. Outler; Nashville: Abingdon, 1987), 4:28–38, 187–200. In the second sermon he goes right over the top, claiming that we will be fitted out with new senses (or supplied with senses that will be made operate) to perceive all sorts of phenomena in eternity now hidden to view. It is in this sermon particularly that we see how insistent Wesley was that faith was a form of perception.

4. I pursue the instability in Wesley's epistemology in "Conversion and Knowledge of God: Is There Anything New," in *Conversion in the Wesleyan Tradition* (ed. Kenneth J. Collins and John H. Tyson; Nashville: Abingdon, 2001), 175–194.

5. For a recent hard-hitting analysis along these lines see A. C. Grayling, *What is the Good?* (London: Weidenfield and Nicholson, 2003), especially ch. 4.

6. Alvin Plantinga, *Warranted Christian Belief* (New York: Oxford University Press, 2000).

7. Plantinga carried out this critique most famously in his "Reason and Belief in God," *Faith and Rationality* (ed. Alvin Plantinga and Nicholas Wolterstorff; Notre Dame: University of Notre Dame Press, 1983), 16–93.

8. See Alvin Plantinga, *Warrant and Proper Function* (New York: Oxford University Press, 1993).

9. It is striking how far divine revelation has dropped out of standard texts in philosophy and philosophy of religion, even in texts written and edited by conservative Christians.

10. See Richard Swinburne, *The Existence of God* (Oxford: Clarendon, 1991).

11. For a splendid introduction see Robert Audi, *Epistemology: A Contemporary Introduction to the Theory of Knowledge* (New York and London: Routledge, 2003).

RESPONSE TO ABRAHAM

D. STEPHEN LONG

William Abraham uses Scripture to make epistemological claims. Hebrews 11:1, he tells us, offers a "wealth of epistemic concepts." This may surprise casual readers of his work, for he argues both here and in *Canon and Criterion* that the Western Christian tradition misleads us by turning Scripture into canon and canon into an epistemic criterion.[1] Has he not participated in this misleading tradition when he offers "an epistemological commentary on Heb 11:1"? If the Western Christian tradition misleads us by turning the Bible into an epistemic criterion, should not the resolution to our problem be "thou shalt not do epistemology" rather than looking to the Bible for "epistemic concepts"? If so, then we could take solace in the Barthian revolution where revelation needs no epistemological justification because, as Karl Barth taught us, "Revelation is the condition that conditions all things without itself being conditioned."[2] But having taken from us the Bible as an epistemic criterion, Abraham will not allow us any Barthian consolation either. In his *Canon and Criterion* he refuses this consolation, stating, "how little Barth has escaped from the epistemological captivity in the West. The situation is this. At one level Barth took the Bible as an epistemic norm."[3] So why is it that Abraham can find a "wealth of epistemic concepts" in Heb 11:1 as a means out of the West's "epistemological captivity," but Barth's use of the Bible as an "epistemic norm" remains captive?

Is this all finally a shell game? How can Abraham at one moment appeal to something like an intratextual scriptural norm against the extratextualists—"look at the wealth of epistemic concepts in Heb 11:1"—and then at another moment use this "epistemic wealth" as something like extratextual evidence, stating "the writer [of Hebrews] clearly sees divine revelation as indispensable to the grounds of the theology embraced and expounded, and he clearly thinks that signs, wonders, and miracles constitute divine testimony pertinent to the proper identification of rival revelation. Thus against Barth, there is no question of shunting aside the problem of rival claims to divine revelation; against the New Yale School, faith is not seen as secured by the persuasive exposition of the internal grammar of coherence or belief . . . "? I do not think this is finally a shell game, but to see this requires an acceptance of Abraham's historical narration of "the history of theology on the nature and status of canon."[4]

This history assumes a "standard Western way of thinking of the role of Scripture" that turns the Bible into the epistemological foundation for theology and church life. This "standard Western" view tempts us to seek a "monothematic and formal vision of rationality, justification, warrant, knowledge and the like," whether this be located in papal infallibility, *sola scriptura*, religious experience, a single philosophy, or a doctrine of divine inspiration. The Western tradition looks for a single epistemic criterion by which theological determinations can be made with certainty. This first emerges when the West has to justify changing the creed by adding the filioque clause. This sets us out on a quest for that "holy grail"—an infallible epistemic foundation. It is this *singular* epistemic foundation that Abraham identifies as problematic, not epistemology *per se*. Thus no contradiction exists in his critique of the extra- and intratextualists. Appearances to the contrary, his work is not a shell game, for this historical quest for epistemic certainty took multiple forms. Some found it in papal infallibility, others in the Bible, others in some framework within which the Bible or the church's authority could be secured, others in experience, etc. But no matter what the secure foundation, it could not avoid two problems. First, it was unable to adjudicate competing material claims. Second, each epistemic foundation could itself be grounded in something else, leading to an infinite regress, or ground itself precisely in that for which it sought to be the foundation, leading to a vicious circularity. (The Bible is the epistemic criterion grounded in divine inspiration grounded in the Bible as the epistemic authority, and the same can be done with papal infallibility or experience.) So what is the result? An unceasing pursuit of epistemology starves the church of its true means of grace and empties it of an adequate authority.

Means of grace function epistemologically in Abraham's work but without serving as a single foundational criterion. Rather than speak of canon, we should speak of our canonical heritage which includes creed, Scripture, liturgy, iconography, the Fathers, and sacraments. These means of grace are, as Abraham puts it, more like the "production of a grand symphony" than a single secure foundation.[5] How does Scripture function as a means of grace within this "grand symphony"? This essay shows us how this works. First we should note that Abraham looks to Scripture itself to show us this production, and what he discovers is "epistemic concepts" and "variety of modes of argument," which have the purpose of "persuasion." These "concepts" and "modes" include:

(1) "a definitive and unsurpassed Word of God in history in his Son,"
(2) a "divine testimony expressed in original and ongoing signs, wonders, and miracles,"
(3) "inward enlightenment,"
(4) "tasting of the goodness of the Word of God and of the powers of the age to come,"
(5) "the infusion of the divine law in mind and heart."

These "epistemic goods" point beyond Scripture alone, and in fact, they point beyond any single contemporary epistemological option. For this reason Abraham "challenges" nearly all contending epistemological options. He rejects the theistic option as present in the philosophy of religion, cartesian epistemologies, nontradition dependent rationalities as one would find in the Enlightenment, modern denouncers of miracles as unwarranted evidence (Hume and the analytical tradition), Barthians and the Yale School, Tillich and Liberal Protestantism, and Swinburne, Plantinga, and philosophical theology. Along with the number of challenges to epistemologies in *Canon and Criterion*, not many schools or churches in the Western tradition are left standing after Abraham's critique.[6]

I find Abraham's appeal to Scripture as a "means of grace" rather than an epistemological criterion enticing, but I am still left wondering how Scripture functions as a means of grace, and more particularly, how Heb 11:1 offers the counter-example to Scripture as epistemic criterion. So let me conclude with four objections or questions:

First, does Abraham finally avoid the perception that he is still looking to Scripture as the "epistemic criterion" when he draws on Heb 11:1 as an "epistemological commentary"? What makes a "means" other than a "criterion"?

Second, (and here I answer in part my first objection) is not a means other than a criterion because a criterion functions as a theory to adjudicate definitively among competing options while "means" function within the context of a practical reason where no such definitive *epistemological* criterion is to be found? But would not this require a reexamination of Aquinas and his incorporation of Aristotle's *phronesis*—thinking—into theology?[7] Why is Aquinas's virtue tradition with its emphasis on practical reasoning and the key role of gifts, beatitudes, and theological virtues so readily rejected in Abraham's work in favor of a call for "a new subdiscipline identified as the epistemology of theology that will engage in a rigorous and comprehensive way the nature of rationality, warrant, justification, and knowledge in theology"? This call confuses me. How is it not asking for a clearer account of criteria?

Third, I would designate the true culprit in the western tradition as Locke who turned miracles into positivist evidence and made possible something like the verification hypothesis.[8] At times I think Abraham would agree, but then I am confused as to the role of "evidence." Abraham notes the wonderful oddness of Heb 11:1 in that it ties faith to "things unseen" rather than things seen. This would seem to be a challenge to the "verification thesis" present in empiricist thought. But then Abraham himself appeals to the importance of "evidence" as part of the wealth of epistemic concepts in Heb 11:1.[9] Why?

Fourth, should we not recognize that "epistemology" is a modern discipline that we must abandon precisely because it assumes our knowledge can only be of the visible and sensible? Is this not how the verification thesis traps us into an immanent world through epistemology? Would a recovery of the importance of illumination and a metaphysics of participation not provide what we need without the invention of a new subdiscipline of the epistemology of theology? And can we not find this in the book of Hebrews more readily than in an epistemology?

NOTES

1. *Canon and Criterion in Christian Theology* (Oxford: Oxford University Press, 1998).

2. *Church Dogmatics*, vol. I.1, *The Doctrine of the Word of God* (trans. G. W. Bromiley; Edinburgh: T. & T. Clark, 1975), 118.

3. *Canon and Criterion*, 383.

4. Abraham does state, "My aim has not been to develop a comprehensive history of canon and criterion in Christian theology, but to provide sufficient information to show the crucial twists and turns in the journey." See his *Canon and Criterion*, 466.

5. *Canon and Criterion*, 55.

6. If I read him correctly, there is a correlation between the epistemic goods in Heb 11:1 and his challenges to these various schools that looks something like this:

Challenges to epistemological options	*Epistemic Goods from Heb 11:1 and how they challenge epistemological options*
1) Theism as present in the philosophy of religion where knowledge of God depends upon theistic claims alone	1) "A definitive and unsurpassed Word of God in history in his Son"—not God in general, but the Triune God is the "object" of knowledge. This assumes the context of creed.
2) Cartesian epistemologies that seek a single reference point as the foundation for knowledge	2) No single epistemic criterion is deployed, but a "wealth of concepts"
3) Nontradition dependent rationalities, as one would find in the Enlightenment, that seek impersonal arguments	3) The importance of "tasting of the goodness of the Word of God and of the powers of the age to come," which requires a specific social location in the church
4) Modern denouncers of miracles as unwarranted evidence (Hume and the analytical tradition)	4) "Divine testimony expressed in original and ongoing signs, wonders, and miracles"
5) Barthians and the Yale School where external adjudication of epistemological matters is eschewed on the basis that revelation or internal grammar suffices	5) Miracles and signs as external evidence available to reasonable persons who do not share in the internal grammar
6) Tillich and Liberal Protestantism where "faith" as a generic form of trust suffices as a form of knowledge	6) The specificity of the Triune God as well as "tasting of the goodness of the Word of God and of the powers of the age to come"
7) Swinburne, Plantinga, and philosophical theology where all that is possible is probability or person-relative assurance	7) "Inward enlightenment" and "the infusion of the divine law in mind and heart," which produces "assurance, conviction, and knowledge" rather than probability

7. Although I find the overarching narrative Abraham tells quite convincing, I am not so convinced that he has been fair to Aquinas.

8. By "positivism" I mean what the tradition of empiricism led to as found in Carnap. I recognize Locke cannot be held accountable for Carnap, but I do think his work set us on a historical trajectory that leads to logical positivism precisely because Locke was so convinced he knew the limits of how our knowledge works. As Simon Critchley puts it, "Carnap's argument against metaphysics is not that its statements are false, but rather that they are simply meaningless. For logical positivists like Carnap, meaning is rooted in the principle of verification, namely that a word or sentence is meaningful only if it is in principle verifiable. But what are the conditions for verification? They are two-fold: logical and empirical." These two-fold criteria assume either "logic" has a "self-referential system that permits the reduction of all propositions to either tautologies or contradictions" or "empirical truth" where propositions are reducible to "facts." See Simon Critchley's lovely little book, *Continental Philosophy: A Very Short Introduction* (Oxford: Oxford University Press, 2001), 100–101. I am indebted to Billy Abraham for pointing this book out to me.

9. He notes that we usually think of "assurance and conviction" in terms of "evidence" and not "faith." One would think this would lead to an epistemology not linked to "evidence," but that does not seem to be the case. Instead we are told that the writer to the Hebrews "allows for retrospective accumulation of evidence from different sources" which includes miracles, contra David Hume. And we are told, "faith yields knowledge. . . . Against [Plantinga] we have an assurance that is tied quite specifically rather than contingently to divine revelation and relevant evidence." Here I admit my confusion. What is the specific relevant evidence that yields assurance? Is this something like Locke's appeal to miracle? His appeal is distinct from Aquinas's willingness to use miracle within a context of gifts and virtues rather than Locke's very different empiricist epistemology where miracle does function as proof.

BINDING AND LOOSING: ASSERTING THE MORAL AUTHORITY OF SCRIPTURE IN LIGHT OF A MATTHEAN PARADIGM

MARK ALLAN POWELL

The authority of Scripture is challenged from many quarters in our present day but arguments over the authoritative function of Scripture seem to obtain a special poignancy in discussions of ethical and moral conduct. Christians have always recognized the Bible as their supreme reference work for knowing right from wrong, indeed for knowing the will of God regarding most, if not all, matters of moral behavior. The Bible contains an abundance of "Thou shalts" and "Thou shalt nots" and, from these, extrapolations may be made and analogies drawn for ethical questions that are not specifically addressed. But today the moral force of Scripture is waning, even within the church, where the simple observation that "the Bible says . . ." no longer ends discussion regarding controversial issues of moral conduct. Of course, naive citations of biblical texts can ignore the complexities of context with which exegetes and theologians must wrestle to determine whether an interpretation or application is valid. Still, respect for the Bible's moral authority becomes suspect when its moral codes appear to be affirmed selectively.

Virtually all Christian sects and individuals will grant that some prescriptions and proscriptions of Scripture are no longer relevant or applicable to Christians in the world today. Such judgments, furthermore, are made not only with regard to OT laws but also with reference to the teaching of Jesus and the apostles. Most Christian churches will allow their members to have bank accounts and pension funds despite the fact that Jesus said, "Do not store up for yourselves treasures on earth" (Matt 6:19). Likewise, most Christian churches allow women to attend worship services unveiled (1 Cor 11:10) and even to speak in their assemblies (1 Cor 14:35–36). The challenge, then, is to recognize that questions of permanent or continuing relevance must be raised and yet to find a way of engaging those questions with a submissive integrity that respects the authority of Scripture over its interpreters. We cannot simply insist on universal and permanent applicability of all scriptural mandates, but we must avoid the temptation of deciding that directives no longer apply to us simply because they are no longer in sync with the shifting values of our age.

The Gospel of Matthew was written within a community that faced similar concerns. Matthew strives to affirm the eternal validity of "the law" (Matt 5:17–19) while also insisting that allegiance to Christ calls for radical reexamination of how some legal precepts should be interpreted and obeyed (Matt 5:20–48). In this paper, then, I want to describe what I take to be a paradigm for how one NT community sought to interpret the Scriptures with regard to ethical matters, and specifically, with regard to matters that had become controversial. It is a paradigm that Matthew has inherited from Judaism but reworked in light of his christological and ecclesiological convictions.

Twice in Matthew's Gospel the words "bind" (*deō*) and "loose" (*luō*) occur in what is apparently a formula that readers are expected to recognize. In Matt 16:19 Jesus says to Peter, "I will give you the keys of the kingdom of heaven, and whatever you bind on earth will be bound in heaven, and whatever you loose on earth will be loosed in heaven." In 18:18 Jesus says to the twelve, "Truly, I tell you, whatever you bind on earth will be bound in heaven, and whatever you loose on earth will be loosed in heaven." The immediate literary contexts for these two passages include the only two texts in Matthew (or anywhere in the NT) where Jesus explicitly refers to "the church" (16:18; 18:17). Thus, we may observe that Matthew closely connects the business of binding and loosing with the mission of the church that is built by Jesus (16:18) and sustained by his continuing presence (18:20). It would not be an overstatement to say that Matthew considers binding and loosing to be a constitutive aspect of the church's mission on earth.

MEANING OF THE TERMS

A majority of scholars now recognize that the terms "to bind" and "to loose" are best understood with reference to a practice of determining the application of scriptural commandments for contemporary situations.[1] The words are used in this regard by Josephus and in targumic materials. Jewish rabbis "bound" the law when they determined that a commandment was applicable to a particular situation, and they "loosed" the law when they determined that a word of Scripture (while eternally valid) was not applicable under certain specific circumstances.

Other interpretations of the terms have been offered.[2] A few scholars have related them to exorcism (binding and loosing of demons—but why would the church ever want to loose a demon?). More often, interpreters throughout church history (including Luther) have thought the terms referred to the church's authority to forgive or retain sins. The scriptural basis for the church having such authority is secure but is better derived from John 20:23. Modern scholarship has cautioned against reading the Matthean texts in light of the Johannine concept. It seems unlikely that the first evangelist would have favored the notion that the church might withhold forgiveness of sins; he seems to guard against such an interpretation of 18:15–20 via the addendum of 18:21–35 (cf. also 18:10–14).

For Matthew, the issue is *identification* of sin. Final authority rests with the community to identify which behaviors constitute sin and which therefore require repentance. As in John, the person who does not heed the church's authority may be excluded from God's eschatological community, but for Matthew the problem is ethical discernment (and lack of respect for the church's role in this) rather than mere obstinacy. This is consistent with Matthew's understanding of the Great Commission as being to teach baptized people to obey the commandments of Jesus (28:20). To fulfill such a commission the church must be able to discern what obedience to those commandments entails, and the baptized persons who are to be made disciples must accept the church's teaching on such matters.

Matthew's Gospel is commonly understood as reflecting a close connection to the world of Second Temple and post-Temple Judaism.[3] Within that milieu debates over the applicability of the law to specific situations were common. They appear already in famous arguments between the first century schools of Hillel and Shammai and continue to be a defining part of the discussions that would ultimately be codified as the Mishnah. For example, the question was raised whether one might be guilty of stealing if one finds something and keeps it without searching for the rightful owner. When is such a search required and how extensive must it be? The Talmud states, "If a fledgling bird is found within fifty cubits of a dovecote, it belongs to the owner of the dovecote. If it is found outside the limits of fifty cubits, it belongs to the person who finds it (*b. B. Bat. 23b*).[4]

To use Matthew's terminology, the decision was that the law ("Do not steal") was *bound* when the bird was found in proximity to its likely owner; one who keeps the bird under such conditions has transgressed the law and is guilty of sin. But the law is *loosed* when the bird is found at a distance from any likely owner; the law against stealing does not forbid keeping the bird in that instance. Matthew's Gospel displays an awareness of such legal discussions when it refers to "the tradition of the elders" (15:2) and when it engages such questions as "Is it lawful for a man to divorce his wife *for any cause*?" (19:3). Matthew's community seems to have been struggling with issues similar to those that exercised the rabbis.

It is important to note that for the rabbis (and for Matthew) loosing the law never meant dismissing Scripture or countering its authority. The law was never wrong when it was rightly interpreted. The issue, rather, was discernment of the law's intent and of the sphere of its application. Thus, in the above example, the rabbis did not decide that in some instances it is all right to steal; rather, they sought to define *stealing* in a way that would determine just what behavior was prohibited. The logic of rabbinic argument does not always hold up to modern critical scrutiny (especially from Gentiles), and at times decisions to loose the law may appear *to us* as simple dismissals of Scripture. Still, they were apparently never intended as such.

Likewise, in Matthew's Gospel, Jesus may seem dismissive of Scripture when he says, "You have heard that it was said, 'An eye for an eye and a tooth for a tooth,' but I say to you . . ." (5:38). Most likely, however, Matthew intended to present Jesus' radical reinterpretations of the law as bringing out its true intent and defining its sphere of applicability in a manner analogous to what was done by other rabbis. Certainly, Matthew does not intend to pit Jesus against Torah, but strives to present Jesus as the one who indicates how Torah is to be fulfilled.[5] Jesus says:

> Do not think that I have come to abolish the law or the prophets; I have come not to abolish but to fulfill. For truly I tell you, until heaven and earth pass away, not one letter, not one stroke of a letter, will pass from the law until all is accomplished. Therefore, whoever breaks one of the least of these commandments, and teaches others to do the same, will be called least in the kingdom of heaven; but whoever does them and teaches them will be called great in the kingdom of heaven (5:17–19).

The word that the NRSV translates "break" in this passage is exactly the same word that is rendered "loose" in Matt 16:19 and 18:18 above. If the latter two verses were absent from this Gospel, we might assume that Jesus is here rejecting the rabbinic practice of "loosing" the law altogether. But in 5:17–19 "loosing" (*luō*) the commandments is contrasted not with binding (*deō*) them but with doing (*poieō*) them and teaching (*didaskō*) them. Clearly then Matthew condemns the practice of loosing the law when this means abolishing the Scriptures rather than fulfilling them through obedience and teaching. But Matt 16:19 and 18:18 present him as commending the practice of (sometimes) loosing the law in some other undefined sense. Most likely, the latter sense is the same as that employed by rabbis—discerning the intent of the law with regard to particular circumstances. Sometimes, Matthew's Jesus allows, the church will be expected to determine that the law (while eternally valid) does not apply to specific circumstances.

We may also note peripherally that the mere existence of the text cited above (Matt 5:17–19) is a fairly strong indication that some people were saying that Jesus (or the Matthean community speaking in his name) *was* abolishing the law. There would be little sense in issuing the disclaimer otherwise. Apparently, then, Matthew's community and possibly Jesus himself were sometimes regarded by their peers as people who "loosed the law" in ways that were dismissive of its intent and authority, though (like other rabbis) they would have maintained that this was not actually the case. We should also note that, if Matthew's Gospel contains warnings about the potential abuse of "loosing" the law, it likewise warns against abuses involved in *not* doing so. One of Jesus' primary accusations against the scribes and Pharisees is that they "bind (*deō*) heavy burdens that are difficult to bear"on the shoulders of those who listen to their teaching (23:3).

EXAMPLES OF BINDING AND LOOSING IN MATTHEW'S GOSPEL

Many passages in Matthew's Gospel can be read as expressive of a concern for the church's responsibility in binding and loosing the law. The Gospel offers both good and bad examples with regard to how this ought to be done. Jesus consistently exemplifies the right way to bind and loose the Scriptures while the scribes and Pharisees consistently exemplify the wrong way to do so.[6]

In 5:21–23 Jesus binds the law prohibiting murder as applicable to anger and insults, and in 5:27–28 he similarly binds the law prohibiting adultery as applicable to lust. The apparent rationale for these decisions is that the "heart" is the locus of human sin, and thus intentions of the heart are judged by the same standard as actions.

In 5:31–32, Jesus binds the prohibition against adultery as applicable to divorce and remarriage and does so with explicit repudiation of scriptural allowance for the latter. This is taken up later in 19:3–9 where he explains that such allowance was merely a concession granted in recognition of "hardness of hearts" and that it never expressed the actual intent of God. (We note in passing that the notion that some biblical prescriptions and proscriptions are concessions to the human condition and do not represent the intent of God is a fairly radical hermeneutical innovation.) But Jesus also looses his own prohibition of divorce and remarriage for those instances involving *porneia* (i.e., when the spouse has been unfaithful or, possibly, when the marriage itself was illegal—the exact situation governed by this exception clause is debated).

In 5:33–37 Jesus binds the prohibition against swearing false oaths (Lev 19:12) as applicable to *all* oaths (without explanation, but possibly because human frailty or unforeseen circumstances can make even an oath that was intended in good faith into a false one).

In 5:43–48 Jesus effectively binds the commandment to "love your neighbor" as applicable also to enemies, or, we might say, he rejects a loosing of the love commandment by which some have indicated that "enemies" are distinct from neighbors and so not covered by the prescription. He does so with an appeal to the nature of God who bestows blessings upon the good and the bad alike.

In 12:1–9 Jesus looses the prohibition against performing work on the sabbath with regard to plucking grain to satisfy one's hunger. He further opines that the Pharisees' attempt to bind the law in such an instance causes them to "condemn the guiltless" (12:7).[7]

In 12:9–14 Jesus looses the prohibition against performing work on the sabbath with regard to works of healing and then declares, "It is lawful to do good on the sabbath." The latter pronouncement would potentially allow sabbath prohibitions to be loosed in many other instances as well (whenever the otherwise prohibited activity can be construed as "doing good").

In 15:1–2 and 10–20 Jesus looses some law (we are not sure which one) with regard to ritual hand washings. By so doing, he rejects a binding of the law that was found in the tradition of the elders. Apparently that tradition interpreted some purity regulation in the law as necessitating such hand washings.[8] Jesus rejects that interpretation and looses the law on the broad observation that "what goes into the mouth does not defile a person."

In 15:3–9 Jesus binds the commandment "Honor your father and your mother" as applicable to caring for one's parents in old age. He strongly rejects the scribes and the Pharisees' attempt to loose the law for those instances in which one might say, "Whatever support you would have had from me is given to God." He denounces this attempt at loosing the law as "making void the word of God for the sake of human tradition" and declares that those who favor such an interpretation teach "human precepts as doctrines."

There are many other instances in which disputes over binding and loosing the law seem to stand in the background. For example, no Mosaic law is mentioned explicitly in 22:15–22, but the question of paying taxes to Caesar turns on an interpretation of the biblical prohibition against idolatry. One might bind that prohibition to forbid offering tribute to a man who claims to be a god; Jesus appears to loose it on the grounds that a person who does not recognize Caesar's divinity may regard the "payment" as a meaningless act.

We may note that overall Jesus binds laws more frequently than he looses them. Yet this observation must be balanced by the fact that he claims—almost programmatically—to offer an "easy yoke" and a "light burden" to those who follow him (11:30; cf. 23:4). Further, although the instances in which he looses the law are relatively few, his justifications for doing so (e.g., "it is lawful to do good on the sabbath"; "what goes into the mouth does not defile a person") set sweeping precedents with potentially radical implications for ways in which laws could be loosed in many other instances (as they obviously were in the developing Christian church).

SOME OBSERVATIONS FROM THE MATTHEAN EXAMPLES

Emerging from this survey of Matthean texts are the potentially contradictory notions that the Scriptures must be properly bound and loosed if God's will is to be discerned and obeyed but that the Scriptures are often bound when they should be loosed and loosed when they should be bound, with the result that God's will is *not* discerned or obeyed.

Matthew's readers are urged to avoid two pitfalls. On the one hand, if the church is cavalier about loosing the law, it will "make void the word of God for the sake of human tradition" (15:6). On the other hand, if the church neglects to loose the law when it should, it will sometimes end up "condemning the guiltless" (12:7). To help readers find the narrow way that lies between these pitfalls, Matthew's Gospel not only offers the good and bad examples cited above but also presents Jesus as articulating a number of principles that might guide the church in its deliberations. These include the Golden Rule (7:12), recognition of the divine preference for mercy over sacrifice (9:13; 12:7), prioritization of love for God and neighbor (22:34–40), and identification of the "weightier matters of the law" as justice, mercy, and faithfulness (23:23).

Notably, all of these principles derive in some sense from Scripture itself, such that acceptable binding and loosing appears to be founded in a hermeneutic that interprets Scripture in light of Scripture. The key, however, is knowing *which* Scripture is to be given primacy. The Matthean Pharisees might have been able to justify their legal interpretations with reference to Scripture as well, but they are mistaken with regard to God's *priorities*. Sacrifice is good, but showing mercy is better; tithing is good but justice is better; and so forth.

THEOLOGICAL CONSIDERATIONS

The authority to bind and loose is securely located in Matthean Christology and in this Gospel's christological understanding of eschatology and salvation history. Jesus possesses this authority because he is a unique manifestation of God's presence (1:23; 11:27). Thus, even apart from the appeal to mercy, his loosing of the sabbath law is justified because "The Son of Man is Lord of the sabbath" (12:8). Matthew seems to want to say (1) that Jesus' legal interpretations are not arbitrary but follow clear principles such as those articulated above, and (2) that, even if they might *seem* arbitrary, they must be accepted because he has been authorized by God to make such pronouncements. This twofold declaration is significant because Matthew also applies it to the church. The church, in Matthew's mind, will not bind and loose Scripture arbitrarily but will follow the example of Jesus, teaching potential disciples to do *his* commandments. Still, the bottom line for those who might not be able to recognize this is that God (through Jesus) has given the church the authority to make such decisions, and, therefore, the church's pronouncements regarding ethical conduct are to be followed even when the rationale is not understood or appreciated (18:15–18).

The ultimate question for Matthew is not simply "on what basis is the law to be bound or loosed" but "who has the authority to do this." God has given the authority to Jesus (and not to the scribes and Pharisees, cf. 7:29), and Jesus in turn has given it to the church. In Matt 16:13–20, the primary concern is not with *how* the church will exercise its authority to bind and to loose, but with the establishment of that authority and its effects. Just as Jesus' authority to bind and loose is attributed in Matthew to his christological identity, so the church's authority is grounded in its acclamation of Jesus as "the Christ, the Son of the living God." Likewise, in Matt 18:15–20 the church is described as possessing the authority to bind and loose the Scriptures, not because Christians are wiser than Pharisees nor even because they possess a repository of Jesus' sayings and teachings, but because Christ is still present among them (18:20). Only Jesus Christ has the authority to bind and loose the law, but Jesus Christ now dwells in the community of believers that gathers to pray in his name. When the community issues its judgment regarding an ethical matter that has become controversial, that decision is to be regarded as a declaration of the risen Christ who acts and speaks through the community.

The most compelling statement theologically is Matthew's claim that "whatever you bind on earth will be bound in heaven and whatever you loose on earth will be loosed in heaven" (16:19; 18:18). The wording of these phrases seems to imply that the church on earth has a role in establishing or influencing the divine will. An analogy might be drawn to prayer (specifically referenced in 18:19). If divine actions can be influenced by the church's prayers, then divine judgments might be influenced by the church's decisions. But how would that work? Are we to imagine God waiting in heaven to receive the church's decision and then conforming the divine will accordingly?

In Matthew, Christ is both one "under authority" (8:9) and one to whom authority has been "given" (9:8; 28:19). In a similar way, the church might function under the authority of Christ and yet be construed as a veritable manifestation of Christ (as Christ is of God), able to act and speak with his authorization. As an antepenultimate embodiment of the presence of God in this world (10:40), the church may be able to speak for Christ in heaven as Christ on earth could speak for God. But such correlations are only analogous, not exact, and in neither case is the connection absolute. Jesus is often able to declare the will of God in Matthew's Gospel, but he also struggles at times to discern that will and is even careful to distinguish it from his own ("not what I want but what you want," 26:39). The same must be true for the church: its identification with Christ cannot be absolute, for the Matthean Jesus issues specific warnings against those who locate his presence on earth with undue precision or enthusiasm (24:23). Although Christ is present with the church (18:20; 28:20), the era of the church is also marked by his paradoxical absence (9:15; 26:11).

BINDING AND LOOSING IN PRACTICE

Matthew 18:15–20 presents the church's ministry of binding and loosing as necessary for the determination of who is to be subject to church discipline. As such, we are given a glimpse of how the process might actually work within the post-Easter community. Notably, the ministry of binding and loosing is no longer the function of a single gifted leader (e.g., Peter) but is now to be exercised by the community as a whole. We notice also that the church does not attempt to bind and loose laws for the world at large but only for its own community. The ministry is exercised with regard to a "sibling" (i.e., a member of the church) who is believed to be sinning. Indeed, the words "against you" in v. 15 call attention to the conflict that such sin generates between community members. If those words are not textually valid (they are missing from many manuscripts), a concern for conflict resolution remains evident nonetheless in the attention to process: first try to resolve the matter in private; then make certain that every word can be confirmed by witnesses; and so forth.

Thus, Matt 18:15–20 appears to offer a perspective on how binding and loosing might function in a situation where there is conflict, where there is some disagreement over culpability for sin. The sinful sibling in this passage is probably not to be understood as one who just stubbornly persists in what he or she acknowledges to be sinful behavior. (Matthew's definition of "brother" and "sister" in 12:50 makes that unlikely.) Rather, the text seems to envision a situation in which a number of church members confront a member of the community concerning behavior that they claim to be sinful but which he or she apparently does not acknowledge to be sinful. Ultimately, the church as a whole is called upon to make a determination. Basically, the church must either *bind* the law by deciding (with the accusers) that some scriptural injunction does apply to the person's behavior, or they must *loose* the law by deciding (with the accused) that the cited Scripture does not apply to this person's behavior.

An example of such a situation (albeit an issue never mentioned in Matthew) would be the dispute elsewhere in the NT regarding food offered to idols (e.g., 1 Cor 8). According to the program presented in Matt 18:15–20, we may imagine that one member of the community might think another is sinning if the latter individual is consuming such food.[9] The proper procedure, then, would be: (1) confront the person privately; (2) consult with two or three others; (3) bring the matter to the community as a whole for resolution. The community would then ask "Is the scriptural prohibition against idolatry applicable to eating food that was once dedicated to idols?" Conceivably, the church might bind or loose the law, but in either case Matthew's Gospel claims that the community speaks with divine authority: "whatever you bind on earth will be bound in heaven, and whatever you loose on earth will be loosed in heaven."

The person who will not listen to the church is to be regarded as "a Gentile or a tax collector," that is, as a candidate for evangelism. Such a person is no longer a sibling, no longer a member of the church, but must now be viewed as someone who still needs to be made a disciple (by being taught to obey Christ's commandments). Notably, the offense that excludes the person from membership in God's eschatological community is not the offense for which he or she was rebuked but the more serious matter of refusing to listen to the church. There is no interest in whether the offense was intrinsically sinful. Matthew does not think in such categories but is more overtly concerned with whether individuals abide by the moral standards of the community of which they are a part. It is sinful to violate those standards regardless of whether the action would be intrinsically sinful or not. In short, Matthew's Gospel seems to depict behavior that goes against the decision of the church as *definitively* sinful. The phrase "whatever you bind on earth will be bound in heaven" suggests that God holds individual Christians accountable for living in accord with the decisions of the church. Violating the community's ethic is sinful in and of itself, apart from any other consideration.

IMPLICATIONS AND PROBLEMS FOR CONTEMPORARY CHRISTIAN PRACTICE

Matthew's paradigm for binding and loosing is presented somewhat casually without the kind of detailed elaboration that would be necessary for the church to follow such a program today. Several concerns may arise regarding application of this paradigm in our contemporary world.

First, the Matthean paradigm for binding and loosing is only one biblical model for approaching questions of biblical ethics, and it needs to be evaluated in light of a fuller canonical understanding.

Second, the question might be raised as to whether Matthew would ever have expected the church to exercise its function of binding and loosing with regard to commandments of Jesus. We might suppose that the church has been authorized to bind and loose Torah (as Jesus did) but that it is expected to teach unquestioning obedience to what Jesus himself commanded without any thought as to continued relevance or applicability of the latter's words (Matt 28:20). In Matt 15:21–28, however, a Canaanite woman seems to be presented as "loosing" a commandment that Jesus himself had given earlier ("Go nowhere among the Gentiles but only to the lost sheep of the house of Israel," 10:5–6). She does not repudiate or invalidate this command but suggests that her case should qualify as an exception to it, and he allows this.

Third, the Matthean paradigm seems to assume that "the church" is a somewhat monolithic entity, and we might wonder what body in our modern world should have the authority that Matthew ascribes to this entity. Clearly, Matthew never envisioned the variety of denominations and ecclesiastical organizations that confront modern Christians. In light of this, the advice simply to take ethical disputes "to the church" for resolution may seem naive or inadequate. We must note, however, that the existence of diverse Christian communities was also characteristic of first century Christianity. Granted this,

Matthew's program does not anticipate unanimity of all Christian communities but calls for submission of individual Christians to the community with which they identify. For Matthew this is probably the local congregation. Applied literally today, such a program would create a radically congregationalist polity that would destroy unity of the church at other levels. A more helpful approach might be to identify the authoritative community for modern Christians as not only the local congregation but also the larger church body of which it is a part. The step-by-step movement that we find in Matt 18 from individual to "two or three others" to congregation might find a modern parallel in a movement from local congregation to synod to national church assembly. The inexact nature of such analogies should be noted, however, and some consideration given to whether what has been lost in the translation of cultures was essential. In this case, for instance, the modern scenario would allow for ultimate decisions to be made by a community (national church assembly) composed of people who have no personal acquaintance with those who will be affected by the decisions. That would not have been the case in Matthew's original first century model.

Fourth, Matthew's Gospel never addresses the question, "What if the church is wrong?" He seems to assume that the church's decision will always (almost by definition) be in keeping with the will of God. We know, however, that church bodies have often made what were later regarded (even by their own admission) as wrong decisions regarding ethical behavior. This existential realization may require churches to render judgments with humility or even offer warrant for churches to defer definitive judgment on certain matters. But what if a church does render a decision that is in error? To explore the ramifications of such a scenario, we must go beyond descriptive exegesis to consider possibilities that Matthew does not appear to have taken into account.

Let us imagine, first, that the church obtusely binds the law and declares behavior to be sinful that would in fact be acceptable to God. In such a situation I think the typical Christian counsel would be for enlightened believers to abide by their community's unfortunately unperceptive decision. We recall the Apostle Paul's dictum that the "strong" must sometimes yield privilege for the sake of the "weak" (1 Cor 8). Matthew ups the ante on that one, suggesting that refusing to listen to the church is, in itself, a sin that excludes one from God's eschatological community. Thus, the expectation on one who feels the church's restrictions are unnecessary, shortsighted, or wrong seems to be adoption of what we might call a vocation of *obedience under protest.*

Yet such a scenario assumes that obedience to the church's decision will not *in itself* constitute an act of sin. The Matthean conflict text (18:15–20) deals with only one type of ethical dispute, namely a unilateral matter in which the community accuses one of its members of sinning. Significantly, Matt 18:15–20 says nothing about a case in which there could be a *countercharge*, that is, a situation in which the one accused of sinning alleges that the church's decision restricts righteousness, that the condemned behavior *must* be practiced for God's will to be accomplished. In church history there have been Christians who felt compelled by conscience to violate the teaching of their community, not simply because they found that teaching to be unnecessarily restrictive, but because they believed that violating the teaching of an errant church was the only way to maintain obedience to God. We cannot say for certain what Matthew would think of such a scenario, but it seems unlikely that he would want the paradigm presented in 18:15–20 to provide the church with a basis for squelching prophetic critique. Still, for Matthew the typical role of a prophet is that of an outcast. All of the prophets (5:11–12; 23:29–35), including Jesus (13:57) were rejected by their communities. Thus, if obedience under protest is not an acceptable option for believers who think the church has erred, those believers will be expected to accept their status as outcasts and bear the suffering that this entails. They will rightly be regarded "as Gentiles and tax collectors" by a church that cannot see the error of its ways, and they will have to hope for vindication either in this life when the church finally reforms or in the life to come when all true prophets receive their ultimate reward. Of course, Matthew's Gospel also contains warnings about *false* prophets, such that individuals who choose to accept ostracism from the community in exchange for condemning its actions would be wise to consider carefully whether they are truly as enlightened as they suppose. Still, any review of ecclesiastical history accentuates the need for such prophets and commends all churches to watch and listen for them.

Basically, then, Matthew only allows two vocations for believers cast in the role of the accused offender of 18:15–18. Once the church has rendered its decision, the accused must either listen to the church, accepting the vocation of obedience under protest, or be regarded as a Gentile or tax collector, accepting ostracism as the consequence of claiming prophetic status. The key factor in deciding which vocation is appropriate appears to be the question of whether the accused believes that acquiescence to the church's decision will necessitate disobedience to God. The Southern Baptist who objects to prohibition of alcohol must ask, "Is it sinful for me *not* to drink alcohol?" The Roman Catholic who objects to prohibition of artificial birth control must ask, "Is it sinful for me *not* to use artificial birth control?" The Missouri Synod Lutheran who objects to prohibition of abortion must ask, "Is it sinful for me *not* to get an abortion?" The ELCA Lutheran who objects to prohibition of premarital sex must ask, "Is it sinful for me *not* to have sex before I marry?" In situations where the answer is negative, Matthew's position is clear. The individual who disagrees with the church is called to a vocation of "obedience under protest." Individual Christians ought to abide by the teaching of their church, when they do not consider it explicitly sinful to do so.

If the church should be wrong in such a situation, then individual Christians are simply called to practice self-denial and sacrifice in areas where this would have been unnecessary if the community had been more discerning. An ethical perspective informed by Matthew's Gospel regards maintaining the unity of the church as a purpose worthy of self-denial and sacrifice, even if the latter are necessitated by the church's own failings. If individuals were only expected to live in accord with those decisions of the church with which they personally concurred, the ideal of an ethical community would be impossible to maintain. Matthew's Gospel, furthermore, sets its ethical program within an eschatological framework that allows Christians to accept what appears to be unfair treatment through radical trust in God's ultimate justice: those who humble themselves through self-denial for the sake of the community may find that they are among those called "the greatest in the kingdom," and their reward in heaven will be appropriate to their sacrifice (18:4; 20:26–27). Thus, even if we recognize that the church can sometimes be wrong in its judgments concerning what is sinful, insistence upon "obedience under protest" as a normative response to those judgments remains existentially necessary and eschatologically just.

Finally, we must consider that the church might also err in the opposite direction, loosing laws unwittingly and, so, condoning or even blessing behavior that God in fact despises. As a corollary to what we have said above, we might construe Matthew's Gospel as implying that, when the church looses the law on a given matter, then those who abide by that decision will not come under the judgment of God, even if the offense would have been regarded as sinful otherwise. If "whatever you bind on earth will be bound in heaven" means that God holds sinners accountable for actions condemned by the church, then, logically, "whatever you loose on earth will be loosed in heaven" could mean that God will not hold sinners accountable for actions approved by the church. Such a proposition obviously holds some potential for theological controversy. At the very least, however, we might affirm that an individual in such a situation would be spared the judgment of God for the sin of "refusing to listen to the church," which Matthew seems to regard as a more serious offense than any specific act of immorality that a church might unwittingly sanction.[10]

Fifth, Matthew's Gospel never considers another basic question: "What if the church is unable to agree?" The scenario described in Matt 18 may seem naive to those experienced at dealing with church conflicts. The expectation in the Matthean account seems to be that the community will clearly side with either the accused or the accusers. The church *as a whole* will either bind or loose. Matthew does not anticipate a situation in which the church will be split in its deliberation over such matters, yet history reveals that, in practice, split decisions are commonplace.

The mere fact that Matthew assumes agreement in the church with regard to such matters is significant. According to Matthew, the church is to be an ethical community as much as a doctrinal one (28:18–20). Perhaps, then, we should identify a church that is fundamentally divided in its understanding of moral behavior as a church in crisis from the Matthean perspective. The divisive ethical issue is symptomatic of a fundamental problem, perhaps a failure at entrance (catechetical) level to articulate its confessional theology as a hermeneutical approach to ethics.

We might be wrong, however, to assume *unanimity* as the only standard for "agreement." Matthew 18:15–20 does not actually say that the decision of the church is a unanimous one. Matthew deftly avoids presenting any specific standard for defining "agreement" (two-thirds majority of those present and voting?). So, we should perhaps conclude that for modern churches "agreement" may be defined in accord with whatever procedures the particular community has adopted.

Further, ecclesiastical decisions that embrace a continuum of options should not be regarded as disagreement in the church but as agreement to respect a given range of diversity. For example, if a church body adopts a statement saying that it "neither advocates nor condemns" conscientious objection to military service, we should not think the church has lacked the ethical clarity to reach a decision. It *has* reached a decision, namely that individuals should be allowed to make up their own minds on this matter. Scriptural precedent exists for such a strategy (Rom. 14:5).

And, finally, neither ecumenical nor global agreement is presumed here, and that raises the question of whether the one who does not agree with the church might not simply change churches. This option is not entirely modern. If the offender in Matt 18:15–20 was a member of the church at Antioch, he might have been able to move to Corinth or Rome to find a community that would permit what his own church had condemned. The proliferation of church bodies in our age merely increases the likelihood of this happening. The problem with such a strategy, however, is that it might require adaptation of confessional perspectives for the sake of more convenient ethical strictures. There is an apparent lack of integrity in, say, a Southern Baptist deciding to become a Lutheran so that he can drink beer or a Roman Catholic deciding to become a Baptist so that she can use artificial birth control. Of course, disagreement with a church's ethical teaching might be symptomatic of fundamental disavowal of the confessional theology in which the ethical teaching is supposedly grounded. Thus, a process similar to that outlined in Matt 18:15–20 could lead an accused sinner to recognize incompatibility with the community at a basic level and so inspire that person to undertake a legitimate spiritual quest that would lead him or her to another church.

CONCLUSION

The overall concern that this paper has hoped to address is the authority of Scripture for contemporary Christian ethics. It is my contention that the Bible continues to have normative authority for such considerations in spite of the fact that the applicability of its mandates to modern situation might not always be immediate or obvious. The Bible itself recognizes a need for the church to consider the continuing relevance of biblical prescriptions and proscriptions and, when there is controversy, to declare whether those directives remain binding or whether they might be loosed. Thus, the Bible does allow for biblical mandates to be declared invalid for specific contemporary situations, but it makes clear that such a loosing of the law is only to be done by a community that is following the example of Jesus and adhering to principles of interpreting Scripture in light of Scripture, as he did. Perhaps most important, this paradigm indicates that such decisions are communal ones and that individuals are to abide by the moral guidance offered for their community, rather than simply deciding for themselves which of the Bible's directives seem applicable and relevant to their individual lives.

NOTES

1. This accords with the definitions offered in *ABD* 1:743–45 and BDAG 222.

2. Dennis C. Duling, "Binding and Loosing: Matthew 16:19; Matthew 18:18; John 20:23," *Foundations and Facets Forum* 3,4 (1987): 3–31.

3. W. D. Davies, *The Setting of the Sermon on the Mount* (Cambridge: Cambridge University Press, 1964); Anthony J. Saldarini, *Matthew's Christian-Jewish Community* (Chicago: University of Chicago Press, 1994).

4. The citation continues with a humorous note: "Rabbi Jeremiah asked: If one foot of the fledgling bird is within the limit of fifty cubits, and one foot is outside it, what is the law? It was for this question that Rabbi Jeremiah was thrown out of the House of Study."

5. Klyne Snodgrass, "Matthew and the Law," in *Treasures New and Old: Contributions to Matthean Studies* (ed. D. R. Bauer and M. A. Powell; Atlanta: Scholars Press, 1996), 99–128.

6. So polemical a presentation obviously reflects the strained relations between church and synagogue. The bias of Matthew's construal is a matter of record and need not concern us here. Even those who question the historical accuracy of his attributions recognize that the reports of legal disputes reveal this evangelist's own ideas regarding what constitutes proper and improper ways of binding and loosing the law.

7. Similar discussions are found in (later) Jewish literature. Plucking grain on the sabbath is forbidden without qualification (as equal to harvesting) in *y. Šabb.* 7.9b.67, but *b. Šabb.* 128a says, "One may pinch with the hand and eat but not with a tool."

8. Jacob Neusner's theory is that the Pharisees (especially after A.D. 70) sought to apply laws for the purity of priests serving in the temple to the people of Israel in general. See *Das pharisäische und talmudische Judentum* (Tübingen: Mohr/Siebeck, 1984), 24–25, 62.

9. We should not take the (textually suspect) words "against you" in 18:5 as implying that one is only to confront a sibling when one has been the direct or obvious target of the individual's wrongdoing. Sin harms the community of God's people, such that the sin of any community member will necessarily be an affront to all community members. Any sin by any member of the Matthean community will have consequences for siblings who seek to agree in prayer with one another (18:19) and who believe that they experience the presence of Christ through fellowship with each other (18:20). In a sense, then, Matthean church members cannot sin

against God without also sinning against each other. Whether explicit or implicit, the words "against you" would always apply.

10. Matthew would not dismiss entirely the role of individual conscience. He also allows that there are false teachers and blind guides and that those who follow them become children of hell or fall into a pit (15:14; 23:15). It is conceivable, then, that some communities (i.e., false teachers and their followers) might be condemned *in toto* (7:15–23). But in a basic sense Matthew, who no doubt knows that different Christian communities have reached different decisions on certain behavioral issues, wants to assure individual believers that if they "listen to the church" and follow the teaching of their particular community with a clear conscience, they will be safe in the final judgment.

THE NARRATIVE SHAPE OF SCRIPTURAL AUTHORITY: PLOTTING PENTECOST

D. BRENT LAYTHAM

AUTHORITY "IN": PUTTING SCRIPTURE WHERE IT BELONGS

Authority is generally exercised within a particular range, realm, or relation.[1] As a teacher, I have authority in my classroom at school but not in the cockpit of the commercial airliner I flew on last year. This fairly obvious point means that it is not inappropriate to ask at a conference on "The Authority and Function of Scripture in the Contemporary World" what the realm of Scripture's authority is.

Scripture has no authority in the contemporary world. Neither does much else, except for advertisements selling satiation, a medical-pharmaceutical industry offering prolonged health, and nation-states promising security. The modern period has been aptly characterized by Jeff Stout as a "flight from authority."[2] My claim that Scripture has no authority is primarily a theological assertion that will be argued in the following paragraphs. Descriptively, of course, there are more than a billion Christians alive today for whom the Bible is in some way authoritative. But we must also recognize that they regularly quibble among themselves about who *really* takes it seriously, who ascribes authority to it in *appropriate* ways.[3] And they are outnumbered four to one by persons who ascribe authority to no scriptures, or whose scriptures are different writings entirely.[4] In the United States there remain vestiges of the social authority that Scripture bore in Christendom: Bibles are used for taking oaths in judicial and political contexts; an Alabama court judge grandstands over a granite replica of the Decalogue. But such vestigial practices are only cheap imitations, neither authorized by Scripture nor authentic to its intended function. In sum, Scripture's *de facto* authority is presently disputed, misunderstood, and misused. Hyperbolically, Scripture has no authority in the contemporary world.

For Christians, that is as it should be, because the Christian Bible is not the world's text but the church's. As Francis Watson reminds us, "The primary reading community within which the biblical text is located is the Christian church."[5] We can make this point in two ways, one general and the other specific. Generically, one of the distinguishing marks of the category 'scripture' as it is used in the study of religions is that scripture is writing that is authoritative for a particular religious community. David Kelsey has famously remarked that authority is analytic to Scripture; to say that Scripture has authority is to speak a tautology.[6] So the Scripture of Christians—our two testament canon—has authority for us, the church whose Scripture it is. It would be odd indeed if it had authority for those for whom it is not Scripture, say Buddhists or Muslims. Specifically, Christian Scripture was written in, for, and by the church. It was received in and read by the church. It was kept and copied, collected and distributed, debated and canonized in and by the church. The Bible is the church's book, and the church is the Bible's audience. This latter point is true both of the book's own communicative intention and of its regular communicative enactment—most centrally in weekly reading in Christian worship. So both generically as the Scripture of Christians and specifically as the Christian Bible, this text's authority is not "in the contemporary world" but in and for the church.

My claim is thus a theological claim about the *de jure* authority of this text. The appropriate realm of scriptural authority is the church. The purpose of the Christian Bible, and thus its theologically intended function, is to announce the gospel, to author Christian identity, and to authorize Christian practice. Scripture does not do this alone; it is one of a constellation of means by which God makes and sustains the church.[7] Nor does Scripture do this automatically; it functions in this way by being taken up into the triune economy of God's saving grace, an economy that always invites and enables our response. God uses Scripture to make and sustain the church. The church is the primary (*de facto*) and the appropriate (*de jure*) realm of Scripture's authority.

This does not mean, however, that there is not a relation of scriptural authority to the "contemporary world." It simply means that the relation is not direct. The authority of Scripture is indirectly related to the contemporary world in two crucial ways. First, the ability of the world to recognize itself as creation in rebellion requires the church and its scriptural story.[8] As Stanley Hauerwas quips, the world would not know it is the world without the church to show it.[9] As God uses Scripture to author and authorize the church, the church serves the world as "sign, herald, and foretaste" (Vatican II) of the coming kingdom of God. Thus, Scripture does not have authority *in* the world; the world is by definition that rebellious realm where God's authority is refused. But Scripture does have authority in the church *for* the world.[10]

Second, because the church is always partially shaped by its surrounding culture, that culture's understanding of and attitude toward authority will have influence in the way that the church understands and enacts the authority of Scripture.[11] Does culture assist or resist, form or deform, scriptural authority in the church? Francis Watson has suggested that the world can be a source of truth for the church.[12] While this may be true in some areas, when it comes to authority, we should scrutinize Watson's claim closely. We should not fail to notice Jesus' explicit refusal of "worldly" understandings of authority (Mark 10:42–45), a refusal that directly correlates with the shape of his own life and the expected shape of the life of his disciples.[13] Thus, the greater possibility and perennial danger is that the church will simply baptize the wider culture's understanding of, or attitude toward, authority.[14] In our "contemporary world" authority has become a debated if not detested concept. As Richard Bauckham summarizes, "Authority is a very dubious notion in much of contemporary culture, both modern and postmodern, but especially postmodern, and, since Christianity is no longer culturally dominant, it is the secular culture's problem with authority that influences many people in the churches today."[15] Rather than sketch the specific discontents of modernity and postmodernity with authority here, I will turn to a constructive proposal of scriptural authority.[16] That proposal will be introduced briefly and then tested by way of theological interpretation of Scripture.

NARRATIVE AUTHORITY

John Goldingay warns that extrascriptural "concepts such as authority, canon, inspiration, inerrancy, infallibility, and revelation," while not inherently distorting, often function to

> . . . obscure Scripture's own implications regarding its nature, and do so in particular with regard to the prominence of narrative in Scripture. Authority, revelation, and inspiration are not concepts well fitted to bring out the theological status of a body of Scriptures that is dominated by narrative (they suit the *Qu'ran* and the *Book of Mormon* rather better).[17]

Does this mean that investigations of the authority of Scripture are to be eschewed altogether? How can they be, when this very text tells us the story of one who "taught with authority" (Matt 7:29), whose closing claim in Matthew's Gospel is that "all authority in heaven and on earth has been given to me" (Matt 28:18)? Rather, Goldingay's warning reminds us that a theologically adequate account of the authority of Scripture must seek to be adequate to what the Bible is, how it is used, and who—and especially Who—uses it. In agreement with Goldingay's own reference to "the prominence of narrative in Scripture," I will propose a narrative account of scriptural authority.

William Placher has offered a suggestive typology of three different ways of conceptualizing biblical authority. They are (1) Scripture as repository of authoritative propositions, (2) Scripture as transforming word, and (3) Scripture as narration of God's identity.[18] Placher suggests that one of the mistakes in discussions of scriptural authority has been a tendency to quantify. For example, proponents of the propositional approach—generally this group includes conservatives and evangelicals—have tended to consider holders of any other position as ascribing *too little* authority to the Bible. And proponents of the more experiential approach—liberals—have charged that their conservative counterparts ascribe *too much* authority to Scripture.[19] Placher quite rightly suggests that it would move us forward to recognize that ". . . there are different ways of thinking about the Bible as authoritative that we cannot rank on a single scale—not less authority or more, but just different, functioning as authority in different ways."[20] Further, he refuses the claim that such approaches are mutually exclusive; rather, each approach can and should learn from the others. This does not mean, however, that the three approaches are equally valid or useful. Placher sees a clear superiority in the third, narrative approach. In this he is a significant representative of a growing number of theologians and Scripture scholars who recommend that the narrative character of Scripture be central.[21]

This recommendation that we conceive the authority of the Bible in narrative terms involves both recognition and recovery. It recognizes the narrative shape and scope of the biblical text as canonically received, and it recovers the narrative hermeneutic of the church's canonical tradition. Specifically, it recovers the *ruled reading* of the biblical canon in terms of the "rule of faith" or "rule of truth." Such recognition had been eclipsed in modernity by other ways of construing the biblical text.[22] But beginning with the work of Hans Frei (or perhaps earlier with Barth), there are glimmers that biblical narrative is emerging from its eclipse in both theology and biblical studies.

My thesis is that the authority of Scripture is a narratively construed, ecclesially embodied practice of the Triune God. Rather than define my terms and delineate their relation, I will turn to a reading of Acts 2 as an exemplification of it. My choice of Acts 2 is rooted in the following considerations. First, an account of the narrative authority of Scripture should look to a narrative for exemplification.[23] Second, Scripture has a role in this story, yet is not central.[24] Further, Scripture's role in the story is not propositional, though certain propositions are related directly to Scripture; rather, in this story Scripture's authority is to authorize a particular telling of the story of Jesus and to authenticate a particular construal of the Pentecost story. Neither is Scripture's role primarily to author transformation, though Scripture does participate in the transformational economy of the Spirit's grace. Third, it is a narrative which displays the reciprocal dependence of story and church: without the church, there is no story, and without the story there is not church. This mutual interdependence of the church's story and the story's church is the necessary corollary of my thesis. Fourth, Acts 2 sets the authority of Scripture in the context of the economy of the triune God—and specifically in the economy of the Holy Spirit—in a way that requires us to ask how Scripture mediates or participates in God's authority and whether Scripture's authority requires the hermeneutic of the church's Trinitarian rule of faith.

I will look at the narrative authority of Scripture under the following heads: plot and the "sense of an ending," character and the rendering of identity, and world and narrative indwelling. In relation to the first, I will note the necessary coinherence of Scripture with the church's rule of faith. The second entails the mutuality of story and church. The third requires more than imagination, an "as if"; it requires "practices of inscription." This way of developing the argument, by way of coordinate concepts, suggests that scriptural authority is a complex interaction which is held together not by intrinsic properties of Scripture *as text*, but by this text's role within the economy of the Triune God.

William Placher has noted that one of the problems with a narrative account of biblical authority is that it struggles to sound as serious about authority as other accounts. "The claims 'This proposition is true' and 'Hear this word and let it transform your life' convey a more dramatic sense of authority than contemporary theologians have yet managed to capture for the claim to witness to the identity of God through narrative."[25] In reading Luke's dramatic account of Pentecost as the story of Scripture's narrative authority, I hope to provide an account that partakes, however partially, in the compelling nature of this story.

PLOT AND RULED READING: PETER (RE)TELLS THE STORY

Acts 2 is a literary whole, telling first the story of what happened one particular day (vv. 1–41, with emphasis on "the day" and "that day" at 1 and 41 respectively) and then summarizing the results of the following days (vv. 42–47).[26] The story has four scenes: the assembled believers are filled with the Holy Spirit (vv. 1–4), which draws a crowd of devout Jews who hear God's mighty acts proclaimed in their own language (vv. 5–13), allowing Peter to proclaim this as fulfillment of Scripture and the fruit of Jesus' resurrection and exaltation (vv. 14–36), which produces the response of the crowd (vv. 37–41). Each scene leads naturally, even causally, to the next. But what is the meaning of the whole?

A Plea for Plot. Literary analysis can tend to undervalue plot, and so has much narrativist theology. There are various reasons why, including the way a story's plot is apprehended differently in a first telling versus subsequent retellings. The first time you hear the story of the gospel, its twists and turns are shocking. But Christians hear and tell this story again and again, to the point that any sense of peripeteia gives way to a sense of predestination.[27] Paul Ricoeur describes the shift which occurs with subsequent renditions of the story: "As soon as the story is well known . . . retelling takes the place of telling. Then following the story is less important than apprehending the well-known end as implied in the beginning and the well-known episodes as leading to this end."[28] The church is a community that already knows how the story ends; moreover, the church is a community that only exists because it knows the ending.

But because we know how the story goes and how it ends, we can tend to skip too quickly to matters of character, environment, or theme. Yet the plot matters, and nowhere more than in the narration of Pentecost. Though the greater part of the passage is given over to Peter's interpretative speech, the central significance lies with the events—resurrection, exaltation, outpouring—that his speech interprets. Something *happens* on the day of Pentecost—something powerful and profound; God acts.[29] This is the basic structural form of the gospel itself: an indicative announcement in narrative form of what God has done. God does something that makes a difference. It makes a difference for the "devout Jews from every nation under heaven living in Jerusalem" (2:5) because it is God's doing *for them*. It matters for Theophilus (1:1) and the rest of Luke's community because it is God's doing *for them*. It matters for us because it is God's doing *for us*—indeed, "the promise is for you, for your children, and for all who are far away, everyone whom the Lord our God calls to him" (2:39). Thus the first form of the narrative authority of Scripture is that it tells the story of what God has done. Furthermore, the encounter with an oral or textual account of what God has done has the potential to become an event in its own right, in which God does something now in and through the reader's encounter with the story of what God has done.[30]

The importance of event in this narrative is highlighted by the Lukan emphasis on witness (1:8; 1:21–22; 2:32). Witnesses testify to what has happened. The central event of Jesus' resurrection-exaltation requires witness; indeed, it is a reality that cannot be known apart from witness. And the same is true of the event of Pentecost. The pentecostal phenomena are not self-interpreting. Other interpretations are possible, from puzzlement (2:12) to "they are drunk" (2:13). The outpouring of the Holy Spirit, like resurrection, requires witnesses, and it enables and empowers the witnesses it requires. It enables the disciples to be witnesses and to bear witness to the resurrection of Jesus (2:32), it empowers the apostles ("Peter, standing with the eleven"; 2:14) to narrate the event of Pentecost as the action of God in Christ, and it enables the 120 to speak "about God's deeds of power" (2:11). Acts 2 tells the story of God's provision in Christ of Spirit-filled witnesses to the gospel. Yet it does more than merely provide for the telling of the story; at Pentecost we see that the telling of the story is part of the story itself. Thus Luke's own activity of seeking out eyewitnesses (Luke 1:2) in order to write his narrative account is witness too, an ongoing fruit of the Spirit's coming.

"What does this mean?" asks the gathered crowd at Pentecost (2:12). That is a plot question; it invites us to set Pentecost in the larger Lukan narrative. In the context of Luke–Acts, Acts 2 can be read both as culmination of the story to this point and as the inauguration of the story from this point.[31] The sense of culmination is expressed in the introductory phrase "When the day of Pentecost was being fulfilled," a phrase emphasizing the fulfillment of prophecies and promises made in Luke–Acts.[32] The coming of the Holy Spirit had been foretold in the narrative of Luke–Acts by John the Baptist (Luke 3:15–17), and more importantly by Jesus himself (Luke 24:49; Acts 1:4–5, 8).[33] The repetition of this promise at the end of Luke and the beginning of Acts serves to further emphasize its significance in the story. Moreover, it fosters a sense that neither the resurrection of Jesus from the dead nor his ascension has brought the story to completion. Thus when the reader encounters "When the day of Pentecost was being fulfilled" (2:1), she already has an expectation that the final episode in the story of Jesus has yet to occur.[34] Thus Peter's claim that Jesus is the author of "this that you both see and hear" (2:33) is a confirmation of culmination, at least for Christian readers who have followed the story. On the other hand, as Pentecost culminates the ministry of Jesus it also inaugurates the mission of the disciples "to the ends of the earth" (Acts 1:8; cf. Luke 24:47). The remainder of Acts is the outworking of this plot that was prophesied at Acts 1:8, but initiated in Acts 2.[35] These are not two different ways to construe Acts 2 in relation to the overall plot of Luke–Acts. Rather, they are complementary renderings of the one narrative purpose of the entire story: the saving economy of the Triune God. And as we shall see shortly, they authorize a renarration of Israel's story, too.

Our Place in the Story. If Acts 2 is the real beginning of the rest of the story, we need to ask how that story ends. In a very real sense the ending of the *discourse* in Acts does not match the ending of the *story* of salvation in Jesus' name.[36] The angel's claim, which we are given no reason to doubt, is that "this Jesus . . . will come in the same way you saw him go into heaven" (1:11). Thus, the story is certainly not finished by its concluding narrative summary of Paul's bold and unhindered ministry in Rome (Acts 28:30–31).[37] The story inaugurated by Pentecost is not yet finished in the time of Luke–Acts, nor in our time either. We are given some sense of its final substance ("this same Jesus") and shape ("will come *in the same way*"), but these are mere foreshadowings. The result is an inaugurated ending to the story of salvation in Jesus' name that opens out to our present participation while continuing to anticipate a final, eschatological fulfillment.

John Goldingay has noted that stories are "written to do something to people. . . . It involves the possibility of there happening to us that which the story had the power to make happen to its audience."[38] We can see that rather clearly in Luke's construction of Peter's speech. First, Peter articulates the present moment as part of the story. The resurrection and exaltation of Jesus (part of the story past) produce "what you *now* see and hear" (the story brought into the present moment, 2:33). Second, when his hearers are cut to the heart and ask "What shall we do," Peter indicates that the story's conclusion lies in their future. He calls them to repent and be baptized, so that they too may receive "the gift of the Holy

Spirit" (2:38). The future holds for them promise of the same fulfillment that the present holds for Peter. In other words, they are invited to become characters in the story that Peter tells.[39] Third, because Luke has Peter reiterate that "the promise is for you, for your children, and for all who are far away, everyone whom the Lord our God calls to him" (2:39), the effect of telling and retelling the story of Pentecost, the effect of writing and reading the story of Pentecost, is to extend the ending of this episode into the present of every hearer and reader, to extend the invitation to be baptized into this story to every reader and hearer, to inaugurate an ongoing invitation to be inscribed into the story that Peter tells—a story that will not end until Jesus comes.[40]

What I have attempted to demonstrate by attention to the literary shape of Acts 2 is something like the regular claim of advocates of narrative theology that scriptural narrative invites us to 'indwell' it, or find our story within its story.[41] In Acts 2 it is a literary feature of the text that manifests this narrative capacity. But from a theological point of view, indeed from the point of view of Acts 2 itself, it is not the literary character of the text alone that produces this effect but the agency of the Holy Spirit. And the Spirit works this invitation to indwell the story in manifold ways not limited to the literary artistry of a particular narrative passage. Most commonly, the Spirit accomplishes this through ecclesial practices of narrative inscription like preaching, sacraments, or Bible study.

The Sense of an Ending. To this point our focus has been largely on the way the larger plot of Luke–Acts helps us to plot the significance of Pentecost. Acts 2 demands that we reverse the flow of interpretation, asking how this particular event functions to construe not only Luke's two volume story, but also the Bible's two testament story. N. T. Wright concludes his massive study of Christian origins with the claim that

> . . . what united early Christians, deeper than all diversity, was *that they told, and lived, a form of Israel's story which reached its climax in Jesus and which then issued in their spirit-given life and task.* Their strong centre . . . was not a theory or a new ethic, not an abstract dogma or rote-learned teaching, but a particular story told and lived.[42]

I would suggest that Peter's Pentecostal sermon is an example of precisely this phenomenon to which Wright refers. For in the speech Peter both tells what has happened at Pentecost and in the life, death, and resurrection of Jesus and retells the story of Israel through a narrative construal of Israel's Scriptures.

It is a commonplace to name Acts 2 "the birthday of the church." It is less common to note the inauguration of *story* in Acts 2.[43] I would suggest that here we find an account of the birth of church and story in mutual dependence: without the church there is no story, and without the story there is no church. I have shown above how Peter tells the story of Jesus as opening into the present and future of his hearers (and Luke's readers). Here I want to concentrate on the way that this telling of Jesus' story is set in the context of a narrative construal of Israel's story, that is, Israel's Scripture narratively rendered as OT.

Admittedly, Peter does not tell Israel's story in these verses (though Stephen's speech in Acts 7 is precisely such a retelling). He interprets the outpouring of the Spirit as the fulfillment of a prophecy in Joel (quoted in 2:17–21), the resurrection of Jesus as warranted by Ps 16 (2:25–28), and his exaltation as fulfillment of Ps 110 (2:34–35). It is possible to take Peter's exegesis as naive, pre-critical prooftexting, a ransacking of the Jewish Scriptures for any text that would support a witness to Christ. To read Peter's speech this way would be a mistake, however, for it would fail to see that already in the telling of the church's story of Jesus Christ there is a particular narrative construal of Israel's Scripture at work. That is to say, Peter's speech reads Israel's Scripture as "a story in search of a conclusion,"[44] and reads Jesus' story as that story's searched-for conclusion.

This has everything to do with the narrative authority of Scripture. Christopher Seitz reminds us of Hans von Campenhausen's claim that "In the early church, the problem was not how to square faith in Christ with an Old Testament regarded as outmoded, but the reverse. How, in the light of a Scripture everywhere regarded as authoritative and a privileged witness to God and his truth, could it be said that Jesus was in accordance and was one with the Father who sent him?"[45] The answer to the question lay in a construal of those Scriptures as a narrative—a story whose *telos* is Jesus Christ. Paul van Buren has recently suggested that the disciples, rendered mute by the death of Jesus, ". . . found the way out of their speechlessness by telling the story of Jesus, especially the most baffling part, his end, as Israel's story. They told his story in the idiom of Israel."[46] And correlately, they read Israel's story in the idiom of Christ crucified and risen. Thus, it is not just Israel's story, but its story told in a particular way, its canon rendered under a particular narrative construal, that authorizes Peter's proclamation of who Jesus is and what he is doing. It is this narrative construal of Israel's story as culminating in Jesus and his church that accounts for the storied claims of the citation of Joel and David. This is an apostolic exemplification of reading "Moses, the prophets, and the psalms" (Luke 24:44) as pointing to Christ. Luke 24:45–47 implies that both Jesus' story (Luke) and the church's story (Acts) are part of the "thus it is written" (24:46), and Acts 2 gives us a major example of reading each story in terms of the OT story.

The key to this new reading, the rationale for taking Jesus as the *telos* of the scriptural story, is the story's end. Students of narrative have long remarked on the way the ending of the story is most responsible for its overall character. Indeed, in stories that end with a major peripeteia the end changes everything, or at least sets it in an entirely new light. This is precisely what happens with the end of Jesus' story: the resurrection changes everything. Dead, Jesus' story was over; there was nothing more to tell. Risen, a radical rethinking of his story was set in motion, a rethinking which could only be done within Israel's larger story. Luke 24 narrates this rethinking as Jesus' own instruction; the risen Christ authorizes christological reading of the Scriptures. The end changes everything. Peter preaches from the perspective of this new and surprising ending to Israel's story. Luke writes from the perspective of this new ending in Christ, retelling Israel's story accordingly.[47]

The early church read Scripture from this same perspective. David Yeago says that patristic interpreters assumed that the church knew something absolutely essential to biblical interpretation: the resurrection.[48] He illustrates this claim by citing Athanasius' remarks on the way Peter quotes Ps 16 in the Pentecost speech. Athanasius writes that ". . . the resurrection that has now taken place has shown that the things that were written pertain to Jesus."[49] Yeago concludes, "Knowing the resurrection that has now taken place, the apostolic company can hardly help reading the scriptures of Israel in a new way. The 'things that were written' are the same—what they say has not changed—but they are understood quite differently, in the light of new insight into what they pertain to, what they are *about*."[50] Knowing the resurrection fundamentally conditions the way we read Scripture. Or it should.

Follow the Rule. By pointing to the way Peter's knowledge of the resurrection reshapes his reading of Israel's story, I intend to suggest a fundamental grammar that underlies both the composition and reception of the NT and the way the church reads the OT.[51] It includes the claim that the God of Israel is the one who sends Jesus and raises him from the dead, and that this one God's one story (eventually told as two testaments) finds its goal in Jesus.

We can see something like this grammar at work in the "rule of faith" (*regula fidei*) of the early church (especially the second century). While it has been common to see the rule as a kind of creed, precursor to the classic creeds, that opinion is questionable. The rule is more like a "basic digest of the Christian story"; it offered a brief summary of the overall plot of the scriptural story, begun in the OT, culminated in Christ, yet continuing in the church. The rule was given and received in baptism, and as a synopsis of the scriptural story it would allow a Christian to read the story whole, to fit individual parts into the overall pattern, and to render the story through performative repetition in corporate and individual life. Thus the rule functioned as a "hermeneutical frame of reference for the interpretation of Christian Scripture and Christian experience."[52] It was the lens through which Scripture was properly read.

It still is, as I see it. George Lindbeck claims that this ruled way of reading the Bible "was constitutive of the Christian canon and has, it would seem, an authority inseparable from that of the Bible itself. *To read the Bible otherwise is not to read it as Scripture but as some other book*. . . ."[53] I do not believe that Lindbeck is overstating the case. Rather, I agree with Trevor Hart that the first rule of reading is "that reading shall be in accordance with the rules."[54] Concerns that this claim undermines the authority of Scripture are misplaced for the following reasons.[55] First, there is a reciprocal relation between the rule and the developing biblical canon: the rule governs the reading of Scripture, yet Scripture is the source and content of the rule. The rule which guides the church's reading of Scripture is "tested and authenticated and corrected through continuous engagement with Scripture." Nonetheless, the rule itself "is prior to every *particular* interpretive engagement with Scripture. . . ."[56] Second, the logic or grammar which the rule inscribes is the generative logic of the NT itself and of the reading of the OT in the New. It is the grammar of the speeches in Acts, it is the grammar of Luke–Acts as a whole, and it is the grammar that collects and canonizes the NT as culmination and conclusion of the one story of God.[57] Wall summarizes that Christian interpretation of the Bible "came with Jesus, but not until his messianic mission was complete and his promised Spirit was given at Pentecost. It is in this wider sense that we can speak of the church's Rule of Faith as existing prior to its Bible; indeed, Scripture took its final canonical shape by analogy to this extant Rule."[58]

In sum, the narrative authority of Scripture presupposes that Scripture is read as the narrative that it is, a narrative governed by the church's rule of faith. Apart from such ruled reading, Scripture may carry some type of authority, but it is not the authority of Scripture *read as Scripture*.

RENDERING IDENTITY: (THE CHURCH'S) STORY OF GOD

Whose Story? God's. Narrativists often remark on the capacity of story to convey identity. William Placher suggests that "the *meaning* of the Bible lies first of all in its narration of God's identity."[59] John Goldingay notes that "biblical narratives portray character. From a theological angle, they concern themselves with two correlative pairs of characters: God and Israel, Jesus and the church."[60] The point is not merely that the story occasionally says something about God. Rather, it is that the story as a whole is God's story, that God's own identity is rendered there in character and incident.

This ability of Scripture to render God's identity accounts significantly for its authority. The ultimate source of authority is God. Therefore "the *ultimate* source of scriptural authority, on nearly any normative account, is God. . . ."[61] The question is how does Scripture bear, mediate, or participate in God's authority. Scripture's capacity to bring God's own character into speech is a key dimension of its authority, and this capacity is narratively enacted.

In this sense the narrative authority of Scripture lies in its ability to render God's character in human speech and thought.[62] Central to this is the narration of God's agency; the biblical story renders God's identity as it tells what God does. Certainly that emphasis on what God has done and is doing is at the heart of Peter's speech and Luke's story. Acts 2 both displays and requires a Trinitarian reading of the Pentecost story (and implicitly, of the whole canon). This is more than finding a triad of "Jesus, Father, and Holy Spirit" in Peter's speech (2:33). It is the entire narrative structure—congruence of plot and *dramatis personae*. Peter's account of the powerful manifestation of God's gift is what the church later came to call "Trinitarian." The Son spoke the Father's promise of the gift of the Spirit (1:4–5). The Son received from the Father and poured out on us the Holy Spirit (2:32–33, also 17–21). The repentant are called by God (elsewhere identified with the Father) to baptism "in Jesus' name," that through baptism they might receive the gift of the Holy Spirit (2:38–39). At multiple points in the account the Trinitarian logic of divine action is evident. David Yeago's summary description of the Spirit's mission in the Trinitarian work of salvation, written as part of an account of the role of Scripture in the divine economy, is perfectly apt as a description of Acts 2: "The Spirit thus bears witness to Jesus as the *Son* of the God of Israel and to the God of Israel as the *Father* of Jesus and in so doing is obliquely revealed as *the Spirit of the Father and the Son*."[63] While neither Peter's speech nor Luke's text spells out a doctrine of the Trinity, something like that doctrine is implicit in the plot of Pentecost.

Such claims are contested. In his discussion of narrative interpretation, John Goldingay claims that "For all its truth and fruitfulness, the doctrine of the Trinity seriously skews our *theological reading* of Scripture. It excludes most of the insight expressed in the biblical narrative's portrayal of the person and its working out of the plot."[64] I would argue, on the contrary, that the narrative authority of Scripture itself demands Trinitarian readings. There are two mutually conditioning reasons for my claim, nicely summarized in Trevor Hart's remark that "The claim that the God revealed in Scripture is the Father of Jesus Christ is not only a claim that arises out of our reading of the text as a whole, it is also one that should provide us with a basic rule for reading it."[65] In other words, the logic is both *from* the text and *to* the text. First, a Trinitarian reading arises out of the scriptural narrative. The NT tells the story of the triune actions of God. Richard Bauckham is right to say that

> . . . the story of God's acting and suffering in the world in the Gospel story of Jesus is Trinitarian in form. That God is Trinitarian emerges, as it were, from the story. A doctrine of the Trinity represents what we need to say about God in God's self for the biblical story about God to be a true story. It is authorized by the story in that it follows from taking the story seriously as authoritative metanarrative.[66]

Second, a Trinitarian rule enables reading of the scriptural narrative. The canon of Christian Scripture comes to us inextricably related to the rule of faith.[67] It authorizes us to read the Bible as one story of the one God who is Father, Son, and Holy Spirit. Thus, the rule of faith is not only narrative in shape, it is Trinitarian in substance.[68]

Yet Our Story Too. There is a second sense in which Scriptural narrative renders a second character—the church. Pentecost as the "birthday of the church" has been overplayed, while Pentecost as the inauguration of story has been underplayed. In fact, the outpouring of the Holy Spirit births church and story in mutual dependence: without the church, there is no story, and without the story, there is no church. James Dunn is quite right that ". . . without the Spirit there would be no story to tell. Without the Spirit there would be no church. . . ."[69] But this claim needs to be supplemented by the recognition that with the giving of the Spirit there is both a story to tell and a church to tell it! The Christian church has been, from the beginning, an "institution of narration."[70] The church is the community authorized and empowered to tell and retell God's story. The coming of the Holy Spirit inaugurates the community of witness, those who will be witnesses to the end of the earth (1:8). In Luke's account the immediate effect is that the crowd which gathers hears the Spirit-filled disciples "speaking about God's deeds of power" (2:11). Note that this is no longer ecstatic glossolalia but speech which is noteworthy precisely because it is understandable; the hearers are amazed and perplexed because they hear the disciples speak "in our own tongues" (2:11).[71] Thus the hearers are hearing about God's deeds of power in understandable speech and in narrative form, for such declaration would be impossible apart from telling, however briefly, the story of God's deeds.

Peter interprets the event in terms of Joel's prophecy (Joel 2:28–32). This is that. Just as his handling of Ps 16 indicates a narrative construal of the OT as a story which leads to the death and resurrection of Jesus, so here we encounter another dimension of that same construal. The story of Israel culminates in Jesus in such a way that the last days are begun. In these last days the restoration of Israel in the form of the church is being accomplished. What Peter announces as a present moment, a beginning, was already for Luke and his readers a past moment that stretched into their present and anticipated an ever more inclusive future. In light of the resurrection of Jesus and the eschatological outpouring of the Holy Spirit, the OT is read under a narrative construal that identifies the church as eschatological Israel. A prophetic passage is narratively construed to identify the "place" of the church in the ongoing story.

Luke Timothy Johnson suggests that we learn to recognize ". . . the New Testament's ability to *author*, that is to create a certain identity in its readers, to bring a Christian community into existence or renew it."[72] He is quite right about this, but the scope of his claim needs to be expanded to include the OT as well. We see the OT—construed in light of Jesus' resurrection—exercising narrative authority to author the identity of the church at Pentecost. Johnson adds that his claim is not merely literary or sociological but is rather a claim about what God does in and through this text: "What is specifically theological is the church's conviction that this authoring power of the Scripture is activated by the Holy

Spirit. All texts can transform, but these texts transform according to the mind of Christ."[73]

The text may also be transformed in the telling. Luke subtly alters the quotation from Joel in a way that emphasizes that not even the least are excluded from full participation in the community that the Holy Spirit forms. Where Joel 2:29 includes both male and female slaves in the gift of the Spirit, Luke adds "and they will prophecy" (2:18). From the greatest to the least, the church is a community with a story to tell. And in the telling Luke, at least, assumes that he is *authorized* to retell that story with some degree of freedom. Thus the narrative authority of Scripture works to authorize the church to offer new readings and new tellings—in Luke's case, even new writings—of the authoritative story.[74] Neither this freedom to reread, nor the novelty of the readings, is putative evidence that the authority of Scripture has been sacrificed. Rather, such qualities may be evidence that the narrative authority of Scripture is working, that the Spirit is working in and through the story.[75]

Yet such (re)telling is never merely a matter of narrational skills alone, of knowing and articulating the plot and the characters and the setting. The reciprocal relation between story and church is crucial here. Stanley Hauerwas has emphasized this connection in terms of truthfulness. Peter tells a good story, but is it truth or tall tale? Peter invites his hearers to judge the truthfulness of the story on the basis of the visible and audible church. He claims that "*this* that you [scoffers] see and hear" (v. 33) is *that* which "was spoken through the prophet Joel" (v. 16). This visible and audible community embodies the fulfillment of the prophetic word that death will be overpowered and the Spirit poured out on all flesh. The church embodies the truth of the apostles' teaching (v. 42) that "God raised up this Jesus" (v. 32); it does this as a community of witness ("of that all of us are witnesses," v. 32). Telling this story truthfully requires a community faithful to the story; retelling this story truly requires a storyteller (church) which conforms to the central character (God).

But integral to the issue of truthfulness is another issue: understanding itself. For the Jews gathered from the nations to judge the truth of Peter's story must understand it. Peter stakes both their understanding of, and their assent to, his story on the visible and audible presence of the church, which makes visible and audible the action of God. And at the same time Peter stakes their understanding of the church on the story which he tells. The church is *hermeneusis* of the gospel story, and the gospel story is *hermeneusis* of the church. Both together render the identity of God. The gathered nations will come to know God—"know" as faith's understanding, assent, and participation—through the dual enfolding of the church's story and the story's church.

In claiming that God's story is our story too I intend to suggest that it is both the story that identifies us and the story that we are called to tell.

WORLD AND NARRATIVE INDWELLING: TAKING OUR PLACE IN THE STORY

Going On. To this point, I have argued that the authority of Scripture is best understood in narrative terms. Doing so, I have tried to show, requires a construal of Scripture as God's story, culminating in Christ, yet open to our presence and participation. It also requires a community of Scripture—Christ's church, a people who live in and by the telling and retelling. It remains in this final section to ask two questions. The first is whether this account of narrative authority is sufficient to guide the church as it moves toward the story's end. Those who favor a more propositional understanding of the authority of Scripture, with its typical correlate of divine command ethics, will surely suggest that my account of the narrative authority of Scripture does not help the church know how to go on.[76] The second question is whether it is really possible for twenty-first century Christians to live within this scriptural narrative at all. If it is—if the Bible's story is to be our story, then how do we get "in"?

The question of how to go on is first a literary question. One of the skills of reading stories with plots is that, as we read through time, we are continually making sense of the story. We do that by configuring the story's shape up to this point and anticipating what is yet to come. That is to say, at any given "now" in the reading of the story, we can give some account both of how the story has gotten to the place it is and of where it might go from here. Where a reader cannot do that, we might say that he has lost the story's plot, or that she is not "following" the story.

The difference between the literary analogy and our own participation in the story lies first in the fact that we are not merely readers *of* the story but are also characters *in* it. As individuals we are minor characters; as church we are a major character, though not the protagonist. The difference lies, second, in the fact that our "now" is given as a gap in the plot, a part of the story between ascension and parousia that the story's author is only now writing. Richard Bauckham calls this the unfinished nature of the biblical story.[77] Thus, for us as characters in the story, following it means not just retracing the sequence and sense of the plot as we retell it but continuing its direction in our common life and daily discipleship.

In a sense, that is what we find going on in Acts. Joel Green suggests that Acts continues the narrative of Jesus begun in Luke, "showing the ongoing achievement of God's aim, through Jesus, in the early church." By writing the second volume, Luke does more than just tell the story of the early church. He provides us with storied examples of what it means to be authorized to follow the story. Green claims that "Following Luke, Christians today may reflect critically and constructively on the degree to which the church persists along the trajectory of God's salvific plan, witnessed in the Scriptures of Israel, clarified and executed in the life and ministry of Jesus, carried on in the first decades of the Jesus movement."[78]

We can see this exemplified in the choosing of Matthias. There is an easily overlooked significance in Luke's introduction to Peter's speech: "But Peter, *standing with the eleven* . . ." (2:14). The implication is that, though Peter is the spokesman, he stands as one of the twelve apostles. If the apostles are among the Spirit-filled disciples, why single them out as a distinct and visible group? Because they are a visible sign of what is being enacted at Pentecost: the restoration of eschatological Israel.[79] Their presence provides a visible, enacted hermeneutic of "the last days" (2:17) which have now dawned. But there are eleven with whom Peter can stand only because in Acts 1 Matthias has been chosen to take Judas' place (1:15–26).

In that incident the narrative authority of Scripture functioned both to account for Judas' betrayal and demise (1:20a quoting Ps 69:25) and to guide the church as it moves forward into the future (1:20b quoting Ps 109:8). The hint that these isolated sentences from the Psalms are being pressed into a larger narrative framework is found in 1:16, which has Peter saying that "the Scripture had to be fulfilled." If Jesus' betrayal and death is "according to Scripture," something that "must be,"[80] then the presence and actions of the betrayer must be also. Thus, Peter's claim that Judas' demise "is written" does not arise first from the particular discovery of an isolated verse that "fits" Judas' circumstances but rather from the general conviction that the entire shape of Jesus' end—including the role of Judas in it—is written in Israel's Scripture. That conviction allows Peter to follow the story to the point where he speaks.

But how should the story go on? Here we might infer that an isolated and arbitrary verse (Ps 109:8) has been chosen for unknown reasons. But if the real logic of the passage is the narrative authority of Scripture read in light of the revealed and revealing ending in Christ's death and resurrection, then this second sentence that "the Holy Spirit through David foretold" is a trope for a larger narrative sense of how the story can and should go on. It acknowledges the storied identity of the twelve as representatives of the twelve tribes of Israel eschatologically renewed and their necessary role as witnesses who are able to tell Jesus' story "during all the time that the Lord Jesus went in and out among us, beginning from the baptism of John until the day when he was taken up from us" (1:21b–22).

Thus the choosing of Matthias suggests how the church is regularly called to "go on." This story exemplifies a general claim that Lesslie Newbigin makes regarding the narrative authority of Scripture in relation to the church:

> The church is not tied to a text in such a way that nothing will ever be done for the first time. In new situations, those who "indwell" the story of which Jesus is the center will have to make new and risky decisions

> about what faithfulness to the Author of the story requires. There can be no drawing of a straight line from a text of Scripture to a contemporary ethical decision; there will always be the requirement of a fresh decision in responsibility to the one whose story it is.[81]

The church is authorized not only to tell the story, but also to do what is necessary to move the story forward along the narrative lines established by its source and goal.[82]

Getting In. Those who indwell the story are authorized—freed and empowered—to go on. This leads us at last to ask how it is that we "indwell" this story. Above I have already suggested one specific way in which Acts 2 tells a story which includes the present moment of any reader/hearer within the promise of Pentecost. This is not the only way we indwell Scripture, nor is it the most common way in which Christians find that the Bible is their story. Claims that we somehow find ourselves in the biblical story are replete in the works of narrative theologians and biblical scholars who emphasize the biblical story.[83] Such claims are seldom concrete, however. Either indwelling is discussed as if it happens merely through close attention to the narrative structure of the text, or the suggestion is that the primary modality for indwelling is an imaginative effort on the part of readers of the biblical story. Neither approach is adequate, for neither pays enough attention to the actual narrative practices of the church.

For example, Richard Bauckham writes, "To accept the authority of this story is to enter it and to inhabit it. It is to live in the world as the world is portrayed in this story." Imagination is required, Bauckham suggests, but inscription in this story will take more than imagination.[84] It takes concrete practices by which the Holy Spirit makes us part of God's story. I believe that a constellation of such narrative practices is found in the church's liturgy.

Why this is so, and why it matters, can be seen by following Stanley Hauerwas' essay "The Gesture of a Truthful Story." It begins with the claim that ". . . the church is a place where the story of God is enacted, told, and heard." Being Christian means learning to find our life in that story, and such learning must be embodied and enacted. "The way we learn a story, after all, is not just by hearing it. Important and significant stories must be acted out. We must be taught the gestures that help position our bodies and our souls to be able to hear rightly and then retell the story." Practices like the creed, baptism, and eucharist all play a role as narrative enactments of God's story, practices that place us in the story. Because Hauerwas is thinking especially about how the mentally handicapped might encounter and indwell God's story, he has less to say about other narrative practices, such as preaching, the lectionary, the church year, and even the way some hymnody works. Hauerwas concludes by claiming that the mentally handicapped "learn the story through its enactment as they feel and are formed by *the liturgy that places us as characters in God's grand project of the creation and redemption of the world.*[85] I would simply add that regardless of our mental ability, we *all* learn the story through such liturgical enactments. This is not the only place where the Holy Spirit engages us in narrative practices. Corporate Bible study and individual practices of *lectio divina* are certainly important. But the church's common life centered in worship continues to be the primary constellation of such practices.

Describing how this is so is the work of another essay. Suggesting that it is necessary is the central conclusion of this one. Luke ends his account of the day of Pentecost with a summary of the common life that the Spirit brought: "They devoted themselves to the apostles' teaching and fellowship, to the breaking of bread and the prayers" (2:42). So should we, for in doing so the Author of life (3:15) continues to write us into his story.

NOTES

1. For a discussion see Richard T. De George, *The Nature and Limits of Authority* (Lawrence: University of Kansas Press, 1985), 15–21.

2. Jeffrey Stout, *The Flight From Authority* (Notre Dame: University of Notre Dame Press, 1981).

3. Alister McGrath, for instance, remarks rather polemically that "the number of Christians who regard Scripture as authoritative is increasing; those who, in sympathy with more liberal trends, have moved away from biblically centred forms of Christianity are in decline" (*A Passion for the Truth: The Intellectual Coherence of Evangelicalism* [Downers Grove: InterVarsity Press, 1996], 57). While his claim rightly reflects the growth of southern Christianity, much of which strongly emphasizes the authority of the Bible, it falsely implies that for liberal Christians Scripture is not authoritative.

4. As Sarah Heaner Lancaster notes in *Women and the Authority of Scripture: A Narrative Approach* (Harrisburg, Penn.: Trinity Press International, 2002), 162: "Fewer people in the world actually accept the Bible's authority than do not."

5. Francis Watson, *Text, Church and World: Biblical Interpretation in Theological Perspective* (Grand Rapids: Eerdmans, 1994), 3. See also David Kelsey, *The Uses of Scripture in Recent Theology* (Philadelphia: Fortress, 1975; republished as *Proving Doctrine* by Trinity Press International, 1999), 90–97.

6. Kelsey, *The Uses of Scripture in Recent Theology*, 97. Kelsey is speaking there of the authority of Christian Scripture. But the claim is generally analytic in the use of "scripture" as a category in the study of religions. See William A. Graham, "Scripture," in *The Encyclopedia of Religion* (ed. Mircea Eliade; New York: Macmillan, 1987), 13:133.

7. William J. Abraham lists the following "ecclesial canons" which functioned as "means of grace and salvation" in early Christianity: "creed, Scripture, liturgy, iconography, the Fathers, and sacraments." See his *Canon and Criterion in Christian Theology* (Oxford: Oxford University Press, 1998), 1.

8. Barry Harvey describes the world as "creation in rebellion" in *Another City: An Ecclesiological Primer for a Post-Christian World* (Harrisburg: Trinity Press International, 1999), 69–70. Stanley Hauerwas notes the consequence of the world's status: "Without the church the world literally has no hope of salvation since the church is necessary for the world to know it is part of a story that it cannot know without the church." See his *After Christendom* (Nashville: Abingdon Press, 1991), 36.

9. By being a servant community, ". . . the church helps the world understand what it

means to be the world. The world is God's world, God's good creation, which is all the more distorted by sin because it still is bounded by God's goodness. For the church to be the church it must show what the world is meant to be as God's good creation. *For the world has no way of knowing it is world without the church pointing to the reality of God's kingdom.*" Hauerwas, "The Servant Community" in *The Hauerwas Reader* (ed. John Berkman and Michael Cartwright; Durham: Duke University Press, 2001), 375, emphasis mine.

10. Francis Watson notes that the world is "the sphere and object of the church's mission." Thus ". . . the biblical story itself refuses to permit its own enclosure and confinement within the walls of the church . . ." (*Text, Church and World*, 10–11). David Yeago says "Scripture is the standing testimony of the Spirit to the church, *for the purpose of forming the church itself as the Spirit's testimony to the nations.*" David Yeago, "The Spirit, the Church, and the Scriptures: Biblical Inspiration and Interpretation Revisited," in *Knowing the Triune God: The Work of the Spirit in the Practices of the Church* (ed. James J. Buckley and David S. Yeago; Grand Rapids: Eerdmans, 2001), 63, emphasis mine. See also N. T. Wright, "How Can the Bible Be Authoritative?" *Vox Evangelica* 21 (1991): 7–32, 21.

11. McGrath briefly summarizes the way some evangelicals reacted to Enlightenment skepticism by embracing key dimensions of the Enlightenment's understanding of authority. *A Passion for Truth*, 58, 166–174.

12. Watson, *Text, Church and World*, 9.

13. See Brian J. Walsh, "Reimagining Biblical Authority," *Christian Scholars Review* 26 (1996): 206-220, 218 for a discussion of this.

14. Lesslie Newbigin notes that "Any discussion of biblical authority runs the risk that we may begin with the concept of authority that operates in our culture and then ask whether the Bible has this kind of authority." See his *Truth and Authority in Modernity*; *Christian Mission and Modern Culture* (eds. Alan Neely, H. Wayne Pipkin, and Wilbert R Shenk; Valley Forge: Trinity Press International, 1996), 79.

15. Richard Bauckham, *God and the Crisis of Freedom: Biblical and Contemporary Perspectives* (Louisville: Westminster/John Knox, 2002), 53.

16. I discuss modern rejection and postmodern evasion of the biblical metanarrative in my doctoral dissertation "(Re)Forming the Image: A Narrative Reading of *Imago Dei*," Duke University, 1999, 28–42.

17. John Goldingay, "Biblical Narrative and Systematic Theology," in *Between Two Horizons: Spanning New Testament Studies and Systematic Theology* (ed. Joel B. Green and Max Turner; Grand Rapids: Eerdmans, 2000), 123–142, 138–139.

18. William Placher, "The Nature of Biblical Authority: Issues and Models from Recent Theology," in *Conservative, Moderate, Liberal: The Biblical Authority Debate* (ed. Charles R. Blaisdell; St. Louis: CBP Press, 1990), 1–19. Perceptive readers will note that these three types correspond to the three models of religion proposed by George Lindbeck in *The Nature of Doctrine* (Philadelphia: Westminster, 1984). They are the cognitive propositional, the experiential expressive, and the cultural-linguistic respectively.

19. This is the overall tone of John Barton's *People of the Book? The Authority of the Bible in Christianity* (Louisville: Westminster John Knox, 1988).

20. Placher, "The Nature of Biblical Authority," 2.

21. Joel B. Green and Michael Pasquarello III, eds., *Narrative Reading, Narrative Preaching: Reuniting New Testament Interpretation and Proclamation* (Grand Rapids: Baker Academic, 2003), see especially "The (Re-)Turn to Narrative" by Green, 11–36. See the citations above: the seminal article by N. T. Wright (n. 10), as well as the contributions of Walsh (n. 13), Bauckham (n. 15), Newbigin (n. 14), Lindbeck (n. 18), and Lancaster (n. 4). See also the theological work of Hans Frei, *Theology and Narrative: Selected Essays* (ed. George Hunsinger and William Placher; New York: Oxford, 1993) and below nn. 22 and 62; Charles M. Wood, *The Formation of Christian Understanding: An Essay in Theological Hermeneutics* (Philadelphia:

Westminster Press, 1981) and n. 61; Stanley Hauerwas, *A Community of Character* (Notre Dame: University of Notre Dame Press, 1981), *The Hauerwas Reader* (see n. 9) and see below n. 85; and Gabriel Fackre, *The Christian Story: A Narrative Interpretation of Basic Christian Doctrine* (3d ed.; Grand Rapids: Eerdmans, 1996); Ronald Thiemann, *Revelation and Theology: The Gospel as Narrated Promise* (Notre Dame: University of Notre Dame Press, 1985). The most germane collection for this topic is Garrett Green, ed., *Scriptural Authority and Narrative Interpretation* (Philadelphia: Fortress Press, 1987). A more difficult collection of essays is *Why Narrative? Readings in Narrative Theology* (ed. Stanley Hauerwas and L. Gregory Jones; Grand Rapids: Eerdmans, 1989; reprint edition Eugene, Oregon: Wipf and Stock, 1997). A highly accessible narrative approach to systematic theology is Michael Lodahl, *The Story of God: Wesleyan Theology and Biblical Narrative* (Kansas City: Beacon Hill Press, 1994).

22. See Hans Frei, *The Eclipse of Biblical Narrative: A Study in Eighteenth and Nineteenth Century Hermeneutics* (New Haven: Yale University Press, 1974).

23. There are other stories that might serve equally well as exemplifications of the narrative authority of Scripture, the walk to Emmaus (Luke 24) being the quintessential candidate. For an excellent reading of the Emmaus story, see R. W. L. Moberly, *The Bible, Theology, and Faith: A Study of Abraham and Jesus* (Cambridge: Cambridge University Press, 2000), ch. 2.

24. Given how rarely it is that Scripture focuses centrally on the authority of Scripture, to take up those passages might be regarded as special pleading. For a discussion of such passages in the NT, see James D. G. Dunn, *The Living Word* (Philadelphia: Fortress, 1987), 89–136; and Paul Achtemeier, *Inspiration and Authority: Nature and Function of Christian Scripture* (Peabody, Mass.: Hendrickson, 1999), 92–99. Achtemeier begins his discussion by noting: "As has often been observed, it is remarkable how little Scripture has to say about itself and about the process by which it was formed" (p. 92).

25. Placher, "Nature of Biblical Authority," 15.

26. For a narrative reading of this summary see Joel B. Green, "Reading the Gospels and Acts as Narrative," in *Narrative Reading, Narrative Preaching*, 37–66, primarily 56–66.

27. This latter sense is quite appropriate to Luke–Acts. Note the careful use of the particle *dei* (it is necessary) to communicate a sense of divine (and consequently scriptural) plottedness.

28. Paul Ricoeur, "Narrative Time," *Critical Inquiry* 7.1 (1980):169–190, 175.

29. John Goldingay emphasizes the significance of the claim that God acts when he says that the New Testament's "gospel is not essentially or distinctively a statement that takes the form 'God is love,' but one that takes the form 'God so loved that he gave. . . .'" Goldingay, "Biblical Narrative and Systematic Theology," 130. See also his discussion in John Goldingay, *Models for Interpretation of Scripture* (Grand Rapids: Eerdmans, 1995), 56–61.

30. For a similar claim, see Trevor Hart, "Tradition, Authority, and a Christian Approach to the Bible as Scripture" in *Between Two Horizons: Spanning New Testament Studies and Systematic Theology* (ed. Joel B. Green and Max Turner; Grand Rapids: Eerdmans, 2000), 202, where he argues that the authority of the text should be seen, not as a property of the text, but as an "aspect of *the event* in which text and reader together are drawn into a relatedness to the living God whereby God 'speaks' or is known in and through the reading" (emphasis mine).

31. Joel Green (*How to Read the Gospels and Acts* [Downers Grove: InterVarsity, 1987], 112) has suggested that ". . . not only is Pentecost the climax of what has gone before, it is also the beginning of something new."

32. Robert C. Tannehill notes the parallel constructions of Acts 2:1 and Luke 9:51, and the way each represents the fulfilling of prophecies from earlier in the narrative. See his *The Narrative Unity of Luke–Acts: A Literary Interpretation*, vol. 2, *The Acts of the Apostles* (Minneapolis: Fortress, 1990), 26.

33. Luke Timothy Johnson notes the use of "literary prophecy" in Luke–Acts, in which "Not texts from Torah, but statements of characters *within the narrative* are explicitly shown to

find fulfillment." See his *The Gospel of Luke* (SP vol. 3; Collegeville: Liturgical, 1991), 16.

34. Though Peter proclaims Pentecost as a fulfillment of Joel's prophecy (2:16), Joel's prophecy has not functioned in the narrative of Luke–Acts as a promise which builds expectation.

35. See Johnson, *The Gospel of Luke*, 16.

36. For the common distinction between story, the "what" of the narrative (events, plot, character, and theme), and discourse, the "way" the narrative is told, see Seymour Chatman, *Story and Discourse: Narrative Structure in Fiction and Film* (Ithaca: Cornell University Press, 1978), 9 and 19.

37. Johnson (*The Gospel of Luke*, 16) suggests that the prior verse—"Let it be known to you then that this salvation of God has been sent to the Gentiles; they will listen"—was a prophecy that had "clearly reached fulfillment among Luke's readers."

38. John Goldingay, "How Far Do Readers Make Sense? Interpreting Biblical Narrative," *Themelios* (1993): 5–10, 6.

39. Paul van Buren, "Acts 2:1–13—The Truth of an Unlikely Tale," in *The Return to Scripture in Judaism and Christianity: Essays in Postcritical Interpretation* (ed. Peter Ochs; New York: Paulist Press, 1993): 295–307, 306–307.

40. Goldingay (*Models for Interpretation of Scripture*, 75–76) suggests that Luke–Acts as a whole works narratively to link our story to the biblical story.

41. See Newbigin, 42; Bauckham, 64–65; Hart, 197.

42. *The New Testament and the People of God,* vol. 1 of *Christian Origins and the Question of God* (Philadelphia: Fortress, 1992), 456.

43. Paul M. van Buren acknowledges the former while emphasizing the latter in "Acts 2:1–13," 295–307. Garrett Green notes the way Peter's sermon in Acts 2 presents the story of Jesus as a focus for reimagining the Jewish Scriptures, so that "the various parts of the story were reconstituted in a new and meaningful whole" (*Imagining God: Theology and the Religious Imagination* [Grand Rapids: Eerdmans, 1989], 124).

44. See Wright (*The New Testament and the People of God*, 217) for this suggestion as the general context of the production of the NT.

45. Christopher R. Seitz, "Scripture and a Three-legged Stool: Is There a Coherent Account of the Authority of Scripture for Anglicans after Lambeth 1998?" in *Figured Out: Typology and Providence in Christian Scripture* (Louisville: Westminster/John Knox, 2001), 49–68, 65.

46. Paul M. van Buren, *According to the Scriptures: the Origins of the Gospel and of the Church's Old Testament* (Grand Rapids: Eerdmans, 1998), 27.

47. Joel Green has argued that we see precisely this rereading of Israel's Scripture at work in Acts, indicated by the hermeneutical motto "in Jesus the resurrection of the dead." See his "Doing Repentance: the Formation of Disciples in the Acts of the Apostles," *Ex Aud* 18 (2002): 1–23, 9–11. He notes that ". . . at a basic level, the use of Israel's Scriptures in Acts is oriented centrally around the presumption of the continuity of the biblical story and the story of Jesus. . . . Accordingly, the missionary and prophetic work of Jesus' witnesses in Acts is oriented around explaining and proving from the Scriptures 'that it was necessary for the Messiah to suffer and to raise from the dead' (Acts 17:3). *The Scriptures of Israel find their decisive exegesis in the messianic career of Jesus*" (9–10, emphasis mine).

48. Yeago, 54–56. For a discussion of how and why knowing the resurrection alone was insufficient, see Moberly, *Bible, Theology and Faith*, ch. 2.

49. Athanasius, *Against the Arians* II, 16, as cited by Yeago, 54.

50. Yeago, 55.

51. On Luke's intention to continue the narrative of the scriptural story, see Moody Smith, "When Did the Gospels Become Scripture?" *JBL* 119 (2002): 3–20; see especially 8–11. Smith reminds us that this "impulse" to write a Gospel in the first place "came from the proclamation of Jesus as the fulfillment of Scripture" (p. 19).

52. Paul M. Blowers, "The *Regula Fidei* and the Narrative Character of Early Christian Faith," *Pro Ecclesia* 6 (1997): 199–228; for the points made in this paragraph see pp. 200, 202, 206, and 208–215.

53. "Scripture, Consensus, and Community," in *Biblical Interpretation in Crisis* (ed. Richard John Newhaus; Grand Rapids: Eerdmans, 1989): 74–101, 77, emphasis mine.

54. Trevor Hart, "Tradition, Authority, and a Christian Approach to the Bible as Scripture," 192. See the entire article for a helpful account of the necessity and fruitfulness of ruled reading.

55. For a brief discussion of the concern that the rule of faith skews exegesis, see Moberly, *Bible, Theology, and Faith*, 42–44. See also Francis Young, *Virtuoso Theology: the Bible and Interpretation* (Cleveland: Pilgrim, 1993), ch. 3, for an argument that the rule of faith is not adequately narrative in shape.

56. Yeago, 59.

57. Note the comment of Wayne Meeks *(The Origins of Christian Morality: The First Two Centuries* [New Haven: Yale, 1993], 210): "By the end of the second century the whole plot had come to be perceived by the Christians who were calling themselves 'catholics,' as a thread holding together the diverse writings that constituted Christian Scripture. A 'canon' was emerging comprising an 'Old Testament' and a 'New Testament,' which together narrated one drama."

58. Robert W. Wall, "Reading the Bible from within Our Traditions: The 'Rule of Faith' in Theological Hermeneutics," in *Between Two Horizons: Spanning New Testament Studies and Systematic Theology* (ed. Joel B. Green and Max Turner; Grand Rapids: Eerdmans, 2000), 88–107; quotation from p. 98.

59. Placher, "Nature of Biblical Authority," 13. See further his *Narratives of a Vulnerable God: Christ, Theology, and Scripture* (Louisville: Westminster/John Knox, 1994).

60. Goldingay, "Biblical Narrative and Systematic Theology," 125–126.

61. Charles M. Wood, "Hermeneutics and the Authority of Scripture," in *An Invitation to Theological Study* (Valley Forge: Trinity Press International, 1994): 55–70, 63.

62. Indeed, Hans Frei's *The Identity of Jesus Christ: the Hermeneutical Bases of Dogmatic Theology* (Philadelphia: Fortress, 1975), goes further than this, suggesting that the Gospel narrative renders not only Christ's identity but also his presence.

63. Yeago, 62, emphasis original. Though the language of "Son" is absent from Acts 2, it is certainly implicit in the use of "Father" at 2:33.

64. Goldingay, "Biblical Narrative and Systematic Theology," 131, emphasis mine.

65. Hart, "Tradition, Authority, and a Christian Approach to the Bible as Scripture," 200.

66. Bauckham, 72. In this sense, then, he can state that ". . . the Bible both does and does not teach the doctrine of the Trinity."

67. David Steinmetz notes that "the meaning of historical texts cannot be separated from the complex problem of their reception. . . ." David C. Steinmetz, "The Superiority of Pre-Critical Exegesis," in *Memory and Mission: Theological Reflections on the Christian Past* (Nashville: Abingdon, 1988), 143–163, 161; this article was originally published in *Ex Aud* 1 (1985): 74–82.

68. Wall ("Reading the Bible from within Our Traditions," 101) says ". . . the church's Rule of Faith is narrative in shape, Trinitarian in substance, and relates the essential beliefs of Christianity together by the grammar of christological monotheism."

69. James D. G. Dunn, *The Acts of the Apostles* (Valley Forge: Trinity Press International, 1996), 22.

70. Eberhard Jüngel, *God as the Mystery of the World: On the Foundation of the Theology of the Crucified One in the Dispute between Theism and Atheism* (trans. by Darrell L. Guder; Grand Rapids: Eerdmans, 1983), 312.

71. An interesting corollary of this, which cannot be pursued here, would be the claim that the narrative authority of Scripture functions in any language. Thus, *translations* of the Bible are the Bible.

72. Luke Timothy Johnson, "The Authority of the New Testament in the Church: A Theological Reflection," in *Conservative, Moderate, Liberal: The Biblical Authority Debate* (ed. Charles R. Blaisdell; St. Louis: CBP Press, 1990), 94. Johnson's claim would include the identity of both church and individual believer.

73. Ibid.

74. Johnson discusses the NT as "authorizer" on pages 95–96. On Luke as writer and re-writer of Scripture, see Smith, "When Did the Gospels Become Scripture?"

75. This is not to say that there are no criteria by which to judge such authorized retellings and rereadings. A key criterion of their *authenticity* would be whether they retain the "sense of an ending" that constitutes this story and whether they retain a clear sense that it is God's story that is being told.

76. Of course, a narrative approach to authority does not ignore the importance of command in Scripture, but places law, commandment, and obedience in the narrative context that gives it meaning and coherence in the first place.

77. "The *unfinished* nature of the biblical story—or, more positively, the eschatological hope as the ultimate future God will give to his world—is what creates the space for finding ourselves and our contemporary world in the biblical story. . . . It is what both keeps the story open to the inclusion of all other stories and invites all other stories to find the ending that will give them meaning in the coming kingdom of God" (Bauckham, 76–77).

78. Joel B. Green, *The Theology of the Gospel of Luke* (Cambridge: Cambridge University Press, 1995), 147.

79. See Gerhard Lohfink, *Jesus and Community* (Philadelphia: Fortress, 1984), 9–12. Note the claim of Luke 22:28–30.

80. On what to make of "it must" (*dei*), including references, see Johnson, *The Gospel of Luke*, 15–16.

81. Newbigin, *Truth and Authority in Modernity*, 45.

82. Note Bauckham's claim (*God and the Crisis of Freedom*, p. 73): "While we often think of authority as obliging us, it is also possible to think of authority as *authorizing* us." E.g., ". . . the Great Commission . . . *authorizes* us to act with the delegated authority of the Lord Jesus in making disciples of all nations for the kingdom of God. Much that we often think of as obedience can also be construed as being authorized. . . ." More generally, the Bible authorizes us "to speak of God." See also Johnson, *The Gospel of Luke*, 95-96; N. T. Wright's much quoted analogy of performing an unfinished play in "How Can the Bible Be Authoritative?" 18–19; and the discussion in Walsh, "Reimaging Biblical Authority," 215–218.

83. E.g., Trevor Hart writes ("Tradition, Authority, and a Christian Approach to the Bible as Scripture," 197): "But treated as 'a whole,' Scripture, in all its diversity of types, offers a narrative world the reader is invited to indwell, and from within which she is now expected to view things. In the familiar parlance of Wittgenstein, Christians are required to take the world 'as' the world that Scripture portrays, to indulge in an imaginative shift. . . ." Placher ("Nature of Biblical Authority," 13) writes ". . . the language and narrative world of the Bible as a whole come to provide a framework within which we understand our own lives as they are and might become. We accept this biblical world, with all its inconsistencies and ambiguities, as the world in which we live."

84. Bauckham, 64-65; quote from 64.

85. For the points made in this paragraph see "The Gesture of a Truthful Story" in *Christian Existence Today: Essays on Church, World and Living In Between* (Durham: Labyrinth Press, 1988), 101–110, specifically pp. 101, 106–107, and 109 (cmphasis in the last quotation mine).

RESPONSE TO LAYTHAM

DANIEL J. TREIER

Rather than a detailed analysis of the debasing of authority in our contemporary world and how it influences the church, Prof. Laytham bravely offers a "constructive proposal" for Scripture's "narrative authority," tested by a theological interpretation of Acts 2.[1] We should appreciate his plea for the value of plot; the relevance of the ending for sensing the whole story and our proper role in it; and therefore our need for the trinitarian rule of faith. We should admire the way this paper helps us grasp such a narrative shape for Scripture's authority while interacting with an important text.

Nevertheless, respondents at conferences are supposed to say nice generalities but then be somewhat disagreeable. In this case my disagreement takes the form of a nagging feeling that Laytham's narrative is too smooth. So skillfully does he lead us that we feel relatively little tension. But maybe the ending would be happier if we faced more dramatic choices, so I will highlight a couple of narrative gaps where the audience might wish to interrupt the storyteller and ask questions.

Gap Number One: Scripture's Nonnarrative Storytelling. It is suggested that "an account of the narrative authority of Scripture should look to a narrative for exemplification." This is a useful starting point, to be sure. But the priority of narrative threatens to eclipse the other literary genres of the Bible, as Paul Ricoeur himself suggests.[2] We must also face the issue of how nonnarrative portions of the Bible relate to Scripture's overall narrative flow, or whether there even is one. Many of our most heated flash points about Scripture's authority concern which psalms we may pray, which commands we must obey, whether prophecies are believable, and what may count as one.

Gap Number Two: Scripture's Nonpropositional Storytelling. We are also told that Scripture's role in the Acts 2 story is "not propositional, though certain propositions are related directly to Scripture; rather, in this story Scripture's authority is to authorize a particular telling of the story of Jesus and to authenticate a particular construal of the Pentecost story." I confess that I fail to see how authorizing a telling of the story is nonpropositional. Once all the proper denials have been made about the horrors of prooftexting individual line items of the Bible, it still seems that telling stories is a truth claiming act. In Acts 2 Peter's "*this* is *that*" sounds like a proposition to me.[3]

Might not these first two gaps run together? Pouring Scripture's diverse content through the modern sieve for extracting only propositional truth claims was surely a mistake that isolated particular verses and often "left behind" entire portions of the Bible. Yet pouring it directly into a narrative mold threatens also to snatch up and transform isolated material into something else, without the necessary moments of conceptual clarification regarding the particulars of literary form.

Gap Number Three: Our Sense of Scripture's Story. A third gap appears where Laytham writes that "Peter's speech reads Israel's Scripture as 'a story in search of a conclusion,' and reads Jesus' story as that story's searched-for conclusion." The next paragraph makes the important point that the OT has priority in this: Jesus filled a gap that the early Christians had come to see in their Scriptures; it is not as if they thought themselves authorized to refashion the OT until it fit him. The resurrection changed everything, but their categories for its significance were OT categories in an important respect (as Tom Wright has freshly shown us).[4]

The gap here though, to my mind, is the immediacy of Peter's engagement with the text from Joel. I have granted elsewhere the difficulty of sorting out Peter's and Luke's voices.[5] But we have here at least a kernel of Peter's speech itself, which correlated the events before their eyes with the events anticipated by the prophet. Yes, Jesus was the beginning of the end for Peter, so that, as Laytham accepts, the rule of faith "is prior to every *particular* interpretive engagement with Scripture. . . ." But it is also true that the textual details *fit*, and so we must say that engagements with Scripture have the capacity to confirm—or falsify—a particular appraisal of the rule of faith.

This is simply a point of emphasis but an important one for how we interact with biblical scholarship on trinitarian readings. In a paper of this size and scope all one can do in responding to John Goldingay's charge is assert the contrary: no, trinitarian readings do not skew the biblical narrative's portrayal of God. Eventually, however, we shall have to wrestle with whether and where the details of trinitarian and other readings work, not simply with the generality of narrative structures. That is true not only to address the public square but simply to explore the meaning of the rule of faith.

The first two gaps were more *literary*; we need to know how to keep narrative from smothering nonnarrative genres or from sidestepping the conceptual questions that stories raise. This third gap is a bit more *grammatical-historical*, to use an old fashioned term. We need to know whether it matters, not that Peter was a critical biblical scholar or interpreted within strict limits of the Old Testament's "human authorial intentions," but that we develop a hermeneutical defense of NT appeals to Joel, Psalms, and other OT writings in the face of textual details. Laytham could probably fill in all these gaps with enough time and space; here we are simply asking whether they would add a bit of unacknowledged tension to his story.

Gap Number Four: Our Sense of our Roles in the Story. Finally, the biggest gap: from the *then* of an OT or even a NT context to the *now* of our own responsibility to indwell it. Two days before receiving this paper I was talking about Acts 2 in my hermeneutics class. At some point every semester I ask the students why it is that many of our church traditions appeal to the narrative of Acts 2:41 for a theology of baptism and church membership, or to Acts 2:42 for a theology of congregational meetings, but only some would expect the miracles narrated in Acts 2:43. Almost no one would mention (let alone practice) the communal economy narrated in Acts 2:44–45 or the daily frequency of congregational gatherings narrated in Acts 2:46.

If the scriptural narrative is meant to shape Christian identity, nevertheless sooner or later identity involves actions, which *character-ize* people. Persons and congregations want, and need, to know their God given role. Since this conference takes place in the shadow of momentous days for the Anglican communion—as only one example—we had better take seriously this ethical getting "in" to the biblical story. Are we Protestants not obligated to offer canonical reasons for playing out some patterns but not others from passages like Acts 2?

Or maybe we cannot. One of my hermeneutics students wrote an editorial in the student newspaper, suggesting that the dominant campus opposition to the Episcopal Church decisions was wrong and ignored the complexity of the issue of homoerotic behavior. On a class day prior to that this same student had opposed any doctrine of the clarity of Scripture since "in the church where I grew up in Kentucky, all the members carry Bibles but are also members of the Ku Klux Klan."

What then shall we say? Laytham is right that a more propositional understanding of Scripture's authority usually correlates with divine command ethics. I think he is also right that, instead, we must take more seriously a narrative shape to Scripture's authority. The obvious corollary would then be an ethic of virtue, fostered by liturgical formation. And this is consistent with the reading we are given of Acts 2. Following a mention of Stanley Hauerwas, we read, "Peter tells a good story, but is it truth or tall tale? Peter invites his hearers to judge the truthfulness of the story on the basis of the visible and audible church." Aside from the canonical uniqueness of that assembly's moment in salvation history, there is the following difficulty with that claim.

In isolation (especially if we apply this sentence to the NT in the same way as the OT) we have described a hermeneutic diffuse enough to accommodate almost anything a professing Christian or church wants to do. Mind you, Laytham does not intend that. But in footnote three he *does* suggest that for liberals and conservatives alike Scripture is authoritative. Yes indeed, but surely not in the same way? Perhaps I am nitpicking, but a later sentence says it better: the "visible and audible community embodies the fulfillment of the prophetic word . . . ." This makes clearer that Peter pointed to the Pentecostal people *because of* the Joel text, because he saw its *details* unfolding before their eyes.

Yes, Scripture's authority has a narrative shape, but we must not leave out the details that shape our discerning the signs of the times. Especially, perhaps, since the current debasing of authority, to which Laytham refers but does not develop, takes the specific form of divorcing divine commands from their role in describing patterns of virtuous living. Without a substantive scriptural account of virtue that helps us recognize what to do or not do in light of particular texts and contexts, it is unclear that Christian persons and congregations worldwide will share any identity except perhaps for a rite such as baptism. Laytham is right to point out the very basic role of liturgical formation in connecting us with God's story, but again the Episcopalian situation shows how far short that can leave us.

So while we are seeing (as Nancey Murphy and others point out[6]) hopeful signs that the conservative-liberal divide is moving toward the middle of a spectrum, we should still acknowledge that all sides in churchly debates, such as the one on homoerotic behavior, can appeal to narrative concepts of authority and ethics of virtue. The question is how to adjudicate them. It is not yet clear whether narrative and virtue offer a Christian language to guide us from common worship, through conversation, toward unity and truth, or whether instead they cover over differences which cry out to be clarified as irreconcilable: clarified by thinking about the truth claims and ethical concerns that emerge variously from each of the literary forms comprising Scripture's Christian story.

Gerhard Sauter quotes the following:

> A farmer met a schoolmaster in the field. "Were you serious yesterday, schoolmaster, when you interpreted for the children the text 'If anyone strikes you on the right cheek, offer him the other as well'?" "I can neither add to it nor subtract from it," the schoolmaster replied, "It is in the Gospel." Then the farmer slapped the schoolmaster on one cheek, and then the other, for the teacher had annoyed him for a long time. While this was taking place a nobleman and his hunter rode by at a distance. The nobleman said to the hunter, "Joseph, go and see what those two over there are up to." As Joseph approached, the schoolmaster, a strong man, struck the farmer twice and said, "It is also written, With whatever measure you measure, you too will be measured. A packed down and overflowing measure will be thrown in your lap." Along with this last verse the schoolmaster added a half dozen slaps more. Then Joseph returned to his Lord and said, "It's nothing, my Lord, they are merely interpreting Scripture to each other."[7]

We should have no desire for that story to ring as true as it does. Arguably, however, what we need is a thicker description of the narrative moves we make with the details of the Bible so no one can *simply* appeal to what seems plain from their experience; instead, at least sometimes, the texts should make clear why someone is plotting wrongly. Biblical authority should have a narrative shape, *along with* filling in enough detail to move beyond a silhouette or shadow and measure virtuous living by the fullness of Christ.

NOTES

1. Thanks to Darren Sarisky and my colleagues Tim Larsen, Laura Miguélez, and Steve Spencer for commenting on a draft of this response.

2. E.g., Paul Ricoeur, *Time and Narrative* (trans. Kathleen McLaughlin Blamey and David Pellauer; Chicago: University of Chicago Press, 1984–1988), 3:272. See also his essays "Toward a Hermeneutic of the Idea of Revelation," in *Essays on Biblical Interpretation* (ed. Lewis S. Mudge; trans. David Pellauer; Philadelphia: Fortress, 1980); and "Biblical Time," in *Figuring the Sacred: Religion, Narrative, and Imagination* (ed. Mark I. Wallace; trans. David Pellauer; Minneapolis: Fortress, 1995).

3. At the conference Prof. Laytham suggested we call what Peter is doing "narrative description." That is helpful and might suggest that individual line items within the narrative do not always function like propositions. However, it might be argued that the narrative on the whole remains a kind of truth claim or proposition.

4. N. T. Wright, *The Resurrection of the Son of God*, vol. 3 of Christian Origins and the Question of God (Minneapolis: Fortress, 2003).

5. Daniel J. Treier, "The Fulfillment of Joel 2:28–32: A Multiple Lens Approach," *JETS* 40 (1997): 13–26.

6. E.g., Nancey Murphy, *Beyond Liberalism and Fundamentalism: How Modern and Postmodern Philosophy Set the Theological Agenda* (Valley Forge, Penn.: Trinity Press International, 1996).

7. Gerhard Sauter, *Gateways to Dogmatics: Reasoning Theologically for the Life of the Church* (Grand Rapids: Eerdmans, 2003), 218–219.

THE OLD TESTAMENT CANON AND ITS AUTHORITY FOR THE CHRISTIAN CHURCH[1]

STEPHEN B. CHAPMAN

PAINFUL REALIZATIONS

Why revisit the abstract matter of scriptural authority at all? Yes, there are indeed external cultural pressures upon traditional Christian notions of biblical authority, but these threats are nothing new. Moreover, a response to such threats taking the form of a theoretical discussion of "authority" is unlikely to be found persuasive by those not already possessing a substantial familiarity with the lived reality of Christian faith and practice. No, the more significant reason to discuss scriptural authority has arisen in recent years from within Christianity itself. In light of newer trends in historical research and more broadly ecumenical dialogue in biblical studies, old arguments are being reevaluated and traditional theological positions reframed. In this inner-Christian reappraisal the fundamental question at issue is not *whether* Scripture has any authority, but rather *how* Scripture functions authoritatively.

This "how" question bears particularly on a traditional dispute within Christian theology, namely the difference between Catholics and Protestants on the relationship between Scripture and tradition. If Catholicism can be said to have taken a major step toward the Protestant position at Vatican II by rejecting a two source theory of revelation and affirming the essential unity of Scripture and tradition, Protestants have increasingly seemed to find their own doctrine of Scripture incoherent and in need of supplementation by ecclesial tradition, as in Catholic theology.

In his 1985 volume on biblical authority Lutheran scholar Robert Gnuse put the matter bluntly: "Protestants . . . are giving up their radical insistence upon *sola scriptura*."[2] He explained further:

> Protestants have come to a number of painful realizations which led to this moderation. The debate over authority has led Protestants to realize that Scripture does not claim to be the exclusive source of faith, the unique deposit of revelation. *Sola scriptura* is not really taught in the

> Bible. The history of canon taught many Protestants that Scripture was a product of the community of faith, the Church. Previously they believed that the Bible came first historically and the Church developed upon its foundation. However, many now admit that the Church established the canon.[3]

Gnuse's assessment of this trend in Protestant scholarship continues to be accurate, especially in relation to contemporary scholarship on the biblical canon. In the intervening years, even more of the leading Protestant researchers in this area have come to approximately the same conclusions that Gnuse earlier sketched.[4] Yet the purpose of the present essay will be to show how a reexamination of the historical evidence for the history of biblical canon formation actually leads in the opposite direction, reinforcing the traditional Protestant view.

In making this case I would like to confess at the outset my own social location as both a Protestant clergyman (Baptist) and a teacher at a university divinity school affiliated with a Protestant denomination (Methodist). I would quickly add, however, that my motivation for mounting the following argument does not stem from any wish to bring confessional categories into the discussion simply for the sake of creating controversy or reviving traditional polemics. The point is rather to show that theological concerns are deeply related to questions of historical reconstruction and cannot simply be avoided. Confessional categories are always present, even (or perhaps especially) when they go unacknowledged. It is a mistake therefore to pretend that differences in historical reconstruction turn solely on data and methodology or that historical proposals are unrelated to theological positions.

While there is no *necessary* reason that views of scriptural authority be tied to the history of Scripture's formation and canonization,[5] in point of fact historical arguments have always been advanced in disputes about the authority of Scripture, and they continue to be influential in current debates.[6] To the extent that historical arguments are ruled germane at all, then, this essay will proceed to evaluate their appropriateness and force.

The scope of the following treatment is therefore somewhat restricted. I intend to examine the way that historical research into the biblical canon is brought to bear upon the larger theological question of scriptural authority, not meaning to imply by this manner of putting the question that historical factors are solely determinative in resolving the theological issues at stake. My goal is rather to offer an evaluation of how historical arguments are in fact used and the extent to which those arguments support or challenge traditional theological positions about Scripture. Questions regarding other kinds of factors that bear on the issue of biblical authority are thus beyond the purview of this particular essay.

However, a major point to be made here will also be that investigations into the general nature of Scripture frequently give insufficient attention to the specific history of OT canon formation. I will contend that a historical understanding of the significance of the OT canon for the early church frames the broader question of scriptural authority in a theologically crucial manner. Conversely, in my judgment, the contemporary retreat from the traditional Protestant position on Scripture occurs, and can only occur, at the expense of the full authority of the OT for Christian faith and practice and entails the loss of an adequate Christian respect for Judaism.

For these reasons I will focus my remarks on the historical formation of the OT canon and the implications of that process for contemporary discussions of scriptural authority.

THE STANDARD THEORY

Despite some variation in its particulars, a standard theory of OT canon formation has existed within biblical scholarship since the end of the nineteenth century and still predominates in textbooks and other secondary materials.[7] In this theory the OT is thought to have been canonized in three discrete, linear stages corresponding to the three main literary divisions within the Hebrew canon: the Law (or Pentateuch); the Prophets; and the Writings. Especially since there are very few extrabiblical sources to consult for the historical contours of this process, H. E. Ryle's idea that the tripartite OT canon bears within itself the most important evidence regarding the history of its own formation has always seemed like an elegant solution to an otherwise intractable problem.[8] Working from this premise, it was Ryle who more than anyone else gave the standard theory its lasting shape and appeal.

When it came to dating, most scholars agreed with Ryle that the account of Ezra's reading of the law in Neh 8 reflected the emergence of the Pentateuch as canonical Scripture in early postexilic Judah. Even with the significant difficulties involved in dating Ezra's mission, the influence of Neh 8 usually led researchers to a mid-fifth century date for the Pentateuch and thus for the beginning of the OT canon as such.[9] The collection of the Prophets was typically dated to the late third or early second century B.C. Here two key factors were the references to the prophetic books found in the deuterocanonical book of Ben Sira (ca. 180 B.C.)[10] and the placement of the book of Daniel (usually dated to 165 B.C. by historical-critical scholars) within the collection of the Writings. Since even within later tradition Daniel had been remembered as a prophet,[11] so the theory went, a book about him would naturally have been placed among the Prophets if that collection had still been open. The Writings themselves were thought to have been closed as a collection, together with the entire Hebrew canon, by a rabbinical "council" in the town of Jamnia (or Yavneh) in approximately A.D. 90. This dating was reached primarily on the basis of three considerations: 1) the supposed lack of clear evidence for a closed and uniform OT canon within the NT; 2) a handful of brief references in rabbinic literature to discussions in Jamnia about certain biblical books at the end of the first century A.D.;[12] and 3) the testimony to a uniform, closed canon by the Jewish historian Josephus, writing in about A.D. 95 (*Against Apion*, 1.37–43).

It should be noted that this historical reconstruction puts the closing of the OT canon after the time of Jesus and the earliest period in the history of the Christian church. According to this reconstruction, moreover, the bulk of the NT would have been written *prior* to the existence of the OT canon as such. In fact, since the canonization of Jewish Scripture at Jamnia occurred after the fall of Jerusalem in A.D. 70 and the subsequent parting of ways between Judaism and Christianity, it must be concluded on the basis of this reconstruction that Christianity engaged in its own process of closing the OT canon, occurring more or less contemporaneously with the canonization of the NT writings. In other words, this standard way of reconstructing the history of canon formation leads directly to the related conclusion that Judaism and Christianity engaged in *separate* processes of canonization, with the Christian OT being a construction of the early church rather than an inheritance from Judaism.[13]

In the time since Ryle's work scholarship has moved toward an even later dating scheme. Citing references in the NT and other early Christian writings to books that were eventually left outside the biblical canon[14] and also taking into account the wide variety of canonical lists found among early Christian authors,[15] recent writers argue that several centuries actually passed before the church could clarify and standardize the contents of its own biblical collection. Scholars continuing to work within the framework of the standard theory have therefore increasingly emphasized that *Christian* definition of the OT canon only really began in the second century A.D., a process that cannot be considered complete until the time of Athanasius' 39th Festal Letter (A.D. 367), at which point the entire Christian Bible had finally stabilized and was invested with full "canonical" status.[16]

LIBERAL PROTESTANT INTERPRETATION

Based upon the standard view of OT canon formation just outlined, liberal Protestant scholars have characteristically found certain implications for a contemporary view of scriptural authority. These implications are articulated in such a particularly clear and comprehensive way by Lee McDonald that he can serve as an exemplary representative for the general viewpoint to be described.

For McDonald, historical evidence calls into question the validity of the narrower Protestant OT canon. He stresses the extent to which the writings of the NT allude to writings later excluded from the Jewish canon.[17] Why is it, he asks, that Christianity should adopt a later Jewish restriction of the Old Testament's literary scope—especially when, as McDonald emphasizes, that restriction was likely made at least partly in response to the threat represented by Christian use of Jewish Scripture?[18] McDonald argues that the later Protestant OT canon "was not the sole canon of scriptures for Jesus and the apostles."[19] To the contrary, according to McDonald the wider canon known in Catholic tradition provides a much better indication of what was considered Scripture within first century Judaism than the (later) Jewish canon does. However, McDonald still views the broader OT canon as not becoming fully closed until the fourth century A.D.

Drawing a distinction between "core" matters and "fringe" concerns, McDonald maintains that, even though the boundaries of the biblical canon were fuzzy within both Judaism and Christianity for some time after the first century A.D., the essential writings of the developing canon and their fundamental teachings found widespread and, for the most part, unquestioned agreement among coreligionists.[20] Yet the fuzziness of the canon's precise scope in this period also reinforces for McDonald the extent to which religious authority was primarily vested in nonscriptural sources throughout the earliest centuries of the church. McDonald maintains that the apostolic memory of Jesus and the living authority of the Holy Spirit both trumped scriptural authority until the biblical canon was finally closed, an event he strongly implies may well have been a theological mistake.[21]

In all this McDonald ostensibly frames his approach christologically. The most appropriate biblical canon, in his judgment, is the one most fully representing the historical canon of Jesus and the apostles. In turn, McDonald's chief worry about a closed scriptural canon arises from his fear that its religious authority may rival the authority properly belonging to Christ alone.[22] McDonald goes so far as to claim at the end of his treatment that "the true canon of faith for the church" is "our Lord Jesus Christ."[23] This sweeping christological formulation represents a protest on McDonald's part against "inappropriate loyalties" present in the modern church, by which he means primarily fundamentalistic bibliolatry—the effort to ground faith in the verbal inspiration of Scripture and biblical inerrancy.

From the perspective of such a protest it can been seen that McDonald not only perceives a direct correlation between the history of the canon and a normative view of biblical authority, but that he also reads the historical evidence in light of a particular theological construal about the contemporary state of the church. Yet left completely unclear in his argument is how christological "loyalty" can be framed *apart* from Scripture and if, in the end, any real authority remains for Scripture within his constructive proposal or whether in its decision-making the church would simply be left with a multitude of christological assertions to adjudicate on some *other* basis (e.g., "what would Jesus do?"). Ironically, McDonald's christological solution also stands on its head a fundamental aspect of the New Testament's witness to Christ, for in the NT it is not the OT that is professed to be "in accordance with" Christ, but Christ who is confessed to be "in accordance with" the OT Scriptures.[24]

In this way, however, McDonald's chief criterion for the authority of Scripture is revealed as not *primarily* christological at all, but historicist. It is the Jesus of history who holds the key to McDonald's canon rather than the Christ of the NT.[25] What McDonald consistently overlooks or minimizes is the extent to which Christ is a "booked" reality for the church. As far as the church is concerned, there is no "Christ" to be found completely apart from the New Testament's testimony to him, neither is there an "Israel" to be discovered that is fully distinct from the OT witnesses.[26] McDonald's argument to the contrary reflects a distinctively liberal Protestant move, involving at one and the same time a deprecation of the scriptural witness and a relocation of revelation to the history "behind" the text.

CATHOLIC INTERPRETATION

While it would certainly be a mistake to presume that only a single interpretation of the historical data pertaining to canon formation can be termed "Catholic," there does appear to be a kind of family resemblance among the views of the most influential Catholic scholars working on the topic.[27] In the following discussion this common interpretive trajectory is represented by Karl Rahner.

In Catholic interpretation, not only can the historical fuzziness of the canon be noted without anxiety, it can even be positively welcomed as a reminder of how it was *tradition* as much as (or perhaps even more than) Scripture that held primary authority for the early church and mediated divine revelation. In this reading of the evidence Scripture itself is seen more as the historical product of tradition than its source,[28] which typically means in turn that Scripture is also treated primarily as the legacy of the church instead of its inheritance.

Such views have found wide acceptance among liberal Protestant scholars,[29] as Gnuse confesses in the quotation found at the beginning of this essay. To reiterate:

> The history of canon taught many Protestants that Scripture was a product of the community of faith, the Church. Previously they believed that the Bible came first historically and the Church developed upon its foundation. However, many now admit that the Church established the canon.[30]

Against the backdrop of the standard historical reconstruction of OT canon formation, it can now be seen how in this trajectory of interpretation the church becomes not only historically responsible for the final details of the canon's official contents but also for actively selecting and arranging its own separate OT canon, as distinct from Judaism.

With an increasingly late date for the OT as such, however, it becomes all the more remarkable to this view's proponents that the early church put together an "Old Testament" for itself at all. Gnuse suggests that the OT writings were retained by Christians because "they explicated the prior assumptions of the Jewish authors of the New Testament writings and because the Jewish ethos helped Christians to maintain their identity in the face of Greek syncretizing heresies like Gnosticism and Docetism."[31] In this way, the Old Testament's retention is explained, but under the condition that it was always conceived as having had a subordinate place within the canon in relation to the NT. The presence of the OT within the Christian Bible is said to be due primarily to the need for the kind of cultural and historical background that would make the NT comprehensible to an increasingly Gentile audience ("prior assumptions"). The OT books had predicted Christ, and, therefore, they continued to depict the shape of the expectation to which Christ had provided the complete fulfillment.[32] Yet this strongly salvation-historical model also begs a critical question about the Old Testament's present ability to speak vertically as well as horizontally—that is, to speak as an urgently contemporary word of God for the church and not only as a now fulfilled prophecy from the past.

Gnuse does assert at one point in his discussion that his way of configuring the data should not be taken to mean that the church *bestowed* authority on the books of the canon but rather that it *recognized* the authority they had already possessed.[33] Unclear, however, is how this assertion is consistent with what Gnuse says in the rest of his treatment, which sounds very much like "bestowal" and not really like "recognition" at all. So, for example, he speaks elsewhere of the canon being "*created* in the fourth century in the wake of the Constantinian revolution" and stresses that scriptural books gained admittance into the canon to the extent "they agreed with . . . the faith as articulated by Christians."[34] In the details of Gnuse's description, then, the direction of authority always runs from the church and its traditions to Scripture, rather than the reverse.

Thus, for Gnuse the "authority" currently possessed by the OT derives from the authority it received historically by virtue of being in agreement with the Christian faith, as the church defined it. Although he ultimately tries to articulate a perspective in which church and Scripture exerted equal and mutual influence upon each other, he persistently refers to Scripture as arising out of the church.[35] While he does claim that Scripture has always been acknowledged by the church to provide the ultimate norm for theology and ecclesiastical tradition,[36] he lays such stress on the harmonious unity of Scripture and church *in theory* that it is extremely difficult to see how *in practice* Scripture could ever really call the church to account, let alone to judgment.

Gnuse's inconsistency appears to stem from his effort to appropriate the insights of Catholic theologian Karl Rahner in a manner that is free of certain difficulties attaching to Rahner's position. For Rahner, the authority of *all*

Scripture consists precisely in its preservation of the faith of the early church: "We regard [Scripture] as the church's book, the book in which the church of the beginning always remains tangible as a norm for us in the concrete."[37] As the "objectification" of the "original" church, Scripture is normative, but also at the same time "derivative" of the "essential nature of the church."[38] Among other effects, this judgment grants a prior authority to historical-critical reconstructions of the "original" meaning *behind* the NT text, since it is the historical reality of the apostolic church that is ultimately granted hermeneutical control.

Yet, it may well be asked, how can this view of Scripture embrace the OT as well as the New? Rahner argued that only when the OT is read in the light of faith in Jesus Christ is it possible to distinguish a similar "historical objectification" of God's "transcendental self-communication" from a "human corruption" of it.[39] In other words, there is a similar "objectification" of normative faith available within the OT as well as in the New, but it too can only be recognized from the prior stance of the faith of the church. On its own terms, the OT lacks unity and overarching structure.

In fact, Rahner maintained, the OT:

> . . . admits of no unified interpretation with regard to its content and its scope except in view of Christ. For except in view of him, this scripture with its slow genesis and the many strata in its tendencies and its theological conceptions could hardly be subsumed under one unified idea, unless it is the idea that a people in its long history knows that it is the partner of the one, living, judging and gracious God, who is the incomprehensible but ever present Lord of its history, and therefore knows that this history is fundamentally open to an unknown but salvific future, and that it is given over to the disposal of the coming God of the future.[40]

What finally makes the OT revelatory for Rahner is therefore not its specific content, which by itself forms a kind of incomplete jigsaw puzzle, but rather its future orientation, which increasingly moves the puzzle along, beyond itself, toward a completed picture of Christ. Rahner's uncompromising stance here should be noted: any reading of the OT other than one viewing its conclusion in Christ *cannot* be said to represent an alternative interpretation with its own hermeneutical integrity but *must* be viewed as a misunderstanding of the literature itself.[41] Such a position problematically refuses legitimacy to Jewish biblical interpretation and to Judaism in general.

Within the various concerns negotiated by Christian theology, other difficulties are created by Rahner's position. Although Rahner was well aware he could not contravene the First Vatican Council by concluding the church had actually "constituted" the canon of sacred Scripture, he still argued that the books of the canon can only be identified and known through the teaching of the church.[42] He admitted that if canonicity were conferred by the church it would mean the books of the canon had been given "from outside a higher value than they have by themselves."[43] However, he went on to claim that to derive the "essence" of Scripture from the "essence" of the church did not fall afoul of the First Vatican Council's decision: ". . . the church objectifies its faith and its life in written documents, and it recognizes these objectifications as so pure and so successful that they are able to hand on the apostolic church as a norm for future ages."[44] In this way, the authority of Scripture is still derived from the prior authority of the church's tradition, to which Scripture gives expression but, in effect, cannot contradict. Scripture can call debased tradition to account, according to Rahner, by reminding the church of its original "essence." But the *genuine* tradition of the church is, by definition, ruled from the outset as always cohering with the content of Scripture and funding its authority.[45] In fact, what calls the church to account here is not really Scripture per se but the "essence" of the church that Scripture "re-presents."[46] In other words, it is the church that calls the church to account.

Among other consequences, this solution to the question of scriptural authority means that it is not the OT per se which holds authority for Rahner, but the OT as mediated through the New Testament's "objectification" of the apostolic faith (i.e., a form of the position described by the technical phrase *Vetus Testamentum in Novo receptum*).[47] As Gnuse perceives, at this point Rahner's position "relegates the entire Old Testament to an inferior status."[48] For Rahner, the Old Testament's role within the canon is ultimately to provide the modern church with the same kind of salvation-historical background information for the Christ event that it once provided the early church. However, here again, just as in liberal Protestantism, the ability of the OT to speak "vertically" to the contemporary church disappears within the strongly "horizontal" framework of salvation history.[49] In the end, Protestant Gnuse and Catholic Rahner are more alike than different, with Gnuse largely agreeing with Rahner in the way that basic issues are to be formulated, but apparently trying to soften some of the unwanted consequences that Rahner quite logically deduced.

Interestingly, both Gnuse and Rahner represent an approach to these issues which is increasingly out of step with mainstream Catholic theology. In an important recent statement by the Pontifical Biblical Commission entitled, "The Jewish People and their Sacred Scriptures in the Christian Bible," a clear effort is made to acknowledge the full authority of the OT per se for the Christian church:

> The Old Testament in itself has great value as the Word of God. To read the Old Testament as Christians then does not mean wishing to find everywhere direct reference to Jesus and to Christian realities. True, for Christians, all the Old Testament economy is in movement towards Christ . . . [but] this is a retrospective perception whose point of departure is not in the text as such, but in the events of the New

> Testament proclaimed by the apostolic preaching. It cannot be said, therefore, that Jews do not see what has been proclaimed in the text, but that the Christian, in the light of Christ and in the Spirit, discovers in the text an additional meaning that was hidden there.[50]

This bold exposition of the fundamental place of the OT *as such* within Christian faith and practice is stunning both in terms of the newness of its direction and the suggestive power of its implications. Especially noteworthy is how the normative hermeneutical proposals found throughout the Commission's statement flow from a partially new historical reconstruction of canon formation, one in which closed collections of Law and Prophets (but not the Writings)[51] were *inherited* by the church: "What the Church seems to have received was a body of Sacred Scripture which, within Judaism, was in the process of becoming canonical."[52] In this way the link between historical reconstruction and hermeneutical program again comes to the fore, but this time in a manner that increases rather than minimizes the Old Testament's authority.

For this and other reasons, the distance from the traditional Protestant view of Scripture seems to narrow in the new Vatican statement, although one major sticking point between Catholic and Protestant positions remains: the issue of the deuterocanonical or apocryphal books. Much effort is expended in the statement to ground the canonical process in tradition, both Jewish and Christian, so that the deuterocanonical books can be accepted as fully authoritative on the same basis. In doing so, however, the statement then seems to slip back into a kind of formulation that stands at considerable tension with the rest of its conceptual framework:

> To determine this canon, [the Catholic Church] based itself on the Church's constant usage. In adopting this canon, which is larger than the Hebrew, it has preserved an authentic memory of Christian origins, since, as we have seen, the more restricted Hebrew canon is later than the formation of the New Testament.[53]

Not only is the OT canon now treated as a later reality, here it is, as with Rahner, the "authentic memory of Christian origins" that provides the ultimate authority for the church, rather than Scripture per se.

Throughout the Vatican statement tradition is said to "give birth to" Scripture, so that the authority of Scripture itself remains derivative. It therefore amounts to a major concession in the statement when it is declared: ". . . early Christians had the Scripture from the very beginning, since as Jews, they accepted Israel's Bible as Scripture." At this point the OT is acknowledged to have been authoritative for the early church precisely as written Scripture, *not* tradition. Then, however, an appeal is also quickly made to oral tradition in the form of "the teaching of the Apostles" (Acts 2:42),[54] as if to deflect the implications of what has just been said. The statement continues with a section entitled, "Tradition completes Scripture," in which it is concluded that "Christianity has in common with Judaism the conviction that God's revelation cannot be expressed in its entirety in written texts."[55] The question as to whether tradition might offer a "material addition" to Scripture is raised and left open.

In all these various ways, then, clear differences remain between Catholic and Protestant views of scriptural authority in the new Vatican statement, yet the two theological traditions may also have moved closer to each other than ever before. Interestingly, striking differences are evident as well between mainstream Catholic theology of the present and the more liberal Catholic trajectory of the past.[56]

IMPRECISE AND MISLEADING TERMINOLOGY

Both of the interpretive trajectories described thus far rely on the standard historical reconstruction of OT canon formation. In fact, however, this reconstruction is now being called into question on historical grounds, opening up the possibility of a reevaluation of the theological conclusions to be drawn from the particular contours of the historical process. Several different aspects of the standard reconstruction have been found to be problematic, ranging from its methodological presuppositions to its handling of the inner and extrabiblical evidence. One key methodological dispute has to do with how the term "canon" is to be defined. A closely related issue deals with the appropriateness of "closing" language to describe the final stage of the canonical process.

"Canon" has two senses, both of which are rooted in antiquity: "norm" and "list." Scholars have usually valorized one of these senses, often without acknowledging or defending their choice. In a very helpful treatment, however, Gerald Sheppard showed not only that both senses have equal historical pedigrees, but that it is a mistake to place the two senses along a strictly linear progression (i.e., as if canons always begin as vague norms and only eventually become specific lists).[57] Sheppard's typological distinction between what he termed "canon 1" (norm) and "canon 2" (list) enabled him to describe the kind of canonical authority held by certain Scriptures that lack a specific enumeration of their scope. He applied this kind of "canon 1" authority to the Scriptures of Israel prior to their actual "closing." Sheppard justified his approach phenomenologically as a means of characterizing more adequately the way Scriptures and canons actually function throughout the various religions of the world.

By contrast, Eugene Ulrich insists on restricting "canon" to its "strict" sense of "list" and avoiding the "broad" sense of "norm" as improper.[58] For Ulrich, the determination of a canon must entail a "conscious decision" that its contents have a "unique status" and are "necessarily binding."[59] What is curious about Ulrich's argument is how he bases his judgment on contemporary usage (e.g., dictionary definitions) and church tradition (e.g., doctrinal positions).[60] This way of approaching the question is curious because Ulrich's handling of canonical issues is otherwise rigidly historicist. Rather than basing a definition upon the historical reality of canon in ancient Israel, however, he takes what is arguably the prevailing sense of canon in later (church) history and then makes it normative for his historical work.

In this move, Ulrich is not alone. Many researchers holding to the standard historical reconstruction of the canon tend to adopt a "strict" view of the canon rather than a "broad" one. Ironically, however, by reifying the one sense of "canon" at the expense of the other they find themselves eventually forced to concede that an officially complete and absolute listing of the canon *never really took place at all* in either Jewish or Christian tradition.[61] Instead of being a minor point, this concession actually goes to the heart of the methodology employed, for why should one adopt as proper a definition of "canon" that does not ever appear to have existed in reality? If "canon" *never* functions exclusively as an exact list or immutable text, then would it not be better to find another, more nuanced, definition? Sheppard's own work moved in this direction, as has the pioneering work of his teacher, Brevard Childs.[62]

Such methodological issues are not merely tangential but are directly related to the results of historical investigations into the process of canon formation. In a brilliant study John Barton has shown how, in reconstructions of the history of NT canon formation, those scholars working with a strict view of "canon" come to advocate much later dates for the canon, while those researchers who understand "canon" more broadly reach correspondingly earlier dates.[63] Increasing awareness of this point has for some time been casting significant doubt upon the standard three stage reconstruction of the OT canon as methodologically compromised.[64]

The language of "closing" is also deeply embedded in the logic of the three stage theory and, although it has not received as much attention as the term "canon," is quite obviously even more imprecise. This language is fatally anachronistic, borrowing the model of conciliar decision from church history and imposing it unfairly upon ancient Judaism.[65] No direct historical evidence confirms the critical theory that at discrete moments in time a representative body within Judaism determined the binding scope of the biblical canon by conscious decision. In fact, much evidence stands against it.[66]

A NONSTANDARD THEORY

If less emphasis is placed upon the strict view of "canon," then crucial building blocks of the standard theory become significantly less compelling. Absolute uniformity in the text of biblical citations at Qumran and in the NT is no longer a necessary precondition of canonical status. Similarly, the possibility that other, extracanonical, writings may be referenced authoritatively at Qumran and in the NT does not exclude the possibility of a "canon," but rather suggests a canonical collection in which the idea of precise boundaries was less important than the perceptible family resemblance shared by diverse Scriptures, which together symbolized the cumulative weight of Israel's tradition.

Admittedly, it is difficult to make a compelling case for a pre-Christian date for the canonization of Jewish Scripture when using the strict definition of "canon,"[67] but the difficulty relates more to the definition than the data. The so-called "Halakhic Letter" from Qumran (4QMMT/4Q394–399), the extant fragments of which were first published in 1994 and dated paleographically from between 75 B.C. and A.D. 50, refers to "the book of Moses [and] the book[s of the pr]ophets and of Davi[d...]" (4Q397).[68] Here is found an early reference to a three part scriptural collection. Scholarly opinion has not only been inclined to the view that the original text of this document antedates the discovered fragments, it has also recognized that, since the Qumran sectarians are referring their *opponents* to Scriptures they all held in common and mutually deemed authoritative, the shared status of the scriptural books referred to must have been previously established.[69] These and other factors have led to a likely date of ca. 150 B.C. for the original text of the letter.[70] Of course, the point is often made that such broad allusions to categories or subcollections within Scripture do not reveal the precise books of Scripture that were included. However, on the basis of the scriptural citations found within the Qumran documents generally and a variety of other factors, a surprising number of scholars are willing to accept the notion of a "core canon" of (at least) Torah, Prophets, and Psalms being in place by the first century B.C.[71]

This idea of a "core canon" at Qumran matches nicely with the evidence provided by the book of Ben Sira, whose prologue (ca. 120 B.C.) refers to "the law, the prophets, and the others that followed them" (Sir Prol 1), to "the law, the prophets, and the other books of our ancestors" (Sir Prol 3), and to "the law itself, the prophecies, and the rest of the books" (Sir Prol 7). It bears repeating that since the references in this prologue are to the Greek *translations* of the Hebrew books (Sir Prol 6), the authority of the books themselves has already been established for quite some time. That the shape of the collection of prophetic books must have been substantially similar to its present form is indicated by references in the body of the book of Ben Sira (dating to ca. 180 B.C.) to the conclusion of the book of Malachi (Sir 48:10) and to the book of The Twelve as a whole (Sir 49:10).

In fact, the real dispute in canonical scholarship has to do with the status of the Writings prior to the turn of the millennium. As John Collins has written, "It is uncertain whether there was a clear distinction at Qumran between the Kethubim [or Writings] and other authoritative writings," by which latter category he means books like Jubilees, which appears to have enjoyed high status at Qumran but was not received into the later biblical canon.[72] Here again, however, the possible acceptance of a book like Jubilees by the Qumran community only excludes the existence of a scriptural canon at that time to the extent that one anachronistically insists on a strict definition of "canon." All of the Writings were known in some form and read as authoritative Scripture by the Qumran community (except perhaps for Esther and Nehemiah, if transmitted separately from Ezra).[73] Emanuel Tov notes that Chronicles is quoted by Eupolemos in the middle of the second century B.C. and that Job is cited by Pseudo-Aristeas at the beginning of the first century B.C.[74] In fact, Tov dates the Greek translations of most of the books now found in the Prophets and Writings to the beginning of the second century B.C., based in part on the evidence provided by the prologue to Ben Sira.[75] This dating strongly suggests that by the turn of the millennium, a Jewish canon of Scripture was largely in place, if not absolutely defined and delimited in scope.

Such a conclusion is also supported by historical data concerning the prehexaplaric recensions of the Greek biblical texts, in which revisions are evident *in the direction of* the (still developing) Hebrew text. If Frank Moore Cross is correct about the existence of a proto-Lucianic recension, for example, then it provides evidence of a revision of the Greek Bible toward a Palestinian Hebrew text already in the late second/early first century B.C.[76] The Naḥal Ḥever scroll (8ḤevXIIgr) and the *kaige*-Theodotionic revision (to which it belongs) both date to the late first century B.C. or very early first century A.D. and represent an effort to produce a Greek translation more closely resembling the proto-Masoretic text.[77] While the history of canonization and the history of the biblical text are not to be viewed as fully identical, they cannot be fully detached from each other either. The realization that the proto-Masoretic text was developing already before the turn of the millennium, enough so that those reading the Greek Scriptures would experience the need for greater correspondence between the two bodies of texts, provides strong circumstantial evidence for the existence of a canon in the broader sense. In fact, Cross has recently argued that a text-critical approach to the question of canonization would favor a date for both the Pharisaic text and canon in the first part of the first century A.D.[78] He bases this conclusion largely on the evidence of the prehexaplaric recensions of the Greek Bible, but also on his judgment that the close textual activity central to the work of Hillel (d. A.D. 10) is highly difficult to imagine without the existence of a stabilized Hebrew biblical text.[79]

In this context it also bears mentioning that in the entire work of Philo there are only a very few references to apocryphal books![80] It is true that the presence and extent of authoritative references in the NT to apocryphal and/or pseudepigraphical books continue to be disputed.[81] In the debate, however, much depends upon exactly how one understands and defines such terms as "authoritative reference" and "citation formula." Even Lee McDonald admits that the NT writers "never specifically call any extracanonical literature 'scripture.'"[82]

In all of this an astonishing factor is the absence of any explicit debate in antiquity relating to the precise contents of the canon until *after* A.D. 70. Even in contexts of religious dispute among Second Temple groups representing quite different streams of Jewish tradition, the scope of the canon is assumed and *never* thematized directly in debate.[83] This is the case both for Jewish groups such as the Sadducees and Samaritans, which sometimes have been described as possessing a canon consisting of only the Pentateuch, as well as for Jesus and early Christianity. Inference alone has led to the ascription of a Pentateuch-only canon to the Sadducees[84] and the Samaritans[85] prior to A.D. 70. Not only do NT accounts of Jesus' disputes with Jewish leaders portray him as sharing without question their authoritative body of Scripture, they also depict Jesus as assuming a common scriptural canon, regardless of whether his interlocutors are Pharisees or Sadducees.[86] In fact, given the quite divergent traditions of faith and practice within Second Temple Judaism generally, the silence about the exact shape of the biblical canon is remarkable and suggests that a shared body of Scripture antedated the later disagreements.[87]

With respect to the relationship between the two testaments of the Christian Bible, an even more decisive hermeneutical consideration arises from another absence—the lack of any "christianizing" of the OT itself through the addition of Christian redaction or commentary. That this kind of redaction was an actual historical possibility is shown by its presence within some of the apocryphal and pseudepigraphical writings. Instead, the OT was taken up and preserved with its own integrity in the two part Christian Bible.[88] As Bernd Janowski and others have also shown, however, this "givenness" of the OT does not mean that the NT was simply "added on" as a new, completely independent, block of material or that Christian understanding of the OT did not involve a wide ranging "rereading."[89] The NT never existed separately from the Old! Considerable reflection on the historical and literary relationship between the OT and the gospel went into the writing of the NT documents themselves. To be sure, some of the results of that reflection are not directly deducible from the OT but introduce a quality of radical newness and the sharpest kind of discontinuity from the past (e.g., 2 Cor 5:17).[90] Yet even here the historical question for the earliest Christians was not what to do with the OT in light of the gospel of Jesus Christ, but rather how to understand the person and work of Christ in light of the OT "oracles of God" (Rom 3:2).[91]

In this way the constructive work of the church was considerable but did not lie in putting together an OT for itself. As is widely acknowledged, the very first "Bible" of the church was the OT alone. Only gradually did the church combine the OT Scriptures *as it had received them* with newer, authoritative writings arising out of a fresh encounter with the one and same God. Tertullian (ca. 155–220) formulated the point this way:

> [The church] knows one Lord God, Creator of the universe, and Christ Jesus, born of the Virgin Mary, Son of God the Creator, and the resurrection of the flesh; she unites the Law and the Prophets with the writings of the evangelists and the apostles; from that source she drinks her faith and that faith she seals with water, clothes with the Holy Spirit, feeds with the Eucharist, encourages to martyrdom; and against that teaching she receives no one.[92]

It was indeed the church that creatively united the Law and the Prophets with the writings of the evangelists and the apostles, but the Law and the Prophets themselves preceded the church and came from the Jews.

BIBLICAL AUTHORITY

When "canon" is understood in a historically broad sense rather than in an anachronistically narrow one, the Christian church can and in fact must be said to have *inherited* a scriptural canon. This OT canon was then expanded through the addition of the NT writings, even as the original canon of "the Law and the Prophets" was preserved within the two part Christian Bible as its first main part.

This way of seeing things functions as a crucial hermeneutical check against the liberal Protestant and liberal Catholic move to locate revelation in the events behind the text. Theologically, it must instead be affirmed that God chose to reveal himself *in* Scripture, that the mysterious course of divine revelation includes the scripturalization of God's encounter with the world and that revelation, for the church, is therefore necessarily Scripture-shaped.[93]

Such a formulation also sets in new relief several old debates between Protestants and Catholics, lending historical support to the traditional Protestant doctrine of Scripture as *norma normans, sed norma non normata*.[94] Protestants do need a greater appreciation for tradition, both for the tradition that gave rise to the biblical text and for the later tradition of biblical interpretation within the church.[95] The challenge is to recover a robust sense of tradition while at the same time preserving Scripture's ability to question and reform tradition. Despite its deep strength, tradition can also distort and corrupt.[96] In the contemporary scene it looks as if mainstream Protestants and Catholics may be able to find greater common ground on this point, over against those within their respective traditions who would all too eagerly diminish the authority of Scripture in order to accommodate Christian theology even further to contemporary culture. In the future much will depend on whether Scripture is treated as the church's creation, which can therefore be reshaped as the church pleases, or as an external and divinely given norm for ecclesial traditions and practices.[97]

Furthermore, an insistence on the "givenness" of the OT for the Christian church is also an insistence on the "givenness" of Judaism for Christianity, an abiding reminder for Christians to embrace the Jewish people as still in covenant with God and therefore a providentially provided dialogue partner.[98] Conversely, any move to replace the OT per se with the OT *in Novo receptum* or, even more broadly, to subordinate Scripture to ecclesiology must be recognized as deeply implicated in the tradition of supersessionist theology, both in terms of internal logic and practical consequences. Based upon supersessionist theology, the typical, tragic move in the history of biblical interpretation has been to justify the retention of an authoritative OT by the need for its historical witness to Israel's "failure."[99] This move saved the husk of the OT but entailed the loss of the church's ability to hear it as a direct word of God and robbed the Jews of their ongoing place in salvation history with horrifying consequences.[100]

When seen from the historical perspective of OT canon formation, the Christian Bible is only partly a creation of the church. It is true that the church was responsible for the shape of the eventual two part Christian Bible. However, while the church creatively combined the Law and the Prophets with the writings of the evangelists and apostles, the church did not create its own OT, nor did it impose the hermeneutical "givenness" of OT Scripture upon itself. In the beginning, the church inherited written Scripture from Judaism. In precisely that sense, therefore, the following (seemingly outlandish) statement is equally true: the biblical canon is not a creation of the church, the church is instead a creation of the biblical canon.[101] *Ecclesia non facit Verbum sed fit Verbo.*[102]

NOTES

1. This essay is dedicated to the memory of Gerald Sheppard, whose insightful and illuminating work on the authority of the biblical canon will continue to serve as both an inspiration and a model for future explorations.

2. R. Gnuse, *The Authority of the Bible: Theories of Inspiration, Revelation and the Canon of Scripture* (New York/Mahwah: Paulist Press, 1985), 116.

3. Ibid., 117.

4. J. Barton, *People of the Book? The Authority of the Bible in Christianity* (Louisville: Westminster/John Knox, 1988), esp. 32.

5. One could, for example, base a view of scriptural authority on what contemporary Christians actually do, regardless of how Scripture developed historically. For a highly influential treatment of scriptural authority from this kind of "functional" perspective, see D. Kelsey, *The Uses of Scripture in Recent Theology* (Philadelphia: Fortress, 1975), esp. 212–216. For a similar treatment, in which, however, the soteriological function of Scripture is stressed, see J. Barr, *The Scope and Authority of the Bible* (Philadelphia: Westminster, 1980), 52–64.

6. See L. M. McDonald and J. A. Sanders, ed., *The Canon Debate* (Peabody, Mass.: Hendrickson, 2002).

7. J. Barton, "The Significance of a Fixed Canon of the Hebrew Bible," in *Hebrew Bible/Old Testament: The History of Its Interpretation*; vol. 1: *From the Beginnings to the Middle Ages (Until 1300), Part 1: Antiquity* (ed. M. Sæbø; Göttingen: Vandenhoeck & Ruprecht, 1996), 67–83; 68.

8. H. E. Ryle, *The Canon of the Old Testament: An Essay on the Gradual Growth and Formation of the Hebrew Canon of Scripture* (London/New York: Macmillan, 1892), 9.

9. The book of Deuteronomy was often viewed as a prior first step in this direction. An original version of Deuteronomy had been dated to 621 B.C. ever since the groundbreaking work of DeWette in the early eighteenth century.

10. See especially the citation of Mal 3:23–24 [Mal 4:5–6] in Sir 48:10 and the reference to the minor prophets as "the twelve prophets" in Sir 49:10.

11. Matt 24:15; see also the Qumran text *4QFlor* (4Q174) 2.3, which reads "as it is written in the book of Daniel the prophet." Cf. Josephus, *Antiquities* 9:267–269.

12. See, e.g., *m. Yad.* 3.5 (with reference to Song of Songs and Ecclesiastes).

13. E.g., A. Budde, "Der Abschluß des alttestamentlichen Kanons und seine Bedeutung für die kanonische Schriftauslegung," *Biblische Notizen* 87 (1997): 39–55.

14. The parade example always given is the reference to Enoch 1:9 in Jude 14–15.

15. Budde, "Abschluß," 45–48.

16. L. M. McDonald, *The Formation of the Christian Biblical Canon* (rev. and exp. ed.; Peabody, Mass.: Hendrickson, 1995), 127.

17. For McDonald's lengthy list of such allusions, see his "Appendix I.A." in *Formation*, 259–267.

18. Ibid., 125–126. Here McDonald bases his conclusions upon the disputed theory of G. F. Moore, "The Definition of the Jewish Canon and the Repudiation of Christian Scripture," reprinted in S. Z. Leiman (ed.), *The Canon and Masorah of the Hebrew Bible: An Introductory Reader* (Library of Biblical Studies; New York: KTAV, 1974), 115–141.

19. McDonald, *Formation*, 128.

20. Ibid., 132.

21. Ibid., 250–257.

22. Ibid., 257.

23. Ibid.

24. On this point, see P. M. Van Buren, *According to the Scriptures: The Origins of the Gospel and of the Church's Old Testament* (Grand Rapids/Cambridge: Eerdmans, 1998), esp. 65: ". . . Jesus is available only as he comes wrapped in Israel's scriptures. . . . It is therefore misleading to say that the church finds Jesus in the scriptures, the so-called Old Testament. What it finds is that the scriptures speak of Jesus, because it was from Israel's scriptures that it first learned how to speak of him." Van Buren later asserts, however, that the church still cannot be claimed to have inherited its OT from Judaism (p. 86)—but only because he sometimes draws too sharp a distinction on other grounds between the "Old Testament" and "Israel's scriptures" (contrast his p. 131).

25. A similar position is sometimes adopted with respect to the OT. Cf. J. Barr, *Holy Scripture: Canon, Authority, Criticism* (Philadelphia: Fortress, 1983), 48: "The pre-Christian basis of the church, though by shorthand we often call it the Old Testament, is in fact Israel. . ."

26. Cf. the rejoinder of B. S. Childs to Barr's position in his "Response to Reviewers of Introduction to the Old Testament as Scripture," *JSOT* 16 (1980): 57: ". . . there is no direct access to the fullness of that extrinsic reality on which the faith was grounded apart from Israel's own testimony."

27. E.g., J. T. Lienhard, *The Bible, the Church, and Authority: The Canon of the Christian Bible in History and Theology* (Collegeville, Minn.: Michael Glazier/Liturgical Press, 1995); K. McDonnell, "Canon and *Koinonia/communio*: The Formation of the Canon as an Ecclesiological Process," *Gregorianum* 79 (1998): 29–54; A. Sand, *Kanon: von den Anfängen bis zum Fragmentum Muratorianum* (Handbuch der Dogmengeschichte 1.3a.1; Freiburg: Herder, 1974); A. Ziegenaus, *Kanon: von der Väterzeit bis zur Gegenwart* (Handbuch der Dogmengeschichte 1.3a.2; Freiburg: Herder, 1974).

28. Note how E. Ulrich readily perceives the relation between this historical view and the traditional Protestant-Catholic debate over Scripture and tradition, yet buries the point within a single footnote in his "From Literature to Scripture: Reflections on the Growth of a Text's Authoritativeness," *DSD* 10 (2003): 3–25; 23.

29. For the most influential attempt to retrieve the significance of tradition within Protestant OT scholarship, see H. Gese, "Tradition and Biblical Theology," in *Tradition and Theology in the Old Testament* (ed. D. A. Knight; Philadelphia: Fortress, 1977), 301–326.

30. Gnuse, *Authority*, 117.

31. Ibid., 108–109.

32. Ibid., 109.

33. Ibid., 110.

34. Ibid., 109. My emphasis.

35. Ibid., 111.

36. Ibid., 112.

37. K. Rahner, *Foundations of Christian Faith: An Introduction to the Idea of Christianity* (trans. W. V. Dych; New York: Crossroad/Seabury, 1978), 371.

38. Ibid.

39. Ibid., 158–159.

40. Ibid., 167.

41. This position is also well known in Protestant theology. Compare the dictum of H. Gese, "Erwägungen zur Einheit der biblischen Theologie," in *Vom Sinai zum Zion: alttestamentliche Beiträge zur biblischen Theologie* (Beiträge zur evangelischen Theologie 64; Munich: Chr. Kaiser, 1974), 11–30; 30: "Das Neue Testament an sich ist unverständlich, das Alte Testament an sich ist mißverständlich." To this point B. Janowski, Gese's student, has trenchantly commented: "Das Alte Testament an sich ist aber *nicht mißverständlich*, sondern *unterschiedlich rezipiert und interpretiert* worden" (his emphases). See his "Der eine Gott der beiden Testamente: Grundfragen einer Biblischen Theologie," in *Die rettende Gerechtigkeit: Beiträge zur Theologie des Alten Testaments 2* (Neukirchen-Vluyn: Neukirchener, 1999), 249–284; 261 n. 57. An English version of this important essay appears as "The One God of the Two Testaments: Basic Questions of a Biblical Theology," *Theology Today* 57 (2000): 297–324.

42. Rahner, *Foundations*, 372–373.

43. Ibid.

44. Ibid.

45. Cf. R. P. McBrien, *Catholicism* (Minneapolis: Winston, 1980), 64–65: "The Catholic Church has always maintained that *there is no other criterion except its own traditions*, and that these, in turn, are vehicles of divine revelation" (his emphasis).

46. Lienhard, *Bible*, 84.

47. Or: "the Old Testament as received in the New." On this formulation, see the important debate between H. Hübner, "Vetus Testamentum und Vetus Testamentum in Novo receptum," *Jahrbuch für biblische Theologie* 3 (1988): 147–162; and B. S. Childs, "Die Bedeutung der hebräischen Bibel für die biblische Theologie," *Theologische Zeitschrift* 48 (1992): 382–390.

48. Gnuse, *Authority*, 54–55.

49. For a related but somewhat different critique of Rahner's salvation-historical emphasis, see K. Lehmann, "Das Alte Testament in seiner Bedeutung für Leben und Lehre der Kirche heute," *Trierer Theologische Zeitschrift* 98 (1989): 161–170; esp. 165–167.

50. Pontifical Biblical Commission, *The Jewish People and their Sacred Scriptures in the Christian Bible* (Città del Vaticano: Libreria Editrice Vaticana, 2002), 49–50 (also available online at http://www.vatican.va/roman_curia/congregations/cfaith/pcb_documents/rc_con_cfaith_doc_20020212_popolo-ebraico_en.html). I am grateful to Reinhard Hütter for bringing this

document to my attention; for his own thoughts regarding its significance, see his "'In': Some Incipient Reflections on *The Jewish People and their Sacred Scriptures in the Christian Bible,*" *Pro Ecclesia* (forthcoming).

51. Ibid., 37–38.

52. Ibid., 39. This "single process" formulation has displaced the theory of a distinct "Alexandrian" canon, which formerly was used both to mitigate the authority of the biblical canon of "Palestinian" Judaism and to underwrite the church's adoption of a wider canon, including the deuterocanonical or apocryphal books. This theory can no longer be sustained historically; see A. C. Sundberg, Jr., *The Old Testament of the Early Church* (Harvard Theological Studies 20; Cambridge, Mass.: Harvard University Press, 1964).

53. Ibid., 41.

54. Ibid., 27.

55. Ibid., 28.

56. Now see P. S. Williamson, *Catholic Principles for Interpreting Scripture: A Study of the Pontifical Biblical Commission's* The Interpretation of the Bible in the Church (*Subsidia biblica* 22; Rome: Pontificio Istituto Biblico, 2001).

57. G. T. Sheppard, "Canon," *Encyclopedia of Religion* (ed. M. Eliade; New York: Macmillan, 1987), 3:62–69.

58. E. Ulrich, "The Canonical Process, Textual Criticism, and Latter Stages in the Composition of the Bible," in *The Dead Sea Scrolls and the Origins of the Bible* (Studies in the Dead Sea Scrolls and Related Literature; Grand Rapids: Eerdmans; Leiden: Brill, 1999), 51–78. Cf. idem, "The Notion and Definition of Canon," in *Canon Debate*, 21–35 (see n. 6).

59. Ulrich, "Process," 55.

60. Ibid., 56. This tendency is even more pronounced in his "Notion," 25–29.

61. E.g., McDonald, *Canon*, 225–227. Cf. J. Barr, *Scripture*, 51–52. This judgment holds true even for the NT since no council of the entire church reached a binding decision on the scope of the canon prior to the separation of Orthodox and Protestant traditions from Catholicism. For a succinct discussion of lesser conciliar decisions, see Budde, "Abschluß," 48–52.

62. Cf. G. T. Sheppard, "Canonization: Hearing the Voice of the Same God through Historically Dissimilar Traditions," *Int* 34 (1982): 21–33, printed also in *Ex Aud* 1 (1985): 106–114; idem, "Canonical Criticism," *ABD* 1:861–866. For some of Childs's best treatments of this topic, see his *The New Testament as Canon: An Introduction* (Philadelphia: Fortress, 1984), 16–33; and "Retrospective Reading of the Old Testament Prophets," *ZAW* 108 (1996): 362–377.

63. J. Barton, *Holy Writings, Sacred Text: The Canon in Early Christianity* (Louisville: Westminster/John Knox, 1997).

64. See, among others, J. H. Lightstone, "The Formation of the Biblical Canon in Judaism of Late Antiquity: Prolegomenon to a General Reassessment," *SR* 8 (1979): 135–142.

65. J. P. Lewis, "What Do We Mean by Jabneh?" *JBR* 32 (1964): 125–132; esp. 127–128. Now cf. idem, "Jamnia Revisited," in *Canon Debate*, 146–162. J. Sanders takes up this topic directly in another article within the same volume, "The Issue of Closure in the Canonical Process" (pp. 252–263), whose main purpose, so far as I can tell, is to argue against the idea of closure as being particularly significant. However, he continues to use "closing" terminology.

66. Just to name two of the most important considerations: those who accept both the strict definition of canon and the three stage theory will usually also concede that although the Pentateuch was rendered "canonical" by Ezra, it continued to sustain editorial revision (typically called "minor") for centuries. To see concessions regarding such revision, consult both J. Wellhausen, *Prolegomena to the History of Israel* (repr. of 1885 ed.; Atlanta: Scholars Press, 1994), 497; and J. Blenkinsopp, *The Pentateuch: An Introduction to the First Five Books of the Bible* (Anchor Bible Reference Library; New York: Doubleday, 1992), 240–241. Yet according to the usual definition of "canon" the Pentateuch was either canonical in the strict sense or not at all.

Thus, at this point the text-history of the biblical literature itself suggests an alternative construal of the entire canonical process, but scholars have chosen instead to harmonize their exegetical findings with the broad contours of the "consensus" reconstruction. Ulrich ("Process," 58) perceives this problem and is at pains to separate the question of canonicity from the stabilization of specific text forms, but obviously these two processes are to be related historically somehow.

A similar problem exists for the standard theory with respect to the prophetic corpus, for why is it necessary to deny canonical status to the prophetic books for 200–250 years after the "canonization" of the Pentateuch, if canonical status does not relate primarily to the attainment of an absolutely final literary form?

67. This difficulty proves to be the central problem with some treatments advocating an early date for the canon, e.g., R. Beckwith, *The Old Testament Canon of the New Testament Church and its Background in Early Judaism* (Grand Rapids: Eerdmans, 1985), D. N. Freedman, "The Law and the Prophets," in *Congress Volume. Bonn 1962* (VTSup 9; Leiden: Brill, 1962), 250–265; and G. Maier, "Der Abschluß des jüdischen Kanons und das Lehrhaus von Jabne," in *Der Kanon der Bibel* (ed. G. Maier; Giessen/Basel: Brunnen; Wuppertal: R. Brockhaus, 1990), 1–24.

68. Although this text has sometimes been restored as having included a final phrase referring to the books of Chronicles ("and the annals of each generation"), such a reading is wholly a reconstruction and thus far too speculative to take as an indication of an early fourfold collection.

69. On this point, see J. VanderKam, "Authoritative Literature in the Dead Sea Scrolls," *DSD* 5 (1998): 382–402; esp. 387–388.

70. See H. Eshel, "4QMMT and the History of the Hasmonean Period," in *Reading 4QMMT: New Perspectives on Qumran Law and History* (ed. J. Kampen, M. J. Bernstein; SBLSS 2; Atlanta: Scholars Press, 1996), 53–65; 64.

71. E.g., VanderKam, "Literature," 401. For a listing of scholars who hold this position along with references to their work, see my "'The Law and the Words' as a Canonical Formula Within the Old Testament," in *The Interpretation of Scripture in Early Judaism and Christianity: Studies in Language and Tradition* (ed. C. A. Evans; Journal for the Study of the Pseudepigrapha: Supplement Series 33; Studies in Early Judaism and Christianity 7; Sheffield: Sheffield Academic Press, 2000), 26–74; 72–73 n. 252.

72. J. J. Collins, "Dead Sea Scrolls," *ABD* II:85–101; 90.

73. For a very helpful index to all the references to biblical books in the Qumran writings, now see D. L. Washburn, *A Catalog of Biblical Passages in the Dead Sea Scrolls* (Society of Biblical Literature Text-Critical Series 2; Leiden/Boston: Brill, 2003).

74. E. Tov, *Textual Criticism of the Hebrew Bible* (Minneapolis: Fortress; Assen: Van Gorcum, 1992), 137, referring to H. B. Swete, *Introduction to the Old Testament in Greek* (rev. ed. R. R. Ottley; Cambridge: Cambridge University Press, 1914), 25–26.

75. Tov, *Criticism*, 137.

76. F. M. Cross, Jr., *From Epic to Canon: History and Literature in Ancient Israel* (Baltimore/London: Johns Hopkins University Press, 1998), 216–217. For criticism of Cross's position, see E. Tov, "Lucian and Proto-Lucian—Toward a New Solution of the Problem," *RB* 79 (1972): 101–113.

77. For the original treatment of this important scroll, see D. Barthélemy, *Les Devanciers d'Aquila* (VTSup 10; Leiden: Brill, 1963); cf. E. Tov, *The Greek Minor Prophets Scroll from Naḥal Ḥever (8ḤevXIIgr)* (DJD 8; Oxford: Clarendon, 1990).

78. Cross, *Epic*, 220–223. In his view, however, this does not also mean that other texts and differing canonical arrangements were immediately rejected, but rather that this process occurred gradually over time (p. 225).

79. Ibid., 216–217.

80. For references and discussion see F. Siegert, "Early Jewish Interpretation," in Sæbø, *Hebrew Bible*, 130–198; esp. 172–176 (see n. 7). Siegert rejects the idea that Philo knew a three part canon, but in my judgment his own evidence argues for a different conclusion. For a helpful index to Philo's scriptural citations, see J. Allenbach, A. Benoît, et al., ed., *Biblia Patristica: Supplément* (Paris: Éditions du CNRS, 1982). Out of all the extra-canonical books, Philo refers only to Ben Sira and the Wisdom of Solomon.

81. As an indication of the current lack of consensus, see the provocatively firm stand taken on this issue by B. S. Childs in his *Biblical Theology of the Old and New Testaments: Theological Reflection on the Christian Bible* (Minneapolis: Fortress, 1992), 62.

82. McDonald, *Formation*, 128.

83. Overwhelmingly, theological differences in the Second Temple period are quite strikingly depicted as being matters of scriptural interpretation, yet the scope of Scripture itself is simply assumed. See M. Fishbane, "Jewish Biblical Exegesis," in *Scripture in the Jewish and Christian Traditions: Authority, Interpretation, Relevance* (ed. F. E. Greenspahn; University of Denver Center for Judaic Studies; Nashville: Abingdon, 1982), 92–110; esp. 95–96. Eventually, of course, the scope of the canon did become a matter of dispute, both within Christianity and between Christianity and Judaism, but no explicit evidence for such disagreement exists prior to A.D. 70. See Beckwith, *Canon*, esp. 63–104; esp. 90–91. Cf. idem, "Formation of the Hebrew Bible," in *Mikra: Text, Translation, Reading and Interpretation of the Hebrew Bible in Ancient Judaism and Christianity* (ed. M. J. Mulder; CRINT 2.1; Assen-Maastricht: Van Gorcum; Philadelphia: Fortress, 1988), 39–86; 49.

84. The idea that the Sadducees' canon consisted of the Pentateuch alone rests on slender references found much later in the writings of Origen (*Against Celsus*, 1.49) and Jerome (*Commentary on Matthew*, on 22:31). Especially given the apparent fusion of the Sadducees with the Samaritans in the second/third centuries A.D., confusion between the two groups would not have been unlikely. The more persuasive explanation for the reported distinctions between Pharisees and Sadducees is that, in contrast to the Pharisees, the Sadducees refused to accept the authority of the oral law. See F. F. Bruce, *The Canon of Scripture* (Downers Grove, Ill.: InterVarsity, 1988), 40–41; cf. Sundberg, *Old Testament*, 77–78 and J. Trebolle Barrera, *The Jewish Bible and the Christian Bible* (trans. W. G. E. Watson; Grand Rapids: Eerdmans; Leiden: Brill, 1998), 217–222.

85. To my knowledge, the earliest explicit reference to a Pentateuch-only Samaritan canon is found in the work of Origen (A.D. 185–253), specifically in his *Commentary on John* 13.26 and in *Against Celsus* 1.49, something which ought to encourage greater caution in making assumptions about the early shape of the Samaritan canon. Contrary to Origen's commentary on John 4, there is no indication in that particular passage of any antipathy toward prophets on the part of Samaritans. In fact, the Samaritan woman is suitably impressed by Jesus' miraculous abilities ("[He] told me everything I have ever done," John 4:29, 39). Interestingly, the woman does assume that a "prophet" will support Judaism's centralization of worship in Jerusalem rather than on Mt. Gerizim. Might this perception have led eventually to a later rejection of the prophetic Scriptures by the Samaritans, who earlier on may have in fact granted at least some of the prophetic writings canonical standing?

For a variety of reasons, there is now a strong case to be made that the later Samaritan canon took the form of a reaction against normative Jewish tradition, rather than being a preservation of the Jewish canon's original shape. For discussion of this possibility and other evidence in support of it, see R. J. Coggins, *Samaritans and Jews: The Origins of Samaritanism Reconsidered* (Atlanta: John Knox, 1975).

86. While it is true that in Matt 22:23–33 Jesus defends a view of resurrection by basing it on a pentateuchal text, the frequent assumption that he is framing his argument with the Sadducees in mind lacks conviction. In later Jewish tradition it is not at all unusual to find textual

warrants for resurrection offered from the Pentateuch (e.g., on Deut 32:39, see Pes. 68a; cf. Sifre Deut 306). Moreover, in Matt 16:1–4 Jesus responds to a request for a sign from the Pharisees and the Sadducees by referring to the "sign of Jonah" without any indication that such a reference would have been ruled inadmissable by the Sadducees. Even if Matthew also added the Sadducees to this narrative scene, as the Lukan parallel suggests, it seems odd that he would have included them if they were known to reject the authority of prophetic Scripture.

87. See M. Simon, "The Bible in the Earliest Controversies Between Jews and Christians," in *The Bible in Greek Christian Antiquity* (The Bible Through the Ages 1; ed. P. M. Blowers; trans. P. M. Blowers, Notre Dame, Ind.: University of Notre Dame Press, 1997), 49–68. See also J. Blenkinsopp, "Interpretation and the Tendency to Sectarianism: An Aspect of Second Temple History," in *Jewish and Christian Self-Definition, Vol. 2* (ed. E. P. Sanders and B. F. Meyer; Philadelphia: Fortress, 1980), 1–26.

88. C. Dohmen, "Die zweigeteilte Einheit der christlichen Bibel," in *Hermeneutik der Jüdischen Bibel und des Alten Testaments* (Kohlhammer-Studienbücher Theologie 1.2; ed. G. Stemberger; Stuttgart: Kohlhammer, 1996), 11–22.

89. Janowski, "Gott," 257.

90. Childs, *Biblical Theology*, 225.

91. H. von Campenhausen, *The Formation of the Christian Bible* (trans. J. A. Baker; Philadelphia: Fortress, 1972), 63–64: "It is quite wrong to say that the Old Testament had no authority in its own right for the first Christians, and that it was taken over purely because people saw that it 'treated of Christ' or pointed toward him."

92. Tertullian, *Prescriptions Against Heretics*, 36; cited by P. Eisenbaum, "The Christian Canon and the Problem of Antisemitism," in *A Shadow of Glory: Reading the New Testament after the Holocaust* (ed. T. Linafelt; New York/London: Routledge, 2002), 3–17; here 8–9.

93. T. Work, *Living and Active: Scripture in the Economy of Salvation* (Sacra Pagina: Grand Rapids: Eerdmans, 2002).

94. Or: "a norming norm, but not a normed norm." See the effort of Catholic scholars R. E. Brown and R. F. Collins to approximate this doctrine in their article, "Canonicity," in *The New Jerome Biblical Commentary* (ed. R. E. Brown, J. A. Fitzmyer, and R. E. Murphy; Englewood Cliffs, N.J.: Prentice-Hall, 1990), 1034–1054; here 1036–1037. In their formulation, the scriptural canon constitutes an "unnormed norm" so long as it functions together with the church's "canon of faith." If, however, this "canon of faith" is itself supersessionist, as argued by R. K. Soulen, *The God of Israel and Christian Theology* (Minneapolis: Fortress, 1996), then its use would not complement the Old Testament's authority but subvert it.

95. G. Ebeling, "'Sola Scriptura' and Tradition," *The Word of God and Tradition* (trans. S. H. Hooke; Philadelphia: Fortress, 1968), 102–147.

96. J. Barr, *The Bible and the Modern World* (London: SCM Press; Philadelphia: Trinity Press International, 1973), 126–127. Barr also criticizes the way Protestants have sometimes demonized tradition, however.

97. If the idea of the church reshaping Scripture seems farfetched, consider the effect of the contemporary lectionary, in which approximately eighty (!) percent of the OT is never read at all. For this figure and for further discussion about the hermeneutical impact of the lectionary, see D. T. Olson, "Rediscovering Lost Treasure: Forgotten Preaching Texts of the Old Testament," *Journal for Preachers* 13 (1990): 2–10. C. C. Black also provides a helpful general evaluation in "Journeying Through Scripture with the Lectionary's Map," *Int* 56 (2002): 59–72.

98. Cf. the words of John Paul II during his 1986 visit to the synagogue in Rome, cited in Pontifical Biblical Commission's *Jewish People*, 196: "The Jewish religion is not 'extrinsic' to us, but in a certain manner, it is 'intrinsic' to our religion. We have a relationship with it which we do not have with any other religion. You are our favoured brothers and, in a certain sense, one can say, our elder brothers."

99. E.g., R. Bultmann, "The Significance of the Old Testament for the Christian Faith," in *The Old Testament and Christian Faith* (ed. B. Anderson; New York: Harper & Row, 1963), 8–35. For a current example of this position in the field, see O. Kaiser, *Der Gott des Alten Testaments. Theologie des Alten Testaments 1: Grundlegung* (Göttingen: Vandehoeck & Ruprecht, 1993), 86–87.

100. Eisenbaum, "Canon." Cf. Pontifical Biblical Commission, *Jewish People*, 50 (Section 22).

101. Cf. M. Hengel, "The Scriptures and their Interpretation in Second Temple Judaism," in *The Aramaic Bible: Targums in their Historical Context* (JSOTSup 166; ed. D. R. G. Beattie and M. J. Mulder; Sheffield: JSOT Press, 1994), 158–175; 175: "In this struggle which probably finds no parallel in earlier history, Judaism 'created' the holy scriptures, but it would be even more correct to say that God's word created Israel and the holy scriptures Judaism."

102. M. Luther, "The Misuse of the Mass," *Luther's Works* (trans. F. C. Ahrens; ed. A. R. Wentz; 55 vol.; Philadelphia: Fortress, 1959), 36:127–230; 144–145: "It is not God's Word just because the church speaks it; rather, the church comes into being because God's Word is spoken. The church does not constitute the Word, but is constituted by the Word."

RESPONSE TO CHAPMAN

CYNTHIA L. MILLER

In his carefully written and well-reasoned paper, Stephen Chapman has presented a fascinating proposal for connecting the *historical* facts concerning the canonization of the OT with the larger *theological* question of the authority of the OT Scriptures within Christianity. In responding to this paper, I do so not as a theologian but instead as a peculiar combination of stodgy Semitic philologist and modern linguist. In other words, I approach the biblical texts from the viewpoint of *language* (that is, how the texts should be read and interpreted), as well as from the viewpoint of *language in society* (that is, how the texts were produced and used within language communities). None of this is to deny the essentially religious nature of the biblical texts nor to minimize my own personal interest in them as Scripture. But my response focuses on the historical and linguistic facts of canon, rather than on the theological ramifications of canon.

Chapman's paper hinges on his definition of "canon." Although the term has historically been used to mean either a "norm" or a "list," Professor Chapman insists that the concept of "canon" should be understood in the sense of a "norm," that is, as defining a sacred text that is accepted by a religious community as authoritative, regulatory, and constitutive.[1] His central claim about the development of the canon can be summarized as follows. By the turn of the millennium a Jewish canon of Scripture was in place (minimally the Law, the Prophets, and Psalms), but, he says, "the idea of precise boundaries was less important than the family resemblance shared by diverse Scriptures, which together represented the cumulative weight of Israel's tradition." As a result, he claims, the early church inherited *written* Scripture (not oral tradition) from Judaism and accepted the "givenness" of the Jewish canon as their OT, while creatively combining it with Gospels and Epistles to form their own Christian Scriptures.

The most interesting feature of Chapman's formulation involves the notion that canon should be understood as a concept with fuzzy boundaries. Rather than viewing membership in the canon as a simple yes or no matter (that is, a "list"), he sees canonicity as a category in which there is a vagueness to the periphery, though the center of the category is clear.[2] In conceptualizing this proposal we can make a helpful analogy to color words and the concepts they denote. Think of the word "blue" for a moment. Imagine the paint department in a home improvement store with a vast array of paint chips. Where exactly does "blue" end and "green" begin? In analyzing words for color in a variety of languages, linguists noticed that, although languages differ with respect to the precise location of the boundaries between "blue" and "green" or "yellow" and "red," different cultures have remarkably similar understandings of what constitutes a prototypical "blue" or "green" or "yellow" or "red." That is, what is most important cognitively is the core of the color; the fuzzy boundaries between colors are less important. A color may be partly blue and partly green, or, as in the case of "teal," there may be disagreement among speakers as to whether a color actually belongs to blue or green.[3] Chapman suggests that we should understand the Jewish canon in a similar way. The prototypical canon—those books that were uncontroversially recognized as Scripture—was surrounded by fluid and fuzzy borders. Books on the borders might be less authoritative for a Jewish community than the core, and Jewish communities need not agree on the borders.

The notion of a prototypical core and a fuzzy periphery helps us with various difficult problems in the history of the development of the canon. At Qumran, for example, we have a category of texts known as "reworked Scriptures." One of these, the Temple Scroll, uses material from Exod 24 through Deuteronomy to produce a new version of Deuteronomy by modifying and rearranging what was later accepted as the biblical text. But the Temple Scroll claims to be the divinely inspired words of God, and the fact that it existed in five copies at Qumran suggests that the Qumran community considered it to be Scripture.[4] In the Second Temple period, then, different Jewish communities seem to have had different boundaries for their canons. The theory for the development of the canon outlined in Chapman's paper works only if we concentrate on the core and ignore the periphery.

Another way in which the analogy to prototype semantics may help us has to do with Chapman's insistence that what the church inherited from Judaism was written Scriptures, not oral tradition. Precisely what he means by "written Scriptures" is not expounded upon, and it is a worthy topic for discussion. The difficulty with the phrase "written Scriptures" is that the textual form of the Hebrew Bible was still pluriform in the first century C.E. Furthermore, the church never adopted the canon of the OT in Hebrew, but rather in Greek. In accepting the written Scriptures of Judaism, then, the church accepted the books considered canonical by Judaism (i.e., their essential content), but not the precise textual form of those books, nor even the language in which they were written.[5]

Finally, the concept of canon as a core with fluid borders may help us to consider the relationship between ongoing revelation to already accepted sacred texts. In the Qumran community it is quite clear that they considered their leader, the Teacher of Righteousness, to be the recipient of ongoing revelation—to him "God made known all the mysteries of the words of His Servants the prophets" (1QpHab VII:4–5).[6] Furthermore, in the sectarian document "The Rule of the Community" (1QS V:8–9) the new initiates of the community were required to swear allegiance both to the precepts of the Torah of Moses and to "all that has been revealed from it to the Sons of Zadoq, the priests."[7] That is, the new supplementary revelation stood side by side with the old.

In the early church, as Chapman has noted, the Jewish canon of Law and Prophets was creatively combined with Gospels and Epistles to form the Christian canon. Although the peripheral boundaries of canon had moved outward, the new Christian canon itself also had fuzzy boundaries, which required some time and effort to define and delimit.

In rabbinic Judaism as well the boundaries of sacred authoritative text moved outward. The oral law, that is, the interpretative judgments of the rabbis, came to be understood to be equivalent to the written law of Scripture—both were given by God to Moses on Sinai and both were transmitted through the centuries to the rabbinic period when the oral law was finally written and codified (*ʾAbot* 1:1). Judaism, then, reconceptualized the history of divine revelation in order to extend the canon beyond its previous boundaries.

As helpful as Chapman's conceptualization of canon is, there remain three areas of his argument that require elucidation. First, if (as Chapman argues) the early church received the core Jewish canon as a "given," then how do we explain the differing OT canons that emerged in the western and eastern churches? Furthermore, how do we explain the fact that Melito, the bishop of Sardis, traveled to Palestine in the late second century in order to ascertain the limits of the Jewish canon?

Second, how does the pluriform nature of the Hebrew text relate to the question of canon? Chapman has suggested that the prehexaplaric recensions provide evidence for canonization. But are these necessarily interconnected phenomena? The fact that the Hebrew text is not standardized until much later suggests that perhaps they are not.

Third, how should we understand ongoing revelation within the various branches of Judaism and early Christianity to relate to the notion of canon?

Attention to these three questions will further refine Chapman's argument reconceptualizing canon as a common core with fuzzy boundaries.

NOTES

1. In Ulrich's careful study of the various notions and definitions of canon, he distinguishes an "authoritative work" (which is not Scripture and not canonical) from a "book of Scripture" (which is canonical); in Ulrich's terms, Chapman's understanding of canon is that of an "authoritative work." See Eugene Ulrich, "The Notion and Definition of Canon," in *The Canon*

Debate (eds. Lee Martin McDonald and James A. Sanders; Peabody, Mass.: Hendrickson, 2002), 21–35, esp. 29–30.

2. For this definition of prototype, see Randy J. LaPolla, "On the Utility of the Concepts of Markedness and Prototypes in Understanding the Development of Morphological Systems," *Bulletin of the Institute of History and Philology* 66 (1995): 1149–1185, esp. 1155–1157.

3. For the initial work on color terms and prototypes, see Brent Berlin and Paul Kay, *Basic Color Terms: Their Universality and Evolution* (Berkeley and Los Angeles: University of California Press, 1967). For a description of protototype semantics generally see the introductory discussion in John Lyons, *Linguistic Semantics: An Introduction* (Cambridge: Cambridge University Press, 1995), 96–101. For a more detailed description of prototype semantics, see John R. Taylor, *Linguistic Categorization: Prototypes in Linguistic Theory* (2d ed.; Oxford: Oxford University Press, 1995).

4. James C. VanderKam, "Questions of Canon Viewed through the Dead Sea Scrolls," in *The Canon Debate* (eds. Lee Martin McDonald and James A. Sanders; Peabody, Mass: Hendrickson, 2002), 91–109, esp. 100–104.

5. Ulrich, "The Notion and Definition of Canon," 31–32.

6. VanderKam, "Questions of Canon Viewed through the Dead Sea Scrolls," 92.

7. Jack N. Lightstone, "The Rabbis' Bible: The Canon of the Hebrew Bible and the Early Rabbinic Guild," in *The Canon Debate*, 163–184, esp. 174.

REREADING *THEIR* SCRIPTURES: AN ANALYSIS OF THE AUTHORITY OF SCRIPTURE AMONG EARLY AFRICAN AMERICANS

RODNEY S. SADLER, JR.

That African Americans came to respect the authority of the Christian Scriptures is a miracle in itself. Their introduction to the Bible frequently came by way of sermons from Eph 6:5–8 directed at ensuring their obedience to their masters. The God they met in these sermons was firmly on the side of their tormentors, opposing their freedom, reifying the status quo. The religion they were offered emphasized, not the love of Christ for their choice of will, but the subjugation of their wills as a divine duty owed to those humans who laid claim to their bodies. In spite of this introduction to the Bible, African Americans have greatly revered the Christian Scriptures throughout their acquaintance with them. But why did African Americans attribute authority to the Bible?

Of course the simple answer is that they fell in love with the God of Scripture. In Christ they found salvation from their sins and reconciliation with the Creator of the universe. Their experience of Christianity resonated with aspects of their pre-Christian religions. They were even able to incorporate cultural particularities into Christianity without compromising their expression of the faith. The Christian God was a source of strength and sustenance to them in the midst of the persistent turmoil that defined their lives. When they were weak, they could be assured that their God was strong and that they were not left to suffer the indignities of slavery alone. No matter what, Scripture testified that God was with them. This was certainly enough to lend authority to these texts; however, I suggest that there may be additional contributing factors as well.

The authority of Scripture for African Americans has at its roots the authority granted to these texts by their ancestors, so it is reasonable to begin this inquiry by reflecting on the works of some notable early authors. Their introduction to Scripture was not a neutral spiritual experience but a hostile activity whereby Holy Writ was used to pacify them and justify their subjugation. But in these texts they found not just an otherworldly God offering spiritual blessings, but a here-and-now God who cared principally for the oppressed, acting in history and eschatologically to deliver the downtrodden from their abusers. They also found Jesus, a suffering savior whose life and struggles paralleled their own struggles. In the narratives that describe these characters they found reasons to believe not only in the liberating power of the God of Scripture, but in the liberating emphasis of Scripture itself.

Because they learned that the Bible did not denigrate African identity, they were able to use it to ground their humanity, to subversively rebut biblically based supremacist readings, and to validate their right to be free and function as equals in this nation. For them Scripture generally had both spiritual and political implications;[1] in fact, it could not have one without the other. Scripture also addressed many dimensions of African Americans' lives. In addition to being a religious document offering spiritual blessing, it also served as the primary document consulted for ethnographic information, a source of myth making for a people with a stolen history, a tool for political empowerment, and a guide for establishing social order. The Bible has been an indispensable part of their lives.

This paper will suggest that there are a number of utilitarian reasons why African Americans attributed authority to the biblical canon. As they became familiar with the Bible texts, it soon became apparent that the same book that was used to justify their oppression also provided hope for African American liberation. Further, recognizing that this collection of ancient texts grounded Western civilization, they realized that by employing the narratives found in the Bible they could find a means to argue for their full equality in terms that their adversaries would have to respect. After all, even their adversaries would have to heed the Word of God. In essence, it would have been counterproductive for this oppressed group to ignore such a valuable resource. Below we will explore several practical reasons why African Americans became faithful adherents of Scripture, developing their own distinctive hermeneutical traditions for reading it. Not just a religious document, early African Americans found that they could benefit from employing the Bible as it:

(1) gave them hope that God would act without human (political) intervention to provide justice for enslaved Africans
(2) grounded subversive arguments against the type of Christianity practiced by southern slaveholders
(3) provided a mythic system that could explain their plight and a symbolic world that resonated with their own, while demonstrating God's fidelity to those similarly situated (slaves, exiles, sufferers)
(4) allowed them the latitude to emphasize or exclude portions of Scripture based upon their needs without compromising the core of the Christian message
(5) envisioned human origins in a manner that allowed them to discern a glorious past for African peoples and discern positive dimensions of African identity
(6) continued to be flexible enough to address their evolving plight in America (slavery, segregation, persistent inequality, etc.).

FREEDOM IN GOD'S HANDS: APOLITICAL SPIRITUAL READINGS

Before we consider texts written by African Americans with a discernable political agenda, it is important to establish that Scripture was from the earliest times understood as the ground of ultimate trust in the Christian God. In this regard some of the earliest African American readers found solace in Scriptures as a source of spiritual transformation, even if it meant that the body would remain enslaved. Such readings were close to what we would identify as fundamentalist readings today. Containing an evangelical zeal for Christ, such readers eschewed this-worldly politics for total reliance on the God of Scripture to rescue them from the evils of slavery and dehumanized status.

Examples of this type of reading can be seen in the work of Jupiter Hammon. One of the first African American authors, Hammon was a devout Christian. As an early enslaved author one might expect him to use his literacy to critique his life situation. However, though his writing addresses the contemporary crisis of North American slavery, it fails to provide a thoroughgoing critique of that institution as would the work of later authors. Hammon instead presents a decidedly mainstream moralistic view of the Christian faith, employing the Bible as a life guide for purposes of self improvement. Though he does subtly argue against slavery, he reserves this-worldly freedom for younger men, not for himself. To him God's Word provided all the freedom that he required as it facilitated access to heaven. Only there can humans find liberation from all that ails them.[2]

In his 1786 "Address to Negroes in the State of New York," Hammon's apolitical sentiments are evident:

> Let me beg of you my dear African brethren, to think very little of your bondage in this life, for your thinking of it will do you no good. If God designs to set us free, he will do it in his own time and way; but think of your bondage to sin and Satan, and do not rest until you are delivered from it.[3]

Here bondage of the flesh is deemed unimportant when compared to spiritual bondage, and the potential for earthly freedom pales in light of the promises of Christ.

A similar all-encompassing reliance on God is echoed in the work of political activist, Maria Stewart. Though she had spent much of her life seeking the abolition of slavery, she had come to the opinion that her efforts were for naught. In her 1832 farewell to her friends in Boston her theological reasons are evident as she states, "It is high time for us to drop political discussions, and when our day of deliverance comes, God will provide a way for escape, and fight his own battles."[4] As with Hammon, she concluded that morality and godliness were to be her goals and that abolitionist political strivings were incompatible with the radical trust in "pure religion." It is up to God alone to determine the time of freedom; political activity seeking social change would be viewed as vain for Hammon and Stewart. As these two authors illustrate, early African American authors were capable of apolitical hermeneutics expressing reliance only on God to provide liberation even during the antebellum period.

SUBVERSIVE POLITICAL READINGS OF BIBLICAL FAITH

Subsequent texts more thoroughly critiqued slavery. Writers like Peter Randolph and Frederick Douglass exemplify the use of the Bible to achieve other ends. Though their faith is apparent, it is not expressed with Hammon's fundamentalist zeal. Instead, their faith could not abide a separation of the spiritual and social dimensions of life. Valid faith must attend to liberation and freedom in order to realize God's promise.

In his 1893 autobiography Peter Randolph demonstrates why it would have been difficult for African Americans initially to believe the Bible, particularly inasmuch as they received it from the hands of less than reliable sources. Randolph critiques slave holders who ironically preached against theft to those they held enslaved, deeming them like Ananias and Sapphira who "betrayed the trust committed to them, or refused to bear true testimony in regard to that trust."[5] For him "[t]he Gospel was so mixed with slavery, that the people could see no beauty in it, and feel no reverence for it."[6] From this statement we could almost conclude that he would reject the Christian God and Scripture.

However, as he attests, it is not the faith with which he had a problem but preachers who would get caught up in the spirit in worship on Sunday morning and then whip an enslaved woman on Monday morning. He declares that, "[s]uch preachers ought to be forbidden by the laws of the land ever to mock again the blessed religion of Jesus, which was sent as a light to the world."[7] For Randolph the "religion of Jesus" was distinct from the expressions seen in the religion of white slaveholders he was forced to endure. He could thus level a critique against slavery in Christian terms, demonstrating the failure of his ideological opponents properly to surmise the scriptural message.

The hypocrisy of white Christianity was also a major theme for Frederick Douglass. In essence he determines that slaveholding religion was different altogether from the Christianity of Christ:

> I assert most unhesitatingly, that the religion of the south is a mere covering for the most horrid crimes, —a justifier of the most appalling barbarity, —a sanctifier of the most hateful frauds, —and a dark shelter under which the darkest, foulest, grossest, and most infernal deeds of slaveholders find the strongest protection.[8]

This statement may on the surface appear to be a rejection of Christianity, but Douglass makes it clear that it is not Christianity that he had problems with but a bastardized version of American religion. He continues:

> What I have said respecting and against religion, I mean strictly to apply to the *slaveholding religion* of this land, and with no possible reference to Christianity proper; for, between the Christianity of this land, and the Christianity of Christ, I recognize the widest possible difference. . . . I can see no reason, but the most deceitful one, for calling the religion of this land Christianity."[9]

Douglass, raised with the hypocrisy of slaveholding Christianity, had ample reason to dismiss the Bible or to conclude that it was nothing more than a tool used to control blacks. However, he does not reject Scripture; instead he uses it to hold those he sees abusing it accountable. Likening southern slaveholding Christians to biblical scribes and Pharisees, he declares that they:

> . . . attend with Pharisaical strictness to the outward forms of religion, and at the same time neglect the weightier matters of the law, judgment, mercy, and faith . . . professing to love God whom they have not seen, whilst they hate their brother whom they have seen."[10]

By finding biblical examples of pious people who were portrayed negatively in the Bible, Douglass was able to redeem the faith of Scripture despite the failings of southern Christianity. Slaveholders, though pious, were not faithful Christians but a central religious hierarchy; like scribes and Pharisees they misconstrued the essence of religion. In this way the Bible's authority could be upheld in spite of the rampant abuses by white Christians.

LIBERATIVE MYTHOPOEIC VALUE OF SCRIPTURE

The story of African American origins is the story of immeasurable loss. Not only were those who were enslaved kidnapped and ripped from their land, but they left behind their societies, their families, their livelihoods, their freedom, their lives. Albert Raboteau suggests:

> In North America a relatively small number of Africans found themselves enslaved amid a rapidly increasing native-born population whose memories of the African past grew fainter with each passing generation. . . . In the United States all these factors tended to inhibit the survival of African culture and religion. It was not possible to maintain the rites of worship, the priesthood, or the "national" identities which were the vehicles and supports for African theology and cult organization.[11]

These losses would have undermined their systems for comprehending the world around them and have had a catastrophic impact on people who had their worlds brutally torn apart. Imagine them having to come to terms with the harsh reality that their lives were no longer their own, that the essential nature of their being had been transformed from that of people into that of property. As a result, there was a need for a new system for understanding the hostile alien world in which they found themselves.

In part the Bible proved useful to African Americans as they realized its liberative mythopoeic value; they found in the pages of Scripture a basis for understanding their new identity and their circumstances. As Albert Raboteau notes:

> Slaves prayed for the future day of deliverance to come, and they kept hope alive by incorporating as part of *their* mythic past the Old Testament exodus of Israel out of slavery. The appropriation of the Exodus story was for the slaves a way of articulating their sense of historical identity as a people. That identity was also based, of course, upon their common heritage of enslavement. The Christian slaves applied the Exodus story, whose end they knew, to their own experience of slavery, which had not ended. In identifying with the Exodus story, they created meaning out of the chaotic and senseless experience of slavery. Exodus functioned as an archetypal event for the slaves.[12]

For many enslaved African Americans the Bible provided a way for them to make sense of the larger world. In the narratives of the Old and New Testaments they could find comfort and assurance that no matter how bleak their lives appeared, God would eventually provide them with the freedom that they deserved as human beings. In this regard narratives about the Exodus from Egypt became the heart of their canon, describing not the lives of a long dead people but their own lives of suffering and subjugation.

In addition to finding comfort in stories about the Exodus, the Gospels also resonated with enslaved African Americans, for they found in Jesus a kindred soul. After all he experienced unmerited suffering throughout his life only to find justice in the resurrection after death. They could identify with Jesus and rest assured that he also identified with their plight. Consider the words of the classic spiritual:

> Nobody knows de trouble I see
> Nobody knows but Jesus
> Nobody knows the trouble I've had
> Glory hallelu![13]

Only the Jesus portrayed in Scripture could know how difficult life was for an enslaved person. As such, his story became archetypal as well, expressing in the person of Jesus the hope of justice and a blessed future after a torturous and violent life. As Kelly Brown Douglas notes:

> Jesus' significance for the slaves was based upon an interpretation of Christianity that stressed the centrality of Jesus' ministry and relationship to the oppressed during his own time. The slaves were drawn, for instance, to Luke's birth narrative. . . . It told them that Jesus was born in a manger, because there was no room for him in the inn. . . . Jesus understood their experience of rejection.[14]

Thus, the Bible proved immeasurably significant for early African American Christians as a resource for understanding their experience in the United States and for providing a sense of hope to a people trapped in seemingly irresolvable circumstances. The texts that they gravitated towards emphasized God as a liberator concerned with the "least of these." In fact, these narratives became the core of their own canon, texts selected because they were "life giving," excluding or de-emphasizing those that were used by "whites" oppressively.

Not just a feature of early African American biblical analysis, the mythic quality of African American appropriations of Scripture played a significant role in the Civil Rights Movement. Martin Luther King, Jr., symbolically employed aspects of the Exodus narratives in the African American struggle for freedom. In his book *Where Do We Go from Here?* King not only draws a parallel between his movement and the Exodus, he identifies them:

> The Bible tells the thrilling story of how Moses stood in Pharaoh's court centuries ago and cried, "Let my people go." *This was an opening chapter in a continuing story. The present struggle in the United States is a later chapter in the same story.*[15]

Pharaoh also appears in King's rhetoric as a symbolic representation of the oppressive system that had taken the people's freedom.[16] King also recognizes his role in this unfolding narrative as that of Moses. It is this role that lends poignancy to his ultimate public address, "I See the Promise Land," delivered the evening prior to his assassination. As Moses, King declares that though he may not enter the promised land God has granted him an opportunity to see it from the "mountaintop."[17] The people he sought to free are likened to the Hebrews escaping bondage, then questioning their allegiance to Moses (read King) and longing to return to Egypt.[18] By employing the Exodus motif King played upon a historic association in the African American cultural imagination; thus he was able to motivate his followers and express the certainty of their victory as an act of God's deliverance. The tangible political benefits of granting authority to Scripture are evident in the positive outcomes of this movement for the African American community.

OUTSIDE THEIR CANON—THE LIMITS OF AUTHORITY

Much can also be learned about the authority of Scripture in African American communities by understanding those texts that they excluded from their canon. Though the Bible was generally deemed authoritative by African Americans, some texts were deemed problematic; thus their authority was rejected, and they were ignored or avoided. The clearest example was the Pauline epistles. Paul's texts were often rejected categorically because this apostle lacked a clear critique of slavery in his writings. "Slaves obey your masters" in Eph 6:9 (attributed by tradition to Paul) was a favorite text of slaveholders and produced no small amount of ire among enslaved Africans in America as would Paul's letter to Philemon, wherein he returns a fugitive to his master.

In his autobiography Randolph also reflects on his life as a slave in Virginia and the sermons that he was forced to endure. He attests to the frequent use of Eph 6:5–8 by preachers who were proslavery advocates. Randolph refers to one preacher in particular, Rev. James L. Goltney, who would frequently expound on this passage, then chastise enslaved Africans by telling them that their dreams of escaping bondage were of the devil and equating leaving slavery to leaving the Christian church.[19] Howard Thurman also recounts that his formerly enslaved grandmother forbid him from reading from the Pauline Epistles because she had frequently been bombarded with sermons from this text.[20]

Amos Jones notes that this tendency was not just prevalent among African Americans during the antebellum period. His 1984 text, *Paul's Message of Freedom: What Does It Mean to the Black Church*, was written as a rejoinder to African American theologians like Howard Thurman and James Cone who in the twentieth century still rejected the authority of Pauline texts. Actually, the book is the result of his efforts to make Pauline literature authoritative for African Americans, to reintroduce Paul to the canon of so many that had rejected his corpus by demonstrating a liberating tendency in Paul's letters. Jones writes:

> I have thought that my most salient task was to vindicate the apostle Paul. The malignant castigation hurled at him by black theologians . . . has made Paul appear to be, in the life and thought of black people, a back number, a byword, and a derision. So I suppose one of the things that is being attempted here is the task of redeeming Paul for the sake of the black church and black theologians."[21]

Though Jones critiques other black theologians and considers himself to be arguing for a traditional view of biblical canon, it is essential to see that his goal is similar to theirs. Even for Jones, African Americans' ability to deem the Pauline corpus authoritative depends upon the extent to which it can provide a message of freedom to this people. Biblical authority for African Americans, it seems, has traditionally been linked to the text's ability to foster liberation!

AFRICAN ORIGINS IN THE EXEGESIS OF GENESIS 9:18–10:32[22]

Not long after African Americans begin to make literary contributions we note the advent of pioneering efforts in exegetical analysis. The first such effort was the work by Robert Lewis. Lewis's work was an initial attempt to use the Bible to demonstrate the humanity of African peoples by highlighting their contributions to biblical history.

This work was a necessary rejoinder to the supremacist work of authors like Josiah Priest who contended that Africans were destined to be an enslaved people. In a very real sense supremacist authors had made the Bible a co-conspirator in one of the greatest hoaxes in human history, the production and perpetuation of race. Though not originating a new idea, these interpreters employed Scripture to reinforce the concept, attempting to invalidate the full humanity of African people, placing them under a divine curse, and subjugating them to whites. Thus, the Bible as source of meaning for the Western world was diametrically opposed to the interests of African peoples.

Their arguments focused on several key passages including Gen 9:18–10:32. Genesis 9:18–27 provided the justification for the subjugation of Africans inasmuch as Ham, who they took to have been cursed, was the progenitor of all African peoples. This text was employed with a very literalist reading of Gen 10, ascribing to it considerable authority as a source of valid and credible information on the origins of racial and ethnic types. Hence, based upon his reading of these two passages, Priest declared that the very name Ham implied that this son of Noah was:

> . . . exceedingly prone to acts of ferocity and cruelty, involving murder, war, butcheries, and even cannibalism, including beastly lusts, and lasciviousness in its worst feature, going beyond the force of these passions, as possessed in common by the other races of men . . . the word signifies deceit, dishonesty, treachery, low mindedness, and malice. What a group of horrors are here, couched in the word Ham, all agreeing in a most surprising manner with the color of Ham's skin, as well as with his real character as a man, during his own life, as well as with that of his race even now.[23]

In contrast to the blackness of Ham, Priest deemed Japheth the "fair white man . . . the progenitor of a race who were to fill the world with their glory . . . for the white man, and the white woman are paramount in all the improvements of the earth.[24]

Priest goes on to deem the Canaanites, as sons of Ham, "black," and to associate all blacks with their disfavored "cursed" position. Hence, he established a biblically-based, theologically-grounded hierarchy of humanity with "negroes" inextricably relegated to the lowest position.[25]

Such arguments posed a particular dilemma for African American authors, for with the advent of Christianity among blacks, the Bible had garnered unparalleled authority as a source of meaning. In response to this line of reasoning Robert Lewis in 1844 published *Light and Truth . . . A Universal History of the Colored and Indian Race*. Lewis begins his analysis *accepting* the supremacist's presumptions that the Bible presents accurate historical genealogical information, and strictly employing the Hamite hypothesis, assumes that all of the sons of Ham were "Ethiopian," hence black in color and race.

Then, Lewis *reverses* the implications of those assumptions and thereby undermines their claims to the text. Employing what amounts to a "one drop" blackness rule popular during his period, he examines the pedigree of countless biblical personalities and concludes that most of the people in the Bible were black or at least "colored," including Ham's brothers Shem and Japheth.[26] Thus, he is able to reappropriate the biblical text, making it palatable for oppressed African Americans.

Using the Bible, he demonstrates that key figures in the history of our faith had a "racial" composition like that of enslaved Africans and that they were indispensable to God's plan of salvation. He thereby subverts the arguments of those who would use similar racial traits as a cause for oppression. As a result we see the antithetical nature of Lewis' work to that of the supremacists who presumed the normative whiteness of the majority of the biblical characters and condemned those few characters they identified as "blacks." Biblical history (and history in general), as he sees it, is not the result of the activities of white peoples as the Supremacists would suggest, but colored or black peoples.

Writing in 1893, Rufus Perry determines that "now the black man must write for black men, and give them proper or merited rank among the historic peoples of the earth."[27] He begins his argument addressing a pattern that had become pervasive in mainstream biblical scholarship.

> [T]he most favored race of men [whites] preach about their own superiority till it becomes a kind of second nature. Then they piously incorporate it in their religion, and put it in their schoolbooks to be imbibed by their children. . . . They have egregiously falsified the true history of the Cushites, or the Hamitic branch of the human family.[28]

Noting this, his clearly political aim is to inspire "the thoughtful Negro to look back to his remote progenitors and trace up his lineage in the hope of finding something of ancestral greatness with which to . . . kindle in his breast a decent flame of pride of race."[29] To accomplish this aim he *accepts* the popularized view of the "Table of Nations" in Gen 10, deeming it to be "the most ancient and reliable ethnographic table known to historians."[30] But Perry's *reversal* comes in two distinct moves. First, in subsequent chapters he uncovers evidence of the glorious past of black people by tracing narratives about the "sons of Ham" in the Bible. This "glorious past" is contrasted with the contemporary status of subjugated African peoples who are debased by the actions of their brothers, the Japhethites and Shemites "who unrighteously conspired against him."[31] Nobility is thus no longer a trait associated with whiteness, for "white" peoples are guilty of a collective crime against the truly noble race of Cushites (Africans). Hence, the nature of the two types of people, both black and white, is contrasted in his hermeneutical system.

And second, instead of seeking to resolve the matter of the "Curse of Ham," he accepts it, determining that it is currently in effect. Like Priest, he determines that the "Curse of Ham" was responsible for the present denigration of African peoples, explaining the contrast between their present status and their glorious past.[32] However, the reversal is manifest inasmuch as he is able to offer hope for modern Cushites in the prophesied moment when, as suggested in Ps 68:31, Cush will "stretch out her hands unto God."[33] With this Ethiopianist move the "Curse of Ham" becomes a temporary disadvantage destined to be reversed by God's providence at a near future moment. This move also illustrates a temporal dualism inasmuch as time has again been bifurcated. The present moment is one of oppression for Cushites (Africans); yet God will intervene to provide great blessing in the subsequent era when:

> . . . the 'Dark Continent' would soon stretch out her hands unto God, and robe herself in a garb more conformed to the Christianity of the New Testament than has hitherto clothed the character of any nation of Europe, Asia, or America.[34]

By employing subversive reading strategies these exegetes were able to maintain the authority of Scripture for their people. Further, they were able to leverage that authority over black and white Christians, not only to redeem the texts from those who sought to use them against the African peoples, but to achieve their own objectives. No longer would it be possible for their adversaries uncritically to employ racist readings; African Americans now had a sure foundation upon which to build their identity and argue for their rights.

CONCLUDING REMARKS

As we have seen, African Americans were able to derive great benefit from their continued acquaintance with the Christian Scriptures. In fact, much of the progress they have made in their struggle for freedom and self-determination has been influenced by the Bible. Due to the unique circumstances surrounding their history in this nation, the Bible has been an appealing partner, providing a divine framework within which they could argue for their rights as human beings and find reassurance that the Creator of the world had not forgotten them during their darkest hours.

The authority that Scripture has enjoyed in the African American community over time is a testament to its relevance, particularly as regards notions of liberation. In fact, as we have seen, one of the criteria historically used to determine whether a text was authoritative is whether it expressed God's tendency to work for the liberation of those who were oppressed. Further, because of its plastic nature, Scripture has continued to be relevant for African Americans throughout their tenure in the New World, being adapted to address the exigent crises of the era. Whether the concern was slavery, Jim Crow, poverty, unequal treatment under the law, job discrimination, or any of a host of other concerns that plagued African Americans, the Bible was both a source for the spiritual strength needed to survive the struggle and for the righteousness/justice needed to engage successfully those who sought to limit their human potential. With a minor modification the words of a popular gospel song succinctly sum up the essential question regarding African American's reliance on Scripture: "If it had not been for the *Word* on our side, where would we be? Where would we be?"

NOTES

1. C. Eric Lincoln notes that there was "no division in African communities between sacred and secular, especially between religion and politics." See his *The Black Church in the African American Experience* (Durham, N.C.: Duke University Press, 1990), 199–200. Aspects of this integration of sacred and secular persist in African American Christian contexts, which determines that the religious character of the Black Church is necessarily political. For a larger discussion of politics and African American religion, see pages 199–204.

2. Jupiter Hammon, "Address to the Negroes in the State of New York," in *African American Religious History: A Documentary Witness* (ed. Milton C. Sernett; Durham, N.C.: Duke University Press, 1999), 34–43.

3. Ibid., 42.

4. Maria Stewart, "Mrs. Stewart's Farewell Address to Her Friends in the City of Boston," in *African American Religious History: A Documentary Witness*, 208.

5. Peter Randolph, "Plantation Churches: Visible and Invisible," in *African American Religious History: A Documentary Witness,* 1999), 64.

6. Ibid.

7. Ibid., 65.

8. Frederick Douglass, "Slaveholding Religion and the Christianity of Christ," in *African American Religious History: A Documentary Witness*, 103.

9. Ibid., 106.

10. Ibid., 108.

11. Albert J. Raboteau, *Slave Religion: The Invisible Institution in the Antebellum South* (New York: Oxford University Press, 1980), 11.

12. Ibid., 311.

13. Ibid., 259.

14. Kelly Brown Douglas, *The Black Christ* (Maryknoll, N.Y.: 1994), 21.

15. Martin Luther King, Jr., "Where Do We Go from Here?" in *A Testament of Hope: The Essential Writings and Speeches of Martin Luther King, Jr.* (ed. James M. Washington; New York: HarperSanFrancisco, 1991), 619 (italics mine).

16. Martin Luther King, Jr., "I See the Promise Land" in *A Testament of Hope: The Essential Writings and Speeches of Martin Luther King, Jr.*, 280–281.

17. Ibid., 286.

18. Martin Luther King, Jr., "The Strength to Love," in *A Testament of Hope: The Essential Writings and Speeches of Martin Luther King, Jr.*, 495. See also Martin Luther King, Jr., "Stride toward Freedom," in *A Testament of Hope: The Essential Writings and Speeches of Martin Luther King, Jr.*, 482.

19. Randolph, "Plantation Churches: Visible and Invisible," 65–66.

20. Howard Thurman, *Jesus and the Disinherited* (Richmond, Ind.: Friends United Press, 1949), 31, as cited in Douglass, *The Black Christ*, 26.

21. Amos Jones, Jr., *Paul's Message of Freedom: What Does It Mean to the Black Church?* (Valley Forge, Penn.: Judson, 1984), 8.

22. Much of the content from this section was presented earlier as "Exegesis in Black and White: Dualism in 19th and Early 20th Century African American Biblical Hermeneutics" at the Symposium on Dualism at Duke University/University of North Carolina, Chapel Hill, in June, 2003.

23. Josiah Priest, *Bible Defence of Slavery* (Louisville: J. F. Brennan for W. A. Bush, 1851), 33.

24. Ibid., 36.

25. Ibid., 63–88.

26. Robert B. Lewis, *Light and Truth; Collected from the Bible and Ancient and Modern History of the Colored and the Indian Race, from the Creation of the World to the Present Time* (Boston: A Committee of Colored Gentlemen, 1844), 13–19.

27. Rufus L. Perry, *The Cushite or the Descendants of Ham as Found in the Sacred Scriptures and in the Writings of Ancient Historians and Poets from Noah to the Christian Era* (Springfield, Mass.: Willey and Company, 1893), ix–x.

28. Ibid., 12.

29. Ibid.

30. Ibid., 13.

31. Ibid., 162.

32. Ibid., 80–85.

33. Ibid., x.

34. Ibid., 170–171.

IT'S ABOUT GOD!
2 TIMOTHY 3:1–5, 10–17; JOHN 5:19–27, 36–44

MICHAEL PASQUARELLO III

To demonstrate to my students that we intend to take seriously the words of our Lord, "You search the Scriptures, because you think that in them you have eternal life; and it is they that bear witness to me . . ." I have moved my preaching classes from our normally assigned seminar room to one of our seminary chapels. I have been pleasantly surprised to see how this change of environment, which locates our work in a very different home, has contributed to a change in students' outlook, attitude, and actual performance of the practice of preaching. They are coming to realize that we are not simply looking at a text to find an idea or two that might be relevant, but rather we are speaking of God as an act of worship with and from the canon of Holy Scripture that measures the faith, life, and witness of the church.

The chapel where we meet has a large, prominent baptismal font, a Communion table, a pulpit flanked by a tall wooden cross, icons of Christ and the Apostles Peter and Paul, and a large, stained glass window with the symbol of a dove. Perhaps I can summarize in just a few simple words what I am trying to articulate in response to my students' questions and struggles to make sense of Scripture and preaching: "It's about God!" And I am continually amazed at how these few words are often the most important I may speak during the course of an entire semester: "It's about God!" I have begun to surmise that for some my words may function as authorization to break with the conventional wisdom of our time, as encouragement to dare to speak of God and the things of God rather than talking about whatever happens to be on our minds or the minds of our listeners.

We have now made a similar move, have we not? We have moved from a place of teaching and learning to this worship space, not only to bring this symposium to a close, but to gather in the Spirit's power and presence of our Risen Lord. We have come to bring the work we have shared over the past few days to completion, to its true end, by offering our thoughts and words as an act of praise and thanksgiving to the One who speaks with such authority that even the dead are raised to life.

We are gathered as students and teachers of Scripture to remember, celebrate, and enact the great story of the Triune God, the mighty works of creation, incarnation, and redemption, the whole economy of salvation, which is the subject of Scripture's wisdom and the narrative into which we have been incorporated by means of our baptism into the death and resurrection of Jesus Christ. For as John's Gospel asserts, our gathering is about the God of Jesus Christ. John 5 therefore begins with an act of healing by Jesus on the Sabbath for the praise and glory of God, a sign of remembrance that his judging and life-giving activity flows from his dependence on the Father, who is still busily at work on behalf of the salvation of the whole world.

Challenged by a group of scholarly opponents who were offended and even infuriated by what appeared to be blatantly blasphemous talk and action, Jesus provides three witnesses to the authority embodied in his speech and form of life: John the Baptist, his own works, and the words of the Father. Finally, he tells those opposed to him that while they have their heads in their Bibles, looking to find eternal life there, they miss the forest for the trees. The Scriptures are all about Jesus. They bear witness to him; and in him, for those who believe, is found the life-giving power of God's Word whose presence manifests divine grace and glory in the world.

In a wonderful sixteenth century homiletic paraphrase of John's Gospel, Erasmus of Rotterdam rendered this great truth in the following manner:

> Of course you believe the scriptures come from God, and yet while you busy yourselves in close study of them and you locate the hope and happiness of your life in them, you do not believe the scriptures on the one thing that is the chief point of all. For the scriptures promise life, but it is through me. Though you always have the books in your hands, the words in your mouths, you still reject him whom those writings promise. There is no path to life except through me, confirmed as I am by so many witnesses; nonetheless you despise them all and refuse to come by me, where with the least trouble you may have life. For the doorway of salvation is: to have believed in the Son whom the Father sent. So your unbelief is not from a lack of witnesses, but from a lack of true love for God.[1]

Perhaps Augustine of Hippo understood as well as anyone how a lack of true love for God is able to distort our vision, desire, and understanding. After his conversion, Augustine wrote in the *Confessions* of the new life and identity to which he had been called. He was now a participant in a new narrative: the story of Christ enacted in the common life of the church. Augustine, who had been an ambitious, highly successful "wordsmith," a teacher of rhetoric, was blessed with the gifts of humility and wisdom, as his whole life was reoriented to become a witness to the Wisdom of God spoken in Jesus Christ. This life and wisdom, however, was not of Augustine's own making, but rather was constituted on the basis of the Word made flesh and a particular way of rendering the world, namely, Holy Scripture. For Augustine, the language of Trinity and Incarnation, learned through his participation in the faith and practice of the church, was derived from the whole scriptural story of salvation which culminated in Christ and the community he calls and creates. This narrative not only offered a disciplined way, but also a compelling nearness in the Word made known through words. The vitality of God's love revealed in Christ had drawn near to him through the life and authority of the church: its sacraments, Scripture, sermons, and testimony of its saints. Augustine writes of how his life was transformed.

> To possess my God, the humble Jesus, I was not yet humble enough. I did not know what his weakness was meant to teach. Your Word, eternal truth, higher than the superior parts of your creation, raises those submissive to him to himself. In the inferior parts he built for himself a humble house of our clay. By this he detaches from themselves those who are willing to be made his subjects and carries them across to himself, healing their prideful swelling and nourishing their love. They are no longer to place confidence in themselves, but rather to become weak. In their weariness, they fall prostrate before this divine weakness, which rises and lifts them up.[2]

Augustine's eyes were opened to see that Scripture's saving wisdom is granted to all who hear and believe. Its power is in authorizing and shaping us to participate in God's saving purposes that are summed up in the humble obedience of Jesus, the fulfillment God's perfect rule of charity. As Augustine wrote in his handbook for preachers, "Whoever then appears to have comprehended the Sacred Scriptures, or even some part of them, yet does not build up with that knowledge the twofold love of God and neighbor, has not yet known as he ought to know."[3]

When you come to the Lord's Table today, remember that through the sending of the Word and Spirit we have been invited to taste and see that the Lord is good and that through this Holy Meal we who call ourselves Christian, who belong to Jesus Christ, are being equipped, skilled, and made wise for every good work. For we are a people called to be holy as God is holy. Through divine grace, the work of the Spirit, we have been caught up into the life of God whose goodness is revealed in Jesus Christ, the One who has called us, through the words of Holy Scripture, to bear faithful witness to him in the world. Amen.

NOTES

1. Desiderius Erasmus, *Paraphrase on John,* trans. Jane E. Phillips, *Collected Works of Erasmus* (Toronto: University of Toronto Press, 1991), 46:72-73.

2. *Confessions*, VII. xviii. 24.

3. *De Doctrina Christiana*, The Works of Augustine: A Translation for the 21st Century (trans. John E. Rotelle, ed. Edmund Hill; Hyde Park: New City, 1996), I.xxii.21.

ANNOTATED BIBLIOGRAPHY
ON THE AUTHORITY OF SCRIPTURE*

Abraham, William J. *Canon and Criterion in Christian Theology: From the Fathers to Feminism.* Oxford: Oxford University Press, 1998. This is one of the most important works on canon and epistemology. Abraham objects to the prioritizing of epistemology and seeks to recover a better biblical and theological procedure for handling canonical materials whose purpose was to initiate people into the life of God.

_____. *The Divine Inspiration of Holy Scripture*. New York: Oxford University Press, 1981. Abraham identifies problems in the evangelical understanding of divine inspiration and seeks to provide a positive account of inspiration that is contemporary, coherent, and credible, one that is more adequate than the "standard orthodox" accounts.

Achtemeier, Paul J. *Inspiration and Authority: Nature and Function of Christian Scripture.* Peabody, Mass.: Hendrickson, 1999. Originally published by Westminister Press in 1980, this book seeks to move past both liberal and conservative approaches to Scripture. Focus is placed on tradition in the composition of books and less on the "prophetic" model of authorship. He rightly emphasizes the role of the community in interpreting and living out the text.

Auerbach, Erich. *Mimesis: The Representation of Reality in Western Literature*. Translated by W. Trask. Garden City, N.Y.: Doubleday, 1957. Beginning with Homer and the Bible Auerbach's seminal work gives profound readings of significant texts, both Christian and pagan, to explore how we in the West see reality through literature. Crucial literary education in reading the Bible and reality for Christians.

Barr, James. *Holy Scripture: Canon, Authority, Criticism.* Oxford: Oxford University Press, 1983. Barr discusses the emergence of Scripture and the relation of church and canon; he then offers an analysis and critique of B. Childs's canonical criticism. Finally he discusses how biblical research relates to canon. Barr views the canon as a necessity, but in the end he asserts that the canon is not very important.

Barth, Karl. *Church Dogmatics*. Vol. 1/2. Edinburgh: T. & T. Clark, 1956. An astounding synthesis of a millenium of Christian thought through the lens of what Scripture says about Christ. *Church Dogmatics* is an essential work in any theological library (especially chapter 3).

Bartlett, David L. *The Shape of Scriptural Authority.* Philadelphia: Fortress, 1983. Bartlett offers a descriptive survey of scriptural authority in relation to the major genres of biblical literature. Successive chapters discuss the authority of words (prophetic), deeds (narrative), wisdom, and witness (Jeremiah and Paul). The final chapter takes up canon and community.

*This bibliography is based on contributions and suggestions made by the participants of the symposium and was augmented, compiled, and annotated by James Amadon and Lars Stromberg, to whom sincere thanks is heartily expressed.

Barton, John. *Holy Writings, Sacred Text: The Canon in Early Christianity*. Louisville: Westminster/John Knox, 1997. This book is a historical study which focuses on the formation and reception of biblical texts both ancient and modern. Barton's concern is with what we mean by canon and how books in a canon are used by believers.

_____. *People of the Book? The Authority of the Bible in Christianity*. Louisville: Westminster/ John Knox, 1988. Barton treats six topics—scriptural tradition in early Christianity, prophecy and fulfillment, the canon, the Bible as evidence, the Bible as a book of faith, and hermeneutical theories. This is a careful and thoughtful work representing the fruit of Barton's scholarship.

Bauckham, Richard. *God and the Crisis of Freedom: Biblical and Contemporary Perspectives*. Louisville: Westminster/John Knox, 2002. The essay entitled "Authority and Scripture" (pp. 50–77) addresses the authority of Scripture in the context of modern and postmodern rejections of authority. He argues for the authority of the biblical story as an underlying metanarrative expressing the authority of God's grace.

Bellis, Alice Ogden. *Helpmates, Harlots, and Heroes: Women's Stories in the Hebrew Bible*. Louisville: Westminster/John Knox, 1994. Although ten years old, Bellis's book is still a useful guide to a substantial amount of feminist exegesis. The book is organized by biblical book and includes questions for discussion.

Berkouwer, G. C. *Studies in Dogmatics: Holy Scripture*. Grand Rapids: Eerdmans, 1975. A technical yet endearing and carefully reasoned commentary on the broader arguments concerning the authority and interpretation of Scripture. Chapter four is particularly helpful.

Blaisdell, Charles R., ed. *Conservative, Moderate, Liberal: The Biblical Authority Debate*. St. Louis: CBP Press, 1990. A helpful collection of essays treating authority from authors who represent various theological perspectives. Of particular note are essays by William Placher, Luke Timothy Johnson, and David Scholer.

Bloesch, Donald. *Holy Scripture*. Downers Grove, Ill.: InterVarsity, 1994. Bloesch provides a fairly comprehensive discussion of issues of authority and inspiration. He also treats heremeneutics and has a chapter on Rudolf Bultmann.

Borsch, Frederick Houk, ed. *The Bible's Authority in Today's Church*. Valley Forge, Pa.: Trinity Press International, 1993. An Episcopalian view concerning the authority and function of the Bible in today's church.

Braaten, Carl E., and Robert W. Jenson, eds. *Reclaiming the Bible for the Church*. Grand Rapids: Eerdmans, 1995. Among severeal significant articles the most relevant is Roy Harrisville's "The Loss of Biblical Authority and Its Recovery" (pp. 47–61). Harrisville places responsibility on the biblical reader, proclaiming forcefully that "the Bible does not need saving."

Bright, John. *The Authority of the Old Testament*. Nashville: Abingdon, 1967. Bright's book has been and still deserves to be an important voice in the biblical authority debate. He seeks to answer the question, "What place does the Old Testament legitimately occupy in the Christian's Bible and in the church's proclamation?"

Bryan, Christopher. *And God Spoke: The Authority of the Bible for the Church Today*. Cambridge, Mass.: Cowley, 2002. This relatively brief book advises Christians about what one should believe and do with the Bible, particularly in the process of making ethical decisions.

Burgess, John P. *Why Scripture Matters: Reading the Bible in a Time of Church Conflict*. Louisville: Westminster/John Knox, 1998. Burgess gives attention to the compelling power of Scripture and to the life of the church as a commentary on Scripture. His thoughts are helpful and can motivate both pastors and lay leaders.

Countryman, L. William. *Biblical Authority or Biblical Tyranny: Scripture and the Christian Pilgrimage*. Valley Forge, Pa.: Trinity Press International, 1994. Countryman offers thought-provoking discussion on the question "What is authority?" and the actual role of Scripture in the church and Christian life. His conclusion is that scriptural authority is intended to produce conversion, a lifelong pilgrimage with God.

Dockery, David S. *Christian Scripture: An Evangelical Perspective on Inspiration, Authority and Interpretation*. Nashville: Broadman and Holman, 1995. Dockery discusses inspiration and interpretation from the context of debates among Southern Baptists. A lengthy appendix provides a history of Southern Baptist views on the inspiration and authority of Scripture from 1845 to 1994.

Dodd, C. H. *The Authority of the Bible*. New York: Harper, 1929. This discussion by one of the leading NT scholars of the twentieth century is a response to biblical criticism and questions of authority. He seeks to root biblical authority not in propositional truth claims but in the life and religious experiences to which it speaks, centered on what he calls "the fact of Christ."

Dunn, James D. G. *The Living Word*. Philadelphia: Fortress, 1987. Among several essays related to themes of NT interpretation two essays are directly concerned with the authority of Scripture. One deals with levels of canonical authority and is a discussion of the relevance of canonical criticism for understanding the NT. The other is an essay on the authority of Scripture in which Dunn argues against the "Princeton" school and its adherents (who argue for inerrancy) and for a more nuanced yet still evangelical view. To this article is appended a letter to Roger Nicole answering Nicole's published response to Dunn's original piece.

Fackre, Gabriel. *The Doctrine of Revelation: A Narrative Interpretation*. Grand Rapids: Eerdmans, 1997. This book treats both general and special revelation and also includes a section on revelation as reception. Fackre discusses, among others, the contributions of Rahner, Tillich, K. Barth, and Carl Henry.

_____. *Ecumenical Faith in Evangelical Perspective*. Grand Rapids: Eerdmans, 1993. Two chapters in this book relate to Scripture: "What Evangelicals Believe about the Bible" (pp. 3–19) and "The Uses of Scripture in Theology" (pp. 37–70). The former analyzes various ways to think of inerrancy and infallibility. The latter addresses issues of pluralism and the finality of Christ regarding salvation within a discussion of the use of Scripture.

Felder, Cain Hope, ed. *Stony the Road We Trod: African American Biblical Interpretation*. Philadelphia: Fortress, 1992. This collection of essays focuses on the Black Church and the way issues of authority and hermeneutics are processed there and also on the resources the Black tradition offers.

_____. *Troubling Biblical Waters: Race, Class, and Family*. Maryknoll: Orbis, 1990. This book is an important voice in the scriptural authority discussion. Felder provides sorely needed correctives regarding the Bible in relation to ancient Africa and Black people today.

Forsyth, P. T. *The Principle of Authority*. London: Hodder & Stoughton, 1913. Although old and much broader in scope than just the authority of Scripture, this classic work should not be forgotten. There is a chapter on authority in the church and Bible, but the whole book is about authority in faith and religion.

Fretheim, Terence E., and Karlfried Froehlich. *The Bible as Word of God: In a Postmodern Age*. Minneapolis: Fortress, 1998. Fretheim and Froehlich mount important, though divergent, analyses of the contemporary situation regarding Scripture and suggest varying strategies to bring scriptural authority into the postmodern mind.

Garrett, Duane A., and Melick, Richard R., eds. *Authority and Interpretation: A Baptist Perspective*. Grand Rapids: Baker, 1987. This collection of essays is an instructive overview of both doctrinal foundations and practical implications of biblical authority and interpretation in the Baptist Church. Among the contributors are Carl Henry and David Dockery.

Gnuse, Robert. *The Authority of the Bible: Theories of Inspiration, Revelation and the Canon of Scripture*. New York: Paulist, 1985. This short book gives an introduction to various models of authority; among those treated are verbal inspiration, salvation history, and a christocentric model. Attention is also given to the rise of the canon and to ecumenical discussion.

Goldingay, John. "Scripture as Authoritative Canon." Pages 83–197 in *Models for Interpretation of Scripture*. Grand Rapids: Eerdmans, 1995. Goldingay treats a few biblical texts where the authority of Scripture is the subject but spends the majority of his time discussing the development and role of the canon.

Green, Garrett, ed. *Scriptural Authority and Narrative Interpretation*. Philadelphia: Fortress, 1987. This collection of ten essays derives from or responds to the theology of Hans W. Frei and considers the authority of Scripture as it intersects with hermeneutical questions about the character of biblical narrative.

Greenspahn, Frederick E. *Scripture in the Jewish and Christian Tradition: Authority, Interpretation, Relevance*. Nashville: Abingdon, 1982. This collection of essays is divided into three sections on the authority, interpretation, and relevance of Scripture. Each section includes an essay by Jewish, Protestant, and Roman Catholic scholars.

Grenz, Stanley J. "Revisioning Biblical Authority." Pages 109–136 in *Revisioning Evangelical Theology: A Fresh Agenda for the 21st Century*. Downers Grove, Ill.: InterVarsity, 1993. Grenz urges seeing the Bible as a source of spiritual sustenance requiring a spirituality of its readers. Accordingly he focuses on the role of the Spirit in the community and on the prominence of a Christian's biblical identity which leads to a true community of faith.

_____. "Scripture and the Genesis of New Evangelicalism." Pages 53–84 in *Renewing the Center: Evangelical Theology in a Post-Theological Era*. Grand Rapids: Baker, 2000. Grenz gives a concise history of evangelical thought concerning biblical authority, and he offers new ideas for "centering" the theological future.

Hauerwas, Stanley. *Unleashing the Scripture: Freeing the Bible from Captivity to America*. Nashville: Abingdon, 1993. Hauerwas asserts that both liberal and fundamentalist approaches to biblical scholarship have corrupted our use of the Bible in the American church. This is an interesting read for pastors and church leaders.

Hays, Richard B. *The Moral Vision of the New Testament: Community, Cross, New Creation*. San Francisco: Harper San Francisco, 1996. This well-known book offers a comprehensive treatment of how the NT can and should be used to shape and inform Christian ethics. Particularly pertinent to the subject of this journal is the third section of the book, in which Hays deals with questions of scriptural authority and hermeneutics in approaching ethical decision making.

Holladay, William L. *The Psalms through Three Thousand Years: Prayerbook of a Cloud of Witnesses*. Minneapolis: Fortress, 1993. Holladay surveys the interpretation and use of the entire psalter and interacts with questions concerning how the psalms are to be used and proclaimed today.

James, Robison B., ed. *The Unfettered Word: Southern Baptists Confront the Authority-Inerrancy Question*. Waco: Word Books, 1987. This is a collection of essays by Southern Baptist scholars such as Charles Talbert, Alan Culpepper, and Edgar McKnight. The articles deal with truth in the Bible, hermeneutical issues, and historical issues (including chapters on both the views of specific scholars and discussion of confessions of faith).

Johnson, Luke Timothy. *Scripture and Discernment: Decision Making in the Church*. Nashville: Abingdon, 1996. In chapter two ("The Authority of the New Testament in the Church"), Johnson, a prolific Roman Catholic NT scholar, discusses three ways in which the NT exercises authority: 1) as author of Christian identity; 2) as "authorizer" of Christian freedom to interpret and reinterpret Scripture; and 3) as a collection of authorities—that is, as a collection of diverse positions and perspectives on a variety of issues.

Johnston, Robert K. *Evangelicals at an Impasse: Biblical Authority in Practice*. Atlanta: John Knox, 1971. Although an older work, Johnston gives a nice overview of the debate over inspiration and carefully defines terms and methods. It is still helpful for pastors and students alike as they seek understanding on the issues of inspiration and appropriation of Scripture.

Jones, Gareth. "The Authority of Scripture and Christian Ethics." Pages 16–28 in *The Cambridge Companion to Christian Ethics*. Cambridge: Cambridge University Press, 2001. Jones briefly describes the issues involved in appealing to Scripture for ethical insights. He concentrates especially on the difficulty of approaching the Bible as a repository of ethical instruction, particularly in light of the cultural and ethical distance between the world of the Bible and today. The essay focuses on the Bible as God's redemptive story, the way communities are part of the ongoing story, and the ways communities may use Scripture to inform ethical choices.

Kelly, Joseph F., ed. *Perspectives on Scripture and Tradition: Essays by Robert M. Grant, Robert E. McNally, George H. Tavard.* Notre Dame, Indiana: Fides, 1976. These six essays derive from lectures at John Carroll University; they explore the relationship between Scripture and tradition from historical and theological perspectives.

Kelsey, David H. *The Uses of Scripture in Recent Theology*. Philadephia: Fortress, 1975. This book is still quite helpful in gaining perspective on different uses of Scripture. Kelsey examines various ways the text is construed (as doctrine, recital, event, and Scripture). He then focuses on authority and theology. He is particularly concerned with the patterns in Scripture and with the use of Scripture in a believing community.

Lancaster, Sarah Heaner. *Women and the Authority of Scripture: A Narrative Approach*. Harrisburg, Pa.: Trinity Press International, 2002. This useful book by a "reformist Christian feminist" places discussion of the authority of Scripture in the context of its role in the oppression of women. It includes chapters that survey the doctrine of Scripture in feminist theology and in Protestant orthodoxy, as well as philosophical descriptions on the nature of authority. Lancaster's argument construes Scripture as a narrative that bears authority because it brings us into a saving relationship with God.

Lazareth, William H., ed. *Reading the Bible in Faith: Theological Voices from the Pastorate*. Grand Rapids: Eerdmans, 2001. These essays were written with the assumption that the crisis within American mainline Protestant churches is neither programmatic or organizational but theological. The authors are all practicing pastors who seek to recover a reading of the Bible that calls people back to a profound engagement with Scripture. Attention is given to theological and doctrinal themes, as well as special sections on the binding of Isaac (Gen 22) and the Passion of Christ (Matt 26–27).

McClendon, James Wm., Jr. *Systematic Theology: Doctrine, Vol. II*. Nashville: Abingdon, 1994. In a concluding essay McClendon sketches the problems emerging in a discussion of authority and then argues that theologically authority rests in God's love, which is God's interactive authority; God's grace, which is God's redemptive authority; and God's fellowship, which is God's unitive authority. From this ultimate authority we find our own authority as Christians.

McDonald, L. M., and J. A. Sanders, eds. *The Canon Debate*. Peabody, Mass.: Hendrickson, 2002. This comprehensive book supplies us with a historical perspective on the development of the canon, and offers insight as to the canon's meaning for us today.

McFarland, Ian A. *Listening to the Least: Doing Theology from the Outside In*. Cleveland: United Church, 1998. With pastoral concerns McFarland argues that any claim to authority by the church must be done in solidarity with those who are on the periphery of the faith. Of particular note are chapters entitled "The Problem of Authority" and "The Church's Authority and the Priority of Scripture."

McKim, Donald K. *The Authoritative Word: Essays on the Nature of Scripture*. Grand Rapids: Eerdmans, 1983. This collection of essays is grouped under three headings: "Sources and Canon"; "Doctrine and its Development"; and "Current Views." The list of contributors is impressive and includes scholars such as Paul Achtemeier, Robert Grant, C. K. Barrett, F. F. Bruce, G. C. Berkouwer, and Avery Dulles.

Miller, Donald. *The Authority of the Bible*. Grand Rapids: Eerdmans, 1972. Scholars and pastors alike will find Miller's work to be a succinct and helpful synthesis of the major issues surrounding the authority of the Bible.

Moberly, R. W. L. *The Bible, Theology, and Faith: A Study of Abraham and Jesus*. Cambridge: Cambridge University Press, 2000. This book offers an introduction to some of the best in premodern, modern, and postmodern approaches to biblical interpretation. Christian leaders will find this book useful as they seek to develop meaningful and truthful speech about God.

Newbigin, Lesslie. *The Gospel in a Pluralist Society*. Geneva: WCC, 1994. Essential reading for Christians wishing to remain faithful in our pagan, pluralist world. Newbigin argues that the Bible is, among other things, "universal history."

______. *Truth and Authority in Modernity*. Valley Forge, Pa.: Trinity Press International, 1996. Newbigin looks at the sources of authority and truth in the modern world, acknowledging that many in society look at all claims of authority with distrust. Newbigin explores how the church can present the gospel to this society and make new use of the Bible, tradition, reason, and experience.

O'Donovan, Oliver. *Resurrection and Moral Order: An Outline for Evangelical Ethics*. Grand Rapids: Eerdmans, 1994. An immensely learned, challenging effort to work out the implications of a biblical worldview for Christian ethics. Christ's resurrection is God's vindication of human life in creation.

O'Neill, J. C. *The Bible's Authority: A Portrait Gallery of Things from Lessing to Bultmann*. Edinburgh: T. & T. Clark, 1991. O'Neill examines how 21 influential thinkers of the twentieth century understood the Bible's authority.

Olson, Roger E. *The Mosaic of Christian Belief: Twenty Centuries of Unity and Diversity*. Downers Grove, Ill.: InterVarsity, 2002. This volume, written specifically for the nonspecialist, traces Christian thought over the last two millennia on the major doctrines of the faith. The chapter on Christian Scripture traces how Christians have understood the Bible, not so much as a historical study but from the perspectives of the major schools of thought and approaches to the text.

Packer, J. I. *Beyond the Battle of the Bible*. Westchester, Ill.: Cornerstone, 1980. This is an informative and thoughtful collection of Packer's writings concerning the authority of

Scripture. Packer seeks to restore the Bible to a place of prominence in the lives of Christians and churches.

_____. "The Bible in Use: Evangelicals Seeking Truth from Holy Scripture." Pages 59–78 in *Your Word is Truth: A Project of Evangelicals and Catholics Together*. Edited by Charles Colson and Richard John Neuhaus. Grand Rapids: Eerdmans, 2002. This essay is meant to inform nonevangelicals about how the Bible is viewed and used in evangelical churches. Packer focuses on evangelicals' devotion to the Bible and their understanding of its centrality to all aspects of faith and life. He includes the negative results that have occurred from evangelical biblical isolationism.

Perry, John. "Dissolving the Inerrancy Debate: How Modern Philosophy Shaped the Evangelical View of Scripture." *Journal for Christian Theological Research* 6 (2001). Available only online at http://home.apu.edu/~CTRF/articles/2001_articles/perry.html. Perry argues that the concept of inerrancy has never been helpful in relation to biblical authority and shows the role modern philosophy has played in helping to define the terms involved in the debate. He seeks to dissolve the debate by making such categories as inerrancy virtual nonissues.

Phillips, Timothy R., and Dennis K. Okholm, eds. *The Nature of Confession: Evangelicals and Postliberals in Conversation*. Downers Grove, Ill.: InterVarsity, 1996. This collection of essays from evangelical and postliberal theologians explores the commonalities and differences of these two groups. Of particular worth to this journal's focus are four essays on the Bible and the church.

Pinnock, Clark H. *Biblical Revelation—The Foundation of Christian Theology*. Chicago: Moody, 1971. Pinnock is a big proponent of the infallibility of Scripture, and he calls the church to renew its vow with the sovereignty of Scripture.

_____. *The Scripture Principle*. San Francisco: Harper and Row, 1984. This is a systematic, evangelical approach to biblical authority. Pinnock presents his argument for biblical authority in a positive way and defends the full authority and trustworthiness of the Bible.

Placher, William C. "Contemporary Confession and Biblical Authority." Pages 64–81 in *To Confess the Faith Today*. Edited by Jack L. Stotts and Jane Dempsey Douglass. Louisville: Westminster/John Knox Press, 1990. This essay is part of a collection that accompanies the publication of the confession of faith of the Presbyterian Church (USA) in 1990. Placher demonstrates that within the Reformed tradition Scripture's authority can be understood as a set of true propositions, as a transforming word, or as the narrative of God's identity. He concludes by arguing that the church must embrace all three to have a better understanding of Scripture's authority and function for the life of the church.

Powell, Mark Allan. *God With Us: A Pastoral Theology of Matthew's Gospel*. Minneapolis: Fortress, 1995. Powell seeks to show how the pastoral concerns of Matthew's community affected the gospel and vice versa.

Ramm, Bernard. *The Pattern of Authority*. Grand Rapids: Eerdmans, 1957. Despite the date of publication, this is still a good book that discusses authority in religion, particularly Christianity, from a broad and evangelical perspective. It is helpful as an introduction as to why the question of authority is so important.

Reed, Esther. *The Genesis of Ethics: On the Authority of God as the Origin of Christian Ethics*. Cleveland: Pilgrim, 2000. Though this book focuses on the authority of God in relation to ethics, it includes chapters such as "The Authority of God: God as Author" and "God's Word in Dialogue" that speak to issues of scriptural authority as they relate to ethical thinking and decision making.

Reventlow, Henning Graf. *The Authority of the Bible and the Rise of the Modern World.* Philadelphia: Fortress, 1985. The author traces the rise of biblical criticism from its roots in the pre-Reformation period to its climax in the rise of English deism. He shows how new ideas about the Bible's authority had large cultural, political, and religious implications for post-Reformation England.

Richardson, Alan, and W. Schweizer, eds. *Biblical Authority for Today.* Philadelphia: Westminster, 1951. Created out of a World Council of Churches symposium on "The Biblical Authority for the Church's Social and Political Message Today," these essays offer seven denominational approaches to the authority of the Bible, six essays on principles of interpretation, and six essays on specific applications to social and political issues.

Rogers, Jack, ed. *Biblical Authority.* Waco, Tex.: Word, 1977. A collection of six essays by evangelical authors examining the debate within evangelical circles about biblical inerrancy, infallibility, and authority.

Rogers, Jack B., and Donald K. McKim. *The Authority and Interpretation of the Bible: An Historical Approach.* San Francisco: Harper and Row, 1979. This book is a comprehensive historical analysis of how the Scriptures have been viewed in various periods and by the most important representatives, with bias toward the Reformed tradition. The authors seek to move past the errors of much American theology and find a way between rationalism and subjectivism. An appendix shows how several Reformed confessions expressed beliefs about Scripture.

Russell, Letty M. *Feminist Interpretation of the Bible.* Philadelphia: Westminster, 1985. One essay in this book, "Authority and the Challenge of Feminist Interpretation," argues for an approach to the Bible that allows it to be authoritative for feminist interpretation by focusing on the way it shapes lives of faith in particular social contexts. In this view the Bible acts as God's Spirit-filled message to a particular community of people. This allows Scripture to retain authority without the need to assent to a more literal interpretive method or model of authority. She focuses instead on the liberating power of the Word. Russel's introductory essay also offers a brief historical sketch of feminist understanding of scriptural authority.

_____. *Household of Freedom: Authority in Feminist Theology.* Philadelphia: Westminster, 1987. This book analyzes the challenge that feminist theology brings to any concept of authority. It is broad in scope and includes a chapter entitled "Power of Naming" that deals more specifically with scriptural authority.

Sauter, Gerhard, and John Barton, eds. *Revelation and Story: Narrative Theology and the Centrality of Story.* Aldershot, England: Ashgate, 2000. This book explores "revelation" and "story" from both theological and philosophical perspectives and connects these concepts with questions of the authority of religious texts, particularly the Bible. The contributors to this volume were purposefully chosen from British and German traditions to illuminate similarities and differences between different theological frameworks.

Schussler Fiorenza, Elisabeth. *Bread Not Stone: The Challenge of Feminist Biblical Interpretation.* Boston: Beacon, 1984. This book critiques the Bible and certain hermeneutical approaches that legitimize patriarchy and oppression, but it also offers a new hermeneutic that sees Scripture as a source of authority that empowers women and points the way forward to liberation.

Seitz, Christopher R. *Word Without End: The Old Testament as Abiding Theological Witness.* Grand Rapids: Eerdmans, 1998. Among several pertinent articles in this collection of essays the most relevant is "Biblical Authority in the Late Twentieth Century" (pp. 83–101). Seitz is particularly concerned about Anglican views of Scripture and canonical criticism. These important essays are grouped under the headings "Biblical Theology," "Exegesis," and "Practice."

_____. *Figured Out: Typology and Providence in Christian Scripture*. Louisville: Westminster/John Knox, 2001. Seitz seeks to move beyond modernity's obsession with historical readings of Scripture in order to recover a figural/typological approach to the Bible that brings about a truly theological understanding of Scripture. He includes a chapter entitled, "Scripture and a Three-Legged Stool: Is There a Coherent Account of the Authority of Scripture for Anglicans After Lambeth 1998?"

Thompson, John L. *Writing the Wrongs: Women of the Old Testament among Biblical Commentators from Philo through the Reformation.* New York: Oxford University Press, 2001. A detailed study of the history of interpretation of four women's stories in the OT: Hagar, Jephthah's daughter, the Levite's wife (Judg 19), and Lot's daughters. The book also interacts with recent feminist criticism and argues for the continuing relevance of precritical exegesis.

Van Buren, Paul M. *According to the Scriptures: The Origins of the Gospel and of the Church's Old Testament.* Grand Rapids: Eerdmans, 1998. This study attempts to show that the OT was not simply used to clarify the early understanding of the gospel. Rather, Van Buren argues the OT was actually constituted by an interpretation of the Scriptures of ancient Israel as read by certain first century Jews and that the gospel came out of this interpretation.

Walsh, Brian J. "Reimagining Biblical Authority." *Christian Scholars Review* 26 (1996): 206–220. Arguing that "the Scriptures are written for our conversion" (219), Walsh offers an account of biblical authority that promotes embodiment in Christian life and community. He helpfully sets biblical authority in the context of modernity (and postmodernity), then explores various dimensions of authority. His constructive proposal is primarily an extension of N. T. Wright's account of narrative authority.

Warfield, Benjamin Breckinridge. *The Inspiration and Authority of the Bible*. Phillipsburg, N.J.: Presbyterian and Reformed, 1948. This old classic has directly or indirectly influenced many conservatives in their view of Scripture. Warfield gives a detailed discussion of types of inspiration and emphasizes the infallibility and sovereignty of Scripture.

Wiise, Maarten. "The Meaning of the Authority of the Bible." *Religious Studies* 36 (2000): 473–487. The author develops J. M. Bochenski's philosophical theory about the nature of authority. He distinguishes between different kinds of authority and applies this discussion to the authority of the Bible. Wiise adds to Bochenski's work the perspective of speech-act theory.

Wood, Charles M. "Hermeneutics and the Authority of Scripture." Pages 55–70 in *An Invitation to Theological Study*. Valley Forge, Pa: Trinity Press International, 1994. A good introductory essay into the issues of hermeneutics and authority. Wood examines the impact that particular hermeneutical approaches to the Bible have in granting authority and relevance to texts.

Woodbridge, John D. *Biblical Authority: A Critique of the Rogers/McKim Proposal*. Grand Rapids: Eerdmans, 1982. A critique of the historical analysis of Jack Rogers and Donald McKim in *The Authority and Interpretation of the Bible: An Historical Approach* (see above) and the implications for authority and inerrancy.

Work, Telford. *Living and Active: Scripture in the Economy of Salvation*. Grand Rapids: Eerdmans, 2002. Work builds a doctrine of Scripture from a theological understanding of God, salvation, and the church to establish the Bible's character, purpose, and role in worship. Work appeals to theological traditions ranging from patristic to postmodern theology to present a doctrine of Scripture that is comprehensive, balanced, and relevant.

Wright, N. T. "How Can the Bible Be Authoritative?" *Vox Evangelica* 21 (1991): 7–32. This seminal essay should be read by every pastor. It critiques typical evangelical views of biblical authority as asserting the authority of evangelical or Protestant theology rather than the authority of the Bible. Wright argues that the Bible is not a set of abstract truths but "an ancient narrative book" whose authority rests in the grand story. This story can be likened to a play in which the church plays the present part. In this view Scripture functions to govern and direct the church's present performance.

_____. *The New Testament and the People of God: Christian Origins and the Question of God*. Minneapolis: Fortress, 1992. Wright's first book in his multivolume NT series offers important help in reading the Bible as a worldview book and in moving beyond the epistemological impasse of positivism or subjectivism in biblical studies.

Yeago, David S. "The Bible." Pages 49-93 in *Knowing the Triune God: The Work of the Spirit in the Practices of the Churches*. Edited by James J. Buckley and David S. Yeago. Grand Rapids: Eerdmans, 2001. In this essay Yeago argues that the context of ecclesial practice both forms and calls for a distinctive practice of interpreting and understanding the Bible.

NORTH PARK THEOLOGICAL SEMINARY

SYMPOSIUM ON THE THEOLOGICAL INTERPRETATION OF SCRIPTURE

SEPTEMBER 25–27, 2003

THE AUTHORITY AND FUNCTION OF SCRIPTURE IN THE CONTEMPORARY WORLD

THE PRESENTERS

WILLIAM J. ABRAHAM
Perkins School of Theology (Theology)

STEPHEN B. CHAPMAN
Duke Divinity School (Old Testament)

MORNA D. HOOKER
University of Cambridge (New Testament)

D. BRENT LAYTHAM
North Park Theological Seminary (Theology)

MICHAEL PASQUARELLO III
Asbury Theological Seminary (Worship Leader)

MARK ALLEN POWELL
Trinity Lutheran Seminary (New Testament)

RODNEY S. SADLER, JR.
Union Theological Seminary (Biblical Studies)

JOHN L. THOMPSON
Fuller Theological Seminary (Historical Theology)

RAYMOND C. VAN LEEUWEN
Eastern University (Old Testament)

THE RESPONDENTS

LINDA BELLEVILLE
North Park Theological Seminary

JIM DEKKER
North Park Theological Seminary

STEPHEN HALL
Trinity International University

KAZI JOSHUA
North Park Theological Seminary

D. STEPHEN LONG
Garrett-Evangelical Divinity School

CYNTHIA L. MILLER
University of Wisconsin, Madison

MICHAEL PASQUARELLO III
Asbury Theological Seminary

DANIEL J. TREIER
Wheaton College

NORTH PARK THEOLOGICAL SEMINARY

SYMPOSIUM ON THE THEOLOGICAL INTERPRETATION OF SCRIPTURE

SEPTEMBER 25–27, 2003

THE AUTHORITY AND FUNCTION OF SCRIPTURE IN THE CONTEMPORARY WORLD

PERSONS IN ATTENDANCE

William Abraham
James Amadon
Phil Anderson
Daniel Bailey
Linda Belleville
Paul Bramer
James Bruckner
Phil Cannon
Richard Carlson
Joy Challenge
Stephen Chapman
Michelle Clifton-Soderstrom
Paul Corner
Jo Ann Deasy
Jim Dekker
Inagrace Dietterich
Walter M. Dunnett
Jeff Ediger
Ryan Eikenbary-Barber
James H. Erickson
Amparo Fernández
Bruce Fields
Linda Forbes
Ricky Georgetown
Stephen Graham
Stephen Hall
Bill Hanson
Morna Hooker
Pam Hubbard
Robert Hubbard
Everett Jackson
Yolanda Jackson
Kazi Joshua
David Kersten
Karl Klockars
Paul Koptak
Brent Laytham
Karen Lichlyter-Klein
Stephen Long
Greg Mesimore
Cynthia Miller
Tom Montgomery
Burton Nelson
Monty Newton
Dave Noreen
Carol Norén
Peter Norland
Amanda Olsen
Mike Pasquarello III
Nathan Pawl
Eric Pement
Jennifer Pope
Mark Allen Powell
Jerry Reed

Amy Rohler
Robert Satterberg
Phillis Sheppard
Tim Sigler
R. J. Snell
Klyne Snodgrass
Lars Stromberg
Robin Swieringa
John Thompson
Sharon Todd
Daniel Treier
Brian Turnbow
Raymond Van Leeuwen
John Weborg
Lois Weborg
Mark Westlind
Everett Wilson
Jonathan Wilson

EX AUDITU

VOLUMES AVAILABLE

EX AUDITU Vol. 1 (1985) consists of selected articles presenting the issues inherent in the theological interpretation of Scripture.

EX AUDITU Vol. 2 (1986) discusses the theme: "Church and State Relationship." In addition there are two lead articles, one by Peter Stuhlmacher on "EX AUDITU and the Theological Interpretation of Holy Scripture," and the second by Ben F. Meyer on "The Primacy of Consent and the Uses of Suspicion."

EX AUDITU Vol. 3 (1987)	The theme:	"Creation."
EX AUDITU Vol. 4 (1988)	The theme:	"The Church and Israel (Romans 9-11)."
EX AUDITU Vol. 5 (1989)	The theme:	"What is Salvation?"
EX AUDITU Vol. 6 (1990)	The theme:	"Prophetic and/or Apocalyptic Eschatology."
EX AUDITU Vol 7 (1991)	The theme:	"Christology and Incarnation."
EX AUDITU Vol. 8 (1992)	The theme:	"Worship."
EX AUDITU Vol 9 (1993)	The theme:	"Resurrection."
EX AUDITU Vol. 10 (1994)	The theme:	"The Church."
EX AUDITU Vol. 11 (1995)	The theme:	"Biblical Law and Liberty"
EX AUDITU Vol. 12 (1996)	The theme:	"Holy Spirit"
EX AUDITU Vol. 13 (1997)	The theme:	"What is a Human?"
EX AUDITU Vol. 14 (1998)	The Theme:	"The Theological Significance of the Earthly Jesus"
EX AUDITU Vol. 15 (1999)	The Theme:	"Idolatry and the Understanding of God
EX AUDITU Vol. 16 (2000)	The Theme:	"The Task of Interpreting Scripture Theologically"
EX AUDITU Vol. 17 (2001)	The Theme:	"Biblical Ethics"
EX AUDITU Vol. 18 (2002)	The Theme:	"Spiritual Formation"
ES AUDITU Vol. 19 (2003)	The Theme:	"The Authority and Function of Scripture"

EX AUDITU Vol. 20 (2004)

The theme will be: "Judgment"

To be published in April 2005

Pickwick Publications
215 Incline Way
San Jose, CA 95139-1526